EPIGRAMS

MARCUS VALERIUS MARTIALIS, known in English as Martial, was born in Bilbilis, Spain, between AD 38 and 41; he claimed Iberian and Celtic ancestry. He moved to Rome sometime around AD 64, and spent most of his life there, composing the witty epigrams for which he is best known. He depended upon wealthy patrons to support his writing, and his first publication was the *Liber Spectaculorum* or *Book of Shows*, written to celebrate the opening of the Colosseum in 80. Two more books of short, gift-tag poems followed before he embarked upon the twelve books of *Epigrams*, which eventually totalled more than 1,500 poems. Satirical and scurrilous, Martial's epigrams bring the city of Imperial Rome and its citizens vividly to life, and he made the Greek literary form his own. He numbered Juvenal and the younger Pliny among his friends, and wrote under the reign of four emperors, whose favour he sought to cultivate. Martial returned to Bilbilis in 98, and died sometime between 101 and 105.

GIDEON NISBET is Reader in Classics at the University of Birmingham. He researches and teaches in ancient epigram and the reception of classical antiquity. His publications include *Greek Epigram in the Roman Empire: Martial's Forgotten Rivals* (2003) and *Greek Epigram in Reception* (2013).

OXFORD WORLD'S CLASSICS

*For over 100 years Oxford World's Classics have brought
readers closer to the world's great literature. Now with over 700
titles—from the 4,000-year-old myths of Mesopotamia to the
twentieth century's greatest novels—the series makes available
lesser-known as well as celebrated writing.*

*The pocket-sized hardbacks of the early years contained
introductions by Virginia Woolf, T. S. Eliot, Graham Greene,
and other literary figures which enriched the experience of reading.
Today the series is recognized for its fine scholarship and
reliability in texts that span world literature, drama and poetry,
religion, philosophy, and politics. Each edition includes perceptive
commentary and essential background information to meet the
changing needs of readers.*

OXFORD WORLD'S CLASSICS

MARTIAL

Epigrams

Translated with an Introduction and Notes by
GIDEON NISBET

OXFORD
UNIVERSITY PRESS

OXFORD

UNIVERSITY PRESS

Great Clarendon Street, Oxford, OX2 6DP
United Kingdom

Oxford University Press is a department of the University of Oxford.
It furthers the University's objective of excellence in research, scholarship,
and education by publishing worldwide. Oxford is a registered trade mark of
Oxford University Press in the UK and in certain other countries

Published in the United States of America by Oxford University Press
198 Madison Avenue, New York, NY 10016, United States of America

British Library Cataloguing in Publication Data

Data available

Library of Congress Control Number: 2014959008

ISBN 978–0–19–964545–9

Printed in Great Britain by
Clays Ltd, Elcograf S.p.A.

CONTENTS

INTRODUCTION

As it is, I live right next door to the Tiburtine Column, where
rustic Flora looks on ancient Jupiter, so I have to scale the steep
stair of the road up from the Subura. The cobbles are dirty, the
steps are never dry; it's next to impossible to cut past the long
mule-trains, and the marble blocks you see being dragged with
lots of ropes . . . (5.22)

MARCUS VALERIUS MARTIALIS, the poet we call 'Martial', is the
ultimate tour guide to Imperial Rome. He brings the sights, sounds,
and smells of the city vividly to life in his witty, often rude, little
poems. He cultivated a genre—the epigram—and made it his own.

Marcus Valerius Martialis

We know very little about Martial's life. Our only independent source
is a letter of Pliny the Younger (*Letters* 3.21) noting his death, some
time in the first few years of the second century AD. For the rest, we
are reliant on what he says about himself in his own books, much
of which cannot be taken at face-value. Nonetheless, from amongst
these scattered hints and allusions we can assemble the bare bones of
a plausible-enough life story.

By Martial's own account, working backwards from statements
of his age in books to which we can assign approximate dates, he was
born some time around AD 40. Although we do not know the exact year
of his birth, his given name or *cognomen*, Martialis, suggests he was
born on 1 March, named after Mars, god of war. His home town was
Augusta Bilbilis in the hinterland of Hispania Tarraconensis, one of
the three provinces into which Spain was divided under the emperors.
Bilbilis had city (*municipium*) status and its inhabitants were Roman
citizens; its imposing ruins, near the modern town of Calatayud, reflect
the wealth it must have enjoyed in Martial's day. Spain did well under
Rome, exporting wine and olive-oil in vast quantities (7.53) and exploit-
ing its considerable mineral resources (12.57); it was already becoming
known for its intellectual and political heavyweights (Lucan and the
two Senecas, whom Martial puffs at e.g. 1.61), and Martial would end
his days under an emperor, Trajan, who was a fellow countryman.

Martial's family must have been people of substance: they could afford to give him an advanced education in rhetoric, and probably expected he would pursue a career in law or public service. By Book 5 he is claiming equestrian status (5.13), and though he still asserts poverty (cf. 5.18) this social rank ordinarily came with a very substantial wealth qualification (400,000 sesterces), some of which is likely to have been family money. His parents' names were probably Fronto and Flaccilla (5.34). Their son left Spain for Rome some time around AD 64, and they may never have seen him again: he did not come home until he was about sixty.

In between, and for a little while after, he wrote epigrams—hundreds and hundreds of them—and made his way in the metropolis as a client of wealthy and powerful patrons. His first publication was a version of the book we call *Liber Spectaculorum* (*Book of Shows*), celebrating the gladiatorial shows and beast-fights that inaugurated the newly built Colosseum (AD 80). Next came two books with Greek titles: the *Xenia* (*Party Favours*) and *Apophoreta* (*Doggy-bags*), both consisting of gift-tag poems that are humorously proposed as substitutes for the gifts they describe, traditionally sent to friends at the December festival of Saturnalia (a custom that continues to this day as part of Christmas). Then, a fresh start: Martial began to publish a series of numbered books, at the rate of about one a year from the mid-80s to late 90s. There are twelve numbered books in all, a total that, whether by accident or design, puts Martial's epigrammatic *magnum opus* on a par with Virgil's *Aeneid*.

Martial's Genre: Epigram

An epigram is a short poem, most often of two or four lines. Its typical metre is the elegiac couplet, which is also the metre of Roman love poetry (elegy) and the hallmark of Ovid. In antiquity it was a distinctively Greek literary form: Roman writers were never comfortable in it as they were in other imported genres, such as epic and elegy. When they dabbled in epigram they often used Greek to do so. Martial's decision to write books of Latin epigrams, *and nothing else*, is thus a very significant departure.

Epigram had emerged as a literary force to be reckoned with in the Hellenistic age, in the centuries after the death of Alexander the Great (323 BC). Its roots were inscriptional—ever since the archaic period, epitaphs and such had occasionally been composed in verse—but it took a library-based culture of scholarship to collate these older texts and turn them into models for literary imitation. Epigram quickly found a home in the Greek symposium, the traditional after-dinner drinking party at which guests ('symposiasts') were expected to contribute a party turn to the evening's entertainment. It soon diversified: poetic epitaphs and praises of athletes (imitating the inscriptions found on the bases of statues of victors at games such as the Olympics) were joined by love-poems, descriptions of works of art ('ekphrases'), mock dedications, and poems about the symposium itself. Epigram bred epigram: from the beginning the genre encouraged proliferation, with 'families' of poems ringing the changes on favourite themes. This is a feature that carries through into epigram as practised by Martial: the reader will see that there are certain topics he keeps coming back to, each time with a slightly different spin.

When Rome subsumed the Hellenistic kingdoms into its growing empire, the literary culture that it encountered—and that so astounded and intimidated it—was one in which epigram was just hitting its peak. Philodemus of Gadara (first century BC), the Epicurean friend of Piso whose literary criticism inspired Horace's *Art of Poetry*, was a witty poet of love epigrams, many of which survive. Around the same time, Philodemus' fellow Gadarene Meleager was composing his own love-poems to boys and girls and assembling the ancient world's first significant anthology of verse: the *Garland*. This inaugurated a tradition that was to culminate in the *Anthologia Palatina*, the Byzantine-era 'Greek Anthology' that is our main source of ancient literary epigram.

Even before Meleager, Romans had begun paying attention to Hellenistic epigram and making home-grown versions. The early epicist Ennius (239–169 BC) is known to have composed several, and the late second and early first centuries saw a noted trio of epigrammatists: Valerius Aedituus, Porcius Licinus, and Lutatius Catulus (with one 'L'). They composed in elegiac couplets, the traditional Greek metre for epigram, and adapted Hellenistic models. Several of their poems have come down to us, the major source being Aulus Gellius' collection of supposed after-dinner conversations, *Attic Nights* (19.9.10).

The most important Latin epigrammatist before Martial, though, is Catullus (with two 'L's). Martial refers back to him frequently as his major model and as a justification for his choices—for instance, the use of strong language, pre-emptively excused in the preface to Book 1: '. . . but that's how Catullus writes, and Marsus, and Pedo, and Gaetulicus, and everyone who gets read all the way through'.

Martial mentions one or other of the Augustan poets M. Domitius Marsus and Albinovanus Pedo a dozen times in his oeuvre (e.g. 2.77); they are pretexts rather than influences for his own style of epigram. The more frequently cited of the pair, Marsus, composed his epigrams in Greek, as did the slightly later Gaetulicus (adduced only here by Martial but known through the Greek Anthology). Catullus, though, is a much more lively presence in Martial. For modern readers of the classics he is one of ancient Rome's most important poets, second perhaps only to Virgil; he was probably read less widely in the first century AD than he is today (he had died nearly a hundred years before Martial was born), but his name still had power, and Martial wields it in almost every book:

If ever I read out a few of my own couplets, you immediately recite some Marsus or Catullus. (2.71)

Just so, perhaps, did tender Catullus dare send his *Sparrow* to great Maro. (4.14)

Please find room for my little books on whatever shelf Pedo, Marsus, and Catullus share. (5.5)

The names of the poet and his notorious mistress, Lesbia, appear often in Martial, although they cannot always point to *that* Catullus and *that* Lesbia, or not straightforwardly (see pp. xiii–xiv on the Lesbia cycle).

Catullus is a genuinely important predecessor for Martial's 'gossipy little books', which he describes in pointedly similar ways. He follows Catullus closely in detailing the qualities of his *libelli* as material objects and in envisaging the squalid uses that may be found for book-rolls that fail to find an appreciative readership (see note on 3.2). When Martial composes in hendecasyllables (a line of eleven syllables), as he does frequently, he is being self-consciously Catullan. Catullus wrote elegiac epigrams as well, but hendecasyllables are his trademark metre: 'Calling all hendecasyllables, wherever you are! . . .' (Catullus 42.1–2). Martial's other significant Latin prototype is the witty and risqué master of Roman elegy, Ovid. Like Catullus, Ovid develops the presence of the author as a raffish character in his own books, and turns his own activity as a poet (particularly his choice of metre and thus of genre) into a heavily ironic serial drama. Martial elaborates on the template he has established. In the instance below we can see him playing with internal organization to create a piquant twist: Ovid had set out his stall at the outset, but Martial holds back until the last of the twelve numbered books is nearly over:

> *Arma graui numero uiolentaque bella parabam*
> *edere, materia conveniente modis.*
> *par erat inferior uersus—risisse Cupido*
> *dicitur atque unum surripuisse pedem.*

I started working on a war poem once—bloody battles set to a solemn beat, a subject that did the metre justice. Line two was the same length—but then Cupid (they tell me) laughed and stole one of its feet. (Ovid, *Amores* 1.1.1–4)

I tried to write an epic once. You started writing one; so I stopped, so my poetry wouldn't compete with yours. Then my Muse redirected herself to the thigh-boots of Tragedy. You tried on the trailing robe yourself . . . I dare Satire; you throw yourself into becoming Lucilius. I unwind with some light elegies; you copy me and unwind just the same. How low *won't* you go? (Martial 12.94)

As well as justification of his choice of genre, Ovid's work also includes explicit editorial comment that talks the reader through the changes he has implemented in revising his poems for a second edition, and Martial adopts his practice at least once and perhaps twice. The second edition of Book 10, and the poet's own commentary on it, are unmistakable Ovidian gestures:

Before, we were five books of Ovid; now we are three. The author preferred this version to the other. You may not enjoy reading us at all, but with two books gone, it'll hurt less. (Ovid, *Amores* 1 epigrammatic preface)

I was in a hurry, before; I didn't pay attention; and my tenth little book wriggled out of my grasp. It was work in progress, and now it's been recalled. You will read some poems you know, but smoothed by fresh revisions; the majority are new. Reader, look kindly on both—reader, in whom I prosper. (Martial 10.2)

Martial shouts Catullus' name; Ovid's he merely whispers. He mentions him very infrequently and never as a model for his own practice, preferring to slip him into lists of well-known authors (1.61, 5.10). It would perhaps have been unwise to advertise indebtedness to Ovid when courting the patronage of a morally minded emperor and Censor (1.4, 6.4) such as Domitian, given that the Augustan poet's naughtiness (on the page and perhaps also in real life) had got him exiled for life to the remote Black Sea.

If Martial is sometimes disingenuous in how he reports his relation to his Latin predecessors, he is silent on his most immediate and substantial models, Lucillius (with two 'L's) and Nicarchus, who were contemporary or near-contemporary Greeks working in Rome. Greek epigram was still very much a living tradition in their time—indeed, the early centuries AD were its heyday—and had recently taken a turn towards a style we would call satirical (the Greek term is 'skoptic'). Roman audiences were aware of their work, and Martial was not their only imitator. We know these poets of the mid-first century AD only through the successive stages of selection that culminated in the *Anthologia Palatina*, so the exact extent of the debt can never be pinned down, but it is clear that they were prolific (hundreds of poems survived the anthologists' winnowing) and that Martial leant on them often. The remaining work of Lucillius in particular is demonstrably the source of many of Martial's pet topics and comic routines.

The skoptic poets profoundly influenced Martial's technique. It was they who refocused epigram as a vehicle for punch-lines and plays on words, and who suggested to Martial the use of stock and made-up names that helped him stay out of trouble:

You think I'm using Athenagoras' real name. Callistratus, I'm damned if I know who Athenagoras is. But suppose I *was* using his real name: I'm not the villain here, it's your friend Athenagoras. (9.95b)

Martial did nonetheless innovate very significantly within his genre. His biggest change was organizational. The standard practice for compiling a book of epigrams in the Greek tradition, whether an anthology or an authored book by a single hand, had always been to arrange the poems by theme under headed categories. Martial rejects this, and instead brings in a characteristically Latin literary principle of organization: variety (*uariatio*), a carefully judged mix of poems that keeps surprising the reader while also allowing the poet to weave unity through the apparent chaos. He experiments with poem length, blurring the division between epigram and elegy (and even epic) in a way that no previous epigrammatist had attempted, allegedly to the annoyance of his more hidebound readers:

Cosconius, you think my epigrams are 'too long'. You're so thick they could use you for axle-grease. By the same reckoning you'd decide the Colossus was 'too tall' . . . (2.77, cf. 6.65)

Martial demands a smarter and harder-working reader who understands that his books are meant as works of literature. Greek epigram had always had a strong performative character from its use as entertainment at symposia, but Martial will have none of that: he deprecates performing poems to an invited audience (who are typically only there for a free meal, e.g. 3.50). In its place he promotes attentive private reading by individuals whose circumstances are often solitary, perhaps even furtive (e.g. 11.3). The very first poem of Book 1 addresses his reader as a *lector studiosus*, the 'Avid Fan' who has Martial's previous work at his fingertips and will read the new material from start to finish (e.g. 3.68).

Having cast aside the straitjacket of thematic categories, Martial finds other ways to guide his readers through the bewildering variety of his books. They have clear beginnings, often with instructions on how to read them, and definite endings. What is more, certain themes (e.g. plagiarism) and characters (or names; the characterizations are not always the same) keep reappearing.[1] These 'cycles' of poems are lifelines for the reader, who is always wondering when and in what guise, for example, Rufus, Postumus, or Lesbia will next make an appearance. The cycles weave through individual books, but also through the twelve-book cycle as a whole, offering the reader a choice of narrative threads to follow from start to finish.

For instance, in the Lesbia cycle the reader is invited to track Martial's relationship with Catullus, whose poetry made her (or her prototype) famous. Whether Martial's Lesbia is Catullus' Lesbia or inhabits the notional here-and-now of Martial's own corpus, the

---

[1] J. Garthwaite, 'Reevaluating Epigrammatic Cycles in Martial, Book Two', *Ramus*, 52 (2001), 46–55; on names, J. Booth and R. Maltby (eds.), *What's in a Name? The Significance of Proper Names in Classical Latin Literature* (Swansea: Classical Press of Wales, 2006).

name always points back to Catullus as a model. The kisses (*basiae*) of 6.34 are a conscious verbal echo of him as well:

Always with the doors open and no lookout posted, Lesbia: that's how you sin . . . (1.34)

I don't want however many [kisses] Lesbia gave tuneful Catullus, when he finally wore her down . . . (6.34, cf. 2.23)

Fair Nemesis brought fame to clear-voiced Tibullus; and *you*, bookish Catullus, took dictation from Lesbia . . . (8.73)

Every time you get up from your chair—and I've noticed it a lot, Lesbia . . . (11.99)

Catullus is also his model for another kind of unifying strand—the frequent use of a personal voice, or perhaps better, voices, that maintain a strong authorial presence. One of the two main characters in Martial's work is Martial himself.

Martial thinks big in his little genre—bigger than any writer of epigrams before or since. His books really are *books*, designed to be read from start to finish, and the twelve numbered books also add up to something larger than the sum of its parts.

Martial's Rome

If Martial's books are an attempt to scale epigram up to epic size, part of the reason must be the vast scope of the subject that they obsessively narrate: the city of Rome itself. The Imperial capital is Martial's stalking-ground *and* his other main character. No other author brings it so vividly to life:

If he's taken his leave of there, is he pacing the temple portico or ambling along the colonnaded walks of the Argonauts? Or maybe he sits or strolls among box-trees warmed by delightful Europa's afternoon sun, free from stinging cares? Or is he washing in the Baths of Titus, Agrippa, or shameless Tigellinus? Or partying at the country villa of Tullus and Lucanus? Or rushing off to that sweet place of Pollio's at the fourth milestone? (3.20)

Rome is the centre of Martial's world, and he finds time in between social engagements to enjoy its superabundance of beautiful free amenities, but it is not an easy city in which to live. It is smelly—a city of industrial pollution and body odour (e.g. 4.4)—and its streets are

an obstacle course (7.61). There is the ever-present danger of fire—
the city had been devastated by fire, perhaps started deliberately, late
in Nero's reign and was again badly damaged in AD 80 under Titus,
taking years to rebuild (5.7). It is noisy:

> The crested cockerels have not yet shattered the silence, and you're already
> laying down a backbeat of furious mutters and smacks . . . We, your neigh-
> bours, ask for some sleep—not a full night's worth, lying awake in the dark
> is no big deal, but being kept up all night is . . . (9.68)

The only ones who get a good night's sleep are the super-rich whose
hilltop villas soar above the hubbub, like the Janiculan eyrie of
Martial's best friend, the suspiciously named Julius Martial (4.64).
Most of all, the city's chaotic streets teem with people he loves to
hate: hypocrites, informers, parasites, perverts, false friends, unwel-
come guests, inept hosts, legacy hunters, and a seemingly endless
parade of social climbers—all easy targets for his pen. As a satirist,
Martial is unabashedly conservative: he attacks people who do not
know their proper place in his world. Martial is proud of his citizen
birthright and resentful of queue-jumpers, especially ex-slaves who
have made a fortune in trade and now propose to lord it over their
betters:

> The cobbler Cerdo threw games for you, fertile Bologna; a fuller funded
> games in Modena; where will a barkeep throw the next ones? (3.59)

> Rufus, do you see that man who always gets a front-row seat, whose sar-
> donyx-studded hand sparkles even from here? . . . Do you not know what
> he is? Peel off those plasters and you can read the answer. (2.29)

Martial himself has found advancement in Rome, having received
lavish gifts (e.g. 7.36) and favours from the emperors themselves, but
that is different; he is the 'right' kind of person, and a discriminating
patron knows as much (e.g. 7.84), although really good patrons are
a dying breed themselves. The system, Martial complains, is not what
it was in the good old days:

> That this age boasts no Pylades, no Orestes—Marcus, do you wonder why?
> Pylades always got the same wine, and Orestes never got served better
> bread or a bigger thrush; the pair of them shared the same menu. But *you*
> gobble down Lucrine oysters while I get by on big, soggy mussels, though
> my taste-buds are every bit as free-born as your own . . . (6.11)

Martial's cultivation of wealthy sponsors has attracted plenty of hostile comment in modern times, and certainly he does not believe in what we would call working for a living. Instead he favours the conventional ideal of *amicitia*, a transactional friendship founded in reciprocity. Ancient Roman friendships are often asymmetrical, but that is what makes them useful to both parties: a well-connected friend can pull strings, a well-resourced friend can give generous presents, but a humbler friend can help out at election time—or maybe write a flattering poem. Romans typically used the terminology of *amicitia* to describe the phenomenon we call patronage, and Martial is no exception (e.g. 6.11), although occasionally he brings out the lopsidedness of the relationship more explicitly and writes of serving a 'master' (2.32).

At the top of the patronage pyramid was the emperor. Martial lived under seven emperors and wrote under four. His early life in Spain was spent under the later Julio-Claudians—Caligula, Claudius, and the infamous Nero—but the Rome he knew at first hand was ruled by the shorter Flavian dynasty: Vespasian (AD 69–79), the canny veteran of the war in Judaea who led Rome out of the chaos of civil war in the 'year of the four emperors'; his elder son and military colleague Titus, who ruled only briefly (79–81) before succumbing to fever, a common hazard; and Domitian, the autocratic and widely disliked younger son, who ruled Rome for longer than any emperor since Augustus' heir Tiberius (81–96) before falling victim to a palace coup. The Senate immediately replaced him with Nerva (96–8), an elderly and unassuming civil servant whose placeholder reign lasted just long enough to appoint an efficient and popular successor, the professional soldier Trajan (98–117), under whom the empire was to reach its widest extent.

By far the largest part of Martial's literary career (twelve or more of his fifteen books) was under Domitian, whom he praises extensively (though not groundlessly) as an effective defender of the empire from external threats and as the imperial builder par excellence (e.g. 5.7, 8.65, 8.80)—much of the grandeur of the ancient Rome experienced by visitors today is Domitianic in origin, including the splendid remains of his palace on the Palatine (8.36, 39). His personal treasury funded the 'bread and circuses' (*panem et circenses*, Juvenal 10.81) that kept the people entertained, and he bankrolled the workfare construction projects that created the splendid amenities which made Romans feel their city was the only place to be:

Going out for a drive, some plays, some little books, the Campus, the portico, a bit of shade, the Virgo, the baths. That's where we'd be . . . (5.20)

After Domitian's fall Martial was careful to distance himself from his former benefactor and begin ingratiating himself with Domitian's successors (e.g. 10.72, 11.5).

We will never know how heavily Martial really relied on particular patrons, or on patronage generally. The text suggests he viewed his gains as *quid pro quo* rather than dependency: he sent people copies of his books, and it would have been rude of them not to send something in return. Numerous wealthy friends or potential friends—for example, in Book 1 alone Stella (1.7 and 44), Quintianus (1.52), Proculus (1.70), and more besides—receive flattering write-ups that in the transactional language of Roman friendship might constitute *beneficia* (favours advanced), *officia* (gifts or services due in return), or both. Titus and Domitian clearly noticed Martial and did him at least one substantial good turn which he is careful to repay with good publicity (as e.g. at 2.92), but nothing in his books suggests he was close to the centre of power. Martial often presents himself as living hand to mouth, but poetic declarations of poverty were a familiar trope:

And then he said: 'Are you him? Are you that Martial, whose dirty jokes anyone knows who doesn't have the ear of a Dutchman?' I flashed him a self-deprecating smile and with a discreet nod of the head conceded that he'd got his man. 'If that's so,' he asked, 'why do you wear such rotten coats?' 'Because I'm a rotten poet,' I replied . . . (6.82)

There is next to no evidence that any ancient author wrote for (in our terms) a living, and it is hard to see how they could in a world with no concept of enforceable copyright (although actual plagiarism was recognized and deprecated, 1.52) and in which every book-roll was a handmade copy from a similarly hand-copied exemplar.

When Martial claims he is bedevilled by plagiarists and imitators, he is at least exaggerating for humorous effect; these characters are perhaps not so much a real-life problem as a thematic pretext for advertising the significance of his contribution to epigram. In other words, we may think of the plagiarism poems as a 'cycle', a literary device. No other ancient poet complains about plagiarism or imitation the way Martial does:

Idiot! Why do you mingle your verses with mine? Wretch! What use to you is a book at odds with itself? Why are you trying to slip foxes into a pride of lions, and make little owls resemble eagles? Moron! . . . (10.100)

There is no obvious reason why cheats should have singled him out, nor do any traces of such imitators survive to corroborate his story. What is more, the theme must carry some irony for the Avid Fan (1.1) who knows how heavily Martial himself relies on unacknowledged sources, in a genre where close adaptation had always been fair game. Significantly, the large majority of these claims fall in his very first numbered book (e.g. 1.38, 1.52), where jealous would-be poets are presented as counterfeiting a literary giant who is already 'famous all round the world' (1.1)—quite a large claim to make in the very first poem of a career that, in the closing sequence of Book 1 (1.113), he insists we should regard as having just now begun again from a blank slate, with his earlier works now comprehensively disowned as juvenilia: 'the hick stuff, the junk, the ones I don't even recognize these days.'

Martial and Roman Satire

These incongruities are not careless accidents, or signs of a ruined text: they are part of Martial's technique. Although Martial's genre is epigram, his individual style as an epigrammatist has much in common with satire (*satura*), a literary form that Romans reasonably considered their distinctive contribution to ancient literature, and in particular satire as practised by his younger contemporary and friend, Juvenal (late first and early second century AD). *Satura* was written in hexameters, the metre more usually associated with heroic and didactic epic, but it was far from heroic and it probably taught nothing. It claimed to castigate social evils, but was carnivalesque in spirit—rude, indignant, and frequently obscene.[2] Its defining features were miscellany and

---

[2] The Romans certainly did have a concept of the obscene; the sexual and scatological language of Martial and of the satirists (excluding Horace) was meant to be humorously outrageous and would have been unacceptable in more serious literary genres: see A. Richlin, *The Garden of Priapus: Sexuality and Aggression in Roman Humor* (New Haven: Yale University Press, 1983).

excess: *satur* in Latin means 'stuffed full', and a *satura lanx* was a platter brimming with assorted foods. Accordingly, the moods and topics of satire are inconstant: its first-person narrators seem determined always to cram more in, at the expense of linear argument and good taste. Juvenal was heir to a tradition stretching back to Lucilius (with one 'L'), of whose work only fragments survive. Since Lucilius' time (second century BC), the tradition had been perpetuated and refined by Horace (first century BC) and Persius (first century AD). Juvenal himself only began writing satire as Martial's own literary career drew to a close, but he displayed such mastery that his work defined the genre for all posterity: if he had not imitated Martial so closely and so often, we would not perhaps see Martial's epigrams as 'satirical' in anything like the same degree. Martial is obviously not a satirist in the strict sense of the term, and knows he is not (12.94): his poems are far too short, and he does not write in hexameters, a metre alien to epigram, except as an isolated experiment (6.65). What is more, his own genre offers salient Greek models (Lucillius and Nicarchus) for satire-esque poems that have no organic connection to the Roman tradition of *satura*. These skoptic epigrammatists teach him techniques not available to Roman satirists proper—most notably, the brevity of epigram enables Martial to sting the reader with a sententious punch-line many times on each page.

However, the spirit of Martial's epigrams is unmistakably aligned with that of satire in the hands of Juvenal. A defining feature of the latter's style is the crafting of a humorously inconsistent poetic self-characterization, or *persona*. The Juvenal of the *Satires* is a bravura performance of the role of 'the satirist': he overreacts, loses his temper and the thread of his argument, and contradicts himself.[3] The same can be said of the Martial of the *Epigrams*. If anything, the role-playing counts for more in his work than in Juvenal's, because Martial performs on a much larger stage. Juvenal wrote fifteen satires; Martial, over 1,500 epigrams. The deliberately ramshackle quality of *satura* is perhaps what motivated Martial's radical departure from the traditional, highly orderly Greek arrangement of epigram-books by thematic category, in favour of Roman poetic miscellany: each of his myriad poems has the potential to present a new and different

---

[3] S. H. Braund (ed.), *Satire and Society in Ancient Rome* (Exeter: Exeter University Press, 1989).

'Martial', opening up unheard-of opportunities for comic incongruity. This has made Martial a frustrating author for scholars who wish to use him as a repository of facts about daily life in ancient Rome, a role to which he superficially seems ideally suited:

Few writers of equal ability show in their work such a total absence of character, such indifference to all ideas or enthusiasms; yet this very quality makes Martial a more perfect mirror of the external aspects of Roman life. The 'candour' noted in him by Pliny is simply that of a sheet of paper which is indifferent to what is written upon it, fair or foul.[4]

This view of Martial notices the dodecalogy's lack of an overriding ethical agenda, implicitly in contrast to a morally outraged Juvenal (in whom modern scholarship no longer really believes), but reads it as evidence of a real-life character flaw rather than a literary performance. However, it is not really possible to extract an actual, flesh-and-blood Martial from the *Epigrams* and interrogate him on his convictions. The Martial of the text can be made to express consistent views on some topics, in keeping with epigram's fondness for variations on a theme, but he is also deliberately inconsistent and shows himself up. For instance, whipping a slave for cooking a bad dinner is monstrous behaviour in an acquaintance (3.94, not in this selection), but fine when Martial does it himself (8.23). Even some quite basic 'facts' of Martial's life are subject to circumstance: most obviously, he shifts from married to single and back again to fit whatever scenario he has conjured up for a particular poem.

The basic problem is that Martial is mostly in the joke business, and whatever they may reveal about broader social attitudes, jokes throw at best an intermittent light on the opinions and experiences of their tellers. They are also a far-from-ideal source of historical facts. Martial's Rome *seems* very real—the bustling variety of the twelve numbered books delivers a visceral impression of the bustling variety of Rome's crowded streets, and the *Book of Shows* puts us in a front-row seat in the newly built Colosseum—but any complex work of literature fashions its own 'reality', and Martial's dodecalogy is increasingly recognized as just such a work.[5]

---

[4] J. W. Mackail, *Latin Literature* (London: Murray, 1895), 194.
[5] W. Fitzgerald, *Martial: The World of the Epigram* (Chicago: Chicago University Press, 2007), 7.

What is more, Martial's urban factoids are inevitably bite-sized: the brevity of individual epigrams makes for a cityscape of sound-bites, of hints and allusions that, in the absence of corroboration, can be maddeningly elliptical. An example is 1.70, where Martial's book is told to go and perform client service for him. Martial's directions steer it through the iconic city-centre, past the gigantic statue (erected by Nero) that will later give its name to the Colosseum:

And please don't linger at the sun-rayed Colossus, that gigantic wonder which delights in surpassing the masterwork at Rhodes. Veer off at the spot where that old soak Bacchus has his dwelling, and where Cybele's rotunda stands with its painted Corybant . . . (1.70)

The standard reference works list this round temple (*tholos*) of Cybele, note its decorative frescos, and locate it at the top of the Sacred Way, somewhere near the Arch of Titus—but the temple hardly exists outside of this one poem by Martial (the archaeology is silent). The 'painted Corybant' (a priest of Cybele) is not *explicitly* a figure in a fresco—perhaps he is even an actual priest, with tattooed or painted skin. The best we can do is make educated guesses about the merely-real Rome of Domitian—and relish the vibrant street scene in the hyper-real Rome of Martial.

A close parallel is instructive: we now know from studies of Roman erotic elegy that those moments when a poem seems most in touch with the real stuff of human intimacy are often its most artificial. Where past generations of scholars took the lovers' Rome of Propertius, Tibullus, and Ovid largely on faith as a prettified version of real ancient life and customs (getting quite hot under the collar at the pagan frolics they unearthed), and saw the points of similarity between the love-poets as confirmation of truth, we now see a network of writers playing with the possibilities of a shared universe—not reality but reality-effect, an elaborate serial fiction. Ovid makes sweet love not (or not primarily) to a flesh-and-blood girlfriend but to the texts of Propertius and Tibullus, his immediate literary predecessors.[6]

This insight has important consequences for Martial. Poem by poem and book by book, he is a relentlessly serial author, forever writing sequels that invite us to reconsider what has gone before

[6] P. Veyne, *Roman Erotic Elegy: Love, Poetry, and the West* (Chicago: University of Chicago Press, 1988); M. Wyke, 'Mistress and Metaphor in Augustan Elegy', *Helios*, 16 (1989), 25–47.

(with the provocative difference that the author he is rewriting is himself). Book by book and poem by poem, he is building up an elaborate literary universe (what Francesca Sapsford has dubbed the 'Martialverse') in which the reader quickly comes to feel at home, an impression confirmed by Juvenal's decision to play in the same literary world.[7] Cycles play an important role in crafting this reality-effect by generating continuity and letting us track characters and situations through time: in the Martialverse, what goes around comes around. The more hyper-real it all seems, though, the more it is actually just commenting on and caught up in itself—*probably*. Martial's books are always teasing us with the hint that bits and pieces *might* be true, if only perhaps by accidental coincidence.

They know they can get away with it. Already in their author's lifetime, Martial's books imagined a far-off readership that depended on him for its fix of the urban action:

My recondite Muse does not beguile just Rome's spare time, nor do these poems reach only the ears of the leisured; no, my book is reread by the tough centurion beside the battle-standard amid Getic frosts. Even Britain is said to have our poems by heart. (11.3)

Cheap flights make it physically easier for modern provincials to drop in on the *Urbs*, but its ancient remains are deaf to our questions. And so our sense of 'what it was really like' remains in Martial's dispensation.

Martial's Books

Fifteen books by Martial survive, or perhaps more accurately, fourteen-and-a-bit: *Liber Spectaculorum*, the *Xenia* and *Apophoreta*, and the series of twelve numbered books, of which one (Book 10) declares itself to be a second edition. A typical book of Martial has around a hundred poems in it, some more, some less—ancient book-rolls were of a fairly uniform length, and books where the poems are longer can fit fewer of them in. The longest is the *Apophoreta*, which at 223 poems is twice as long as usual. At the other end of the scale, the *De Spectaculis* or *Liber Spectaculorum* stands at a mere thirty-four poems and is clearly not a complete book. In all, the books contain 1,559

---

[7] F. Sapsford, 'The "Epic" of Martial', Ph.D thesis, Birmingham University (2012), 40.

poems, or 1,562 if one counts the epigrams that conclude a couple of the prose prefaces (one in Book 1 and two in Book 9, the second nested within the first).

The traditional ordering of the books places the *Liber Spectaculorum* first (in those manuscripts that have it: see the Note on the Text); then Books 1–12; then the *Xenia* ('Book 13'), and finally the *Apophoreta* ('Book 14'). This arrangement is clearly not right: the *Xenia* and *Apophoreta* were written before the twelve numbered books (i.e. they and the *Liber Spectaculorum* are the 'gossipy little books' that Martial alleges in 1.1 are 'famous all round the world'). However, it has been preserved here as the sequence transmitted in the manuscripts and familiar to generations of readers.

Martial's typical term for his books is *libellus* (plural *libelli*), a diminutive form: 'little book'. A regular book is a *liber* (plural *libri*), but Martial only occasionally calls his books *libri*, and then typically when he is talking about them as physical objects. There will have been nothing materially 'small' about the *libelli* when compared to other books that were in circulation; their author took up much the same amount of papyrus as anyone else. So why does Martial call them 'little'?

There is an older theory, not now given much credence, that Martial meant *libellus* quite literally. Martial's 'little books', the story went, were not the books of Martial as we have them, but pamphlets written to please particular patrons. Once a pamphlet had achieved its purpose in the gift-economy of *amicitia* it became redundant, but the Martial of the '*libellus* theory' hated waste: whenever he had collected several such leftover *libelli* he blended their content into a bigger book, a *liber*, for the reading public at large. This process of auto-plagiarism from multiple sources was also believed to explain the apparent miscellaneity of the surviving books.

Anyone who invested in this theory (which for much of the twentieth century went unquestioned) had to accept that the number, content, individual internal arrangement, and collective chronological sequence of Martial's actual 'little books' (the pamphlets for patrons) were thus forever lost to posterity; effectively, he could not be read as a literary author. Practically all he was good for was as raw material for source-books, a role to which, as we have seen, he is not ideally suited.

The likely explanation is less convoluted. As with so much in Martial, '*libellus*' is a self-conscious allusion to Catullus, who inspires

Martial's practice of making his books talk about themselves, both as works of literature and as smartly presented gifts for friends:

To whom am I giving my smart new *libellus*, freshly buffed up with dry pumice? (Catullus 1.1–2)

Whose present, little book, do you wish to be? (3.2)

I entrust my little books to your care, Quintilianus—if I can still call them mine . . . (1.52)

The one significant difference, playing into his humorous self-deprecation as a poet inferior to his high-living Republican model, is that Martial also admits to writing with an eye on the market:

For five denarii, out of the first or second book-case, smoothed down with pumice and elegant in purple . . . (1.117)

Martial's little books make their literary ambition explicit. They begin elaborately, with programmatic prefaces, opening sequences, or both:

Sure, you could have borne three hundred epigrams, but then who would bear *you*, book-roll, and read you from start to finish? It's time you learned what's good about a concise little book. First: I waste less paper . . . (2.1)

They have definite endings:

A little book this long *could* satisfy your appetite, reader, but still you ask me for a few couplets more; but Lupus wants his interest, and my boys, their rations. Reader, clear my slate. Nothing to say? Pretending you're deaf? Get lost. (11.108)

In between there is marvellous variety, but variety was the characteristic strength of Latin poetry-books. Twice in Book 3 Martial talks explicitly about structure for the supposed benefit of a particular kind of reader:

Up to this point, Madam, this little book has been written for you. You want to know for whom the bits further in were written? For me . . . (3.68)

I warned you in advance, bashful lady. I told you: there's part of my naughty little book you shouldn't read. But look, you're reading it . . . (3.86)

Martial's miscellaneity is, then, a carefully planned effect rather than true randomness. We have seen that he creates connections between poems through recurring themes and phraseology, or the appearance of familiar names—the repertoire of techniques that underpin his 'cycles'. He also puts care into juxtaposition and sequencing. The position of an individual epigram within its book affects how it is read. Martial knows that we are never looking at just *one* epigram: the reader's gaze simultaneously takes in a swarm of others on the same page and facing page (for us, reading the poems in a codex). Most of his original readers will have met the epigrams in a papyrus book-roll, where their peripheral vision will have taken in adjoining columns (forward *and* back); and every reader, then and now, retains recent poems in memory.

Consider, for instance, a sequence late in Book 3 that opens with intimations of oral sexual service, a practice that Romans claimed to consider demeaning to the person giving pleasure (see note on 2.12):

You don't whine about anyone, don't speak ill of anyone; all the same, Apicius, rumour has it you're bad-mouthing. (3.80)

Poem 3.81 continues the theme, and it reappears at the climax of 3.82, an extraordinarily long epigram even by Martial's standards (thirty-three lines of hendecasyllables):

. . . That's the kind of ill-treatment we put up with from the vicious bastard, and we can't pay him back, Rufus: he *likes* the taste of cock. (3.81.32–3)

The immediate sequel to this very long poem is a couplet that comments metapoetically on poem size, while also developing the oral-sex theme (Chione the fellatrix is a figure known to Martial's readers, cf. 1.34):

You urge me to make my epigrams more concise, Cordus. 'Do me like Chione does': I can't get more concise than that. (3.82)

Martial keeps up the pressure: 3.84 perpetuates the theme of oral sex, and 3.87–8 circle back round to it. In the meantime (3.86), the joke has been on a particular kind of reader: Martial has told off the prudish Roman matron who ignored his earlier warning (3.68) and now finds herself hemmed in by perverts. Sequencing matters, by design.

It remains possible that Martial sometimes sent shorter collections of poems to friends he wanted to impress as part of the give-and-take of *amicitia*, effectively anthologizing himself—but we have no way of knowing what such collections were like, if they ever existed. Martial's books are Martial's books; they are how he wanted to be read, and they are what made him (if anything did at the time) 'famous all round the world'.

Martial from Then to Now

Pliny the Younger, our only contemporary witness to Martial's life and death, mourned his passing (Martial had written kindly about him in lines he can quote from memory, 10.20) but was unconvinced his little books would stand the test of time: '. . . because he gave me everything he could, and would have given more, if he'd been able. Then again, what greater gift can a man give than glory and praise and eternity? "But they won't last forever, the things he wrote." Perhaps they won't, but he wrote them as if they would' (*Letters* 3.21).

The two centuries after Martial's death appeared to ratify Pliny's scepticism: we have next to no evidence that the epigrams were being read at all. When Hadrian's adoptive heir Aelius Verus (AD 101–38) called Martial 'his Virgil',[8] he declared himself as an attentive reader of the dodecalogy and was perhaps trying to outrage respectable opinion. No one else we know of was paying Martial any heed. When Latin authors (principally Ausonius) do finally engage with epigram again, it is in a very different world—the North Africa of the third and fourth centuries AD; they know Martial's work, but feel no obligation to imitate it extensively. Instead their understanding of epigram is predicated on the standard Greek models of the Hellenistic world, to the extent that Ausonius' poetry sometimes switches into Greek (the Greek epigrammatic tradition flourished in the early centuries AD as never before). Martial may have been Aelius Verus' Virgil, but he was no one else's.

Afterwards, the heartbeat of the *libelli* is weak and erratic for a millennium and more. They are a gold-mine of pithy adages for the Christian authors of late antiquity, but descend through the Middle Ages in near-silence.[9] Only with the Renaissance did Martial really find the readership he had always laid claim to. At long last, the self-advertisement

---

[8] *Scriptores Historiae Augustae*, Life of Aelius Verus 5.9, adding that the pleasure-loving heir-apparent (praised as a man of wide reading) kept copies of Apicius and Ovid's *Amores* next to his bed.

[9] M. T. Crane and J. Goodrich, 'Martial', in A. Grafton, G. W. Most, and S. Settis (eds.), *The Classical Tradition* (Cambridge, Mass.: Harvard University Press, 2010), 565.

of the preface to Book I came true: he really *was* 'famous all round the world' (or enough of it to count) 'for his gossipy little books of epigrams'. The European Baroque world of letters became Martial's Avid Fan: any self-respecting Humanist could and did issue endless epigrams and quasi-epigrams inspired by Martial's wit and concision (though not his obscenity), in letters of friendship and recommendation, book-dedications, and anywhere else they could be squeezed in.[10]

The ubiquity of epigram after the manner of Martial in the cosmopolitan literary culture of Baroque Europe grew out of his omnipresence in an educational pattern common across the continent, Britain included. Schooling meant Latin, and Latin very often meant epigram, certainly as fodder for exercise-books: Martial's brevity (when he *was* being brief) made his poems ideal teaching texts and models for verse composition, although of course many poems had to be avoided because of unacceptable phrasing and content. (Much the same was happening on the Greek side, for the minority-within-a-minority who acquired that language as well; selections from the Greek Anthology were a mainstay of the more prestigious private schools.) However, Martial's convenience as a pedagogic tool bore no relation to his standing in the world of art and morals. His literary influence fell away in the last decades of the eighteenth century, eclipsed by the manly moralist Juvenal.[11]

Foul-mouthed, a flatterer of an odious tyrant, and at the last (Book 12) a fading gigolo battening onto a country widow: new readerships did not like the cut of Martial's jib. Byron called him 'nauseous'.[12] The final nail in the coffin was driven in by, of all people, Napoleon.

---

[10] This part of Martial's story is simply too big to tell here, but is treated with great erudition by J. Sullivan, *Martial: The Unexpected Classic* (Cambridge: Cambridge University Press, 1991), and more recently in S. de Beer, K. A. E. Enenkel, and D. Rijser (eds.), *The Neo-Latin Epigram: A Learned and Witty Genre* (Leuven: Leuven University Press, 2009). For numerous period instances of Martial in English translation and adaptation, see J. P. Sullivan and A. J. Boyle (eds.), *Martial in English* (Harmondsworth: Penguin, 1991).

[11] D. Hopkins, 'Roman Satire and Epigram', in S. Gillespie and D. Hopkins (eds.), *The Oxford History of Literary Translation in English*. Volume 3: *1660–1790* (Oxford: Oxford University Press, 2005), 236; G. Nisbet, 'Revoicing Imperial Satire', in S. Braund and J. Osgood (eds.), *A Companion to Persius and Juvenal* (Malden, Mass.: Blackwell, 2013), 486–512.

[12] J. Talbot, 'Latin Poetry', in P. France and K. Haynes (eds.), *The Oxford History of Literary Translation in English*. Volume 4: *1790–1900* (Oxford: Oxford University Press, 2006), 196.

Martial's style of epigram, always striving for point and effect, made him a favourite author of the French—or at least, the British convinced themselves it did. Britain therefore allied itself with Martial's rivals, the Greek epigrammatists, who were Wordsworthian Romantics long before the fact—or at least, the British now convinced themselves they had been. The French, they decided, were incapable of apprehending the divine simplicity and 'serenity' of Greek epigram; their preference for Greek epigram's Latin imitator betrayed a flaw in national character.[13]

Although the French threat receded, Martial remained an unwelcome interloper in the canon: too foul-mouthed, too obsequious, too lightweight, too late, too short (the poems), too long (the corpus). Readers continued to enjoy him privately, in his own Latin (with the naughty bits) or in winnowed translations, but his stock as a poet stayed low, and until the 1990s he was not considered a viable candidate for serious academic study. Traces of this old attitude still linger: a new wave of scholarship takes Martial seriously as a literary author, but he is still largely absent from university syllabuses—'he is probably the last of the post-Augustan poets to remain "trash"', and some of that trashy reputation is likely always to stick.[14]

All to the good: that reputation was hard-earned, and we would do Martial a disservice by conferring respectability on the epicist of smut and snark. Martial himself embraces the label of trashiness; he reclaims trash for art (2.1, 4.10, 4.72). When a devoted benefactor proposes to place a portrait of the poet in his new library, Martial proposes the following epigram as its subtitle, to fix his reputation for posterity:

'It is I, second to none in my reputation for trash; you're not impressed by me but, reader, I think you love me. Let greater poets pour forth greater themes; I speak of small ones, and am content to come back often into your hands.' (Book 9 prologue)

In a cosmopolitan and multicultural world of disposable culture and streamed media, in a blogosphere that runs on celebrity gossip and sound-bites, Martial's epigrams seem as fresh and alive today as when he wrote them, nearly two thousand years ago.

---

[13] G. Nisbet, *Greek Epigram in Reception: J. A. Symonds, Oscar Wilde, and the Invention of Desire, 1805–1929* (Oxford: Oxford University Press, 2013), 26–7, 44.

[14] V. Rimell, *Martial's Rome* (Cambridge: Cambridge University Press, 2008), 3.

NOTE ON THE TEXT AND TRANSLATION

THE Latin text of Martial's books is securely attested, much more so than that of some more famous ancient authors (prominent among them Martial's declared literary model, Catullus). Three families of manuscripts survive, all deriving from a single ancient source. The text presented facing the translation is based on sources in the public domain; it is peculiar to the present volume, but will present no surprises to readers of Martial's Latin in any modern edition. I follow the numbering used in the Loeb edition by Shackleton Bailey, since this is the version to which readers of Martial are overwhelmingly likely to refer. Where alternative numbers appear in brackets, these are the previously accepted numbers.

The only significant textual riddle is the 'Book of Shows', which survives in only one of the three manuscript families. It comes down without a distinctive title—*De Spectaculis* and *Liber Spectaculorum* are merely reasonable guesses at what Martial or his readers may originally have called a publication of this kind—and its content appears uneven in date, suggesting that it may be the remains of a second edition, or perhaps a posthumous assemblage. The introduction to Coleman's commentary (2006: xxi–xxv) sets out what can be known of its textual history.

The Martial of this little book is *my* Martial—the Martial I hear when I read his Latin. He is frank about what he wants and swears shockingly. This is the Martial we can reflect honestly in the twenty-first century. My translation occasionally borrows a doggerel verse rhythm but is in prose, because Martial is conversational rather than poetic (though he has moments of elegiac tenderness), because I am not a poet, and because attempts to put Martial into verse typically blunt his concision and point. Translators often want to make Martial rhyme, and the results can be very enjoyable, but they lose too much of his devilish detail and struggle to convey his deft comic timing.

Anthologization began with ancient epigram, and modern readerships invariably meet Martial through a selection; the present volume is no different. Martial himself ironically licensed the impatient reader to skim or cut as he or she saw fit: 'If short ones are your thing, just read the two-liners . . .' (6.65).

Selection gives tremendous power to the translator, but also imposes impossible demands—impossible because mutually contradictory. A 'good' selection from Martial ought to emphasize his originality, *and* illustrate his literary influences. It needs to make his world excitingly different, *and* make him seem like 'one of us'. It should represent his versatility by avoiding duplication, *and* illustrate his method as an epigrammatist by including variations on a theme.

The selection tries to do all these and to communicate a sense of Martial's structural gambits. In the Introduction we have seen that the meaning of an individual epigram does not begin and end with its first and last lines, and as far as possible I have tried to show links between poems, in my choices and in the notes at the back of the book.

I am most grateful to Judith Luna and Emily Brand, my editor and production editor at Oxford University Press, and to Jeff New, my copy-editor. This *libellus* is much the better for their help and guidance.

SELECT BIBLIOGRAPHY

Commentaries on Martial in English

Coleman, K., M. *Valerii Martialis Liber Spectaculorum. Edited with Introduction, Translation, and Commentary* (Oxford: Oxford University Press, 2006).

Galán Vioque, G., *Martial, Book VII: A Commentary* (Leiden: Brill, 2002).

Henriksén, C., *A Commentary on Martial, Epigrams Book 9* (Oxford: Oxford University Press, 2012).

Howell, P., *A Commentary on Book One of the Epigrams of Martial* (London: Athlone Press, 1980).

—— *Martial: The Epigrams, Book V. Edited with Introduction, Translation and Commentary* (Warminster: Aris & Phillips, 1995).

Kay, N. M., *Martial, Book XI: A Commentary* (London: Duckworth, 1985).

Leary, T. J., *Martial, Book XIV: The Apophoreta* (London: Duckworth, 1996).

—— *Martial, Book XIII: The Xenia. Text with Introduction and Commentary* (London: Duckworth, 2001).

Moreno Soldevila, R., *Martial, Book IV: A Commentary* (Leiden: Brill, 2006).

Williams, C. A., *Martial: Epigrams, Book 2. Edited with Introduction, Translation, and Commentary* (Oxford: Oxford University Press, 2004).

Martial's Influences and Technique

Booth, J., and Maltby, R. (eds.), *What's in a Name? The Significance of Proper Names in Classical Latin Literature* (Swansea: Classical Press of Wales, 2006).

Braund, S. H. (ed.), *Satire and Society in Ancient Rome* (Exeter: Exeter University Press, 1989).

Fowler, D. P. F., 'Martial and the Book', *Ramus*, 24 (1995), 31–58.

Freudenberg, K., *Satires of Rome: Threatening Poses from Lucilius to Juvenal* (Cambridge: Cambridge University Press, 2001).

Gaisser, J., *Catullus and his Renaissance Readers* (Oxford: Oxford University Press, 1993).

Garthwaite, J., 'Reevaluating Epigrammatic Cycles in Martial, Book Two', *Ramus*, 52 (2001), 46–55.

Hinds, S., 'Martial's Ovid/Ovid's Martial', *Journal of Roman Studies*, 97 (2007), 113–54.

Lorenz, S., 'Waterscape with Black and White: Epigrams, Cycles, and Webs in Martial's *Epigrammaton Liber Quartus*', *American Journal of Philology*, 125 (2004), 255–78.

Nisbet, G., *Greek Epigram in the Roman Empire: Martial's Forgotten Rivals* (Oxford: Oxford University Press, 2003).

Putnam, M. C. J., *Virgil's Epic Designs: Ekphrasis in the Aeneid* (New Haven: Yale University Press, 1998).

Rimell, V., *Martial's Rome* (Cambridge: Cambridge University Press, 2008).

Roman, L., 'The Representation of Literary Materiality in Martial's Epigrams', *Journal of Roman Studies*, 91 (2001), 113–45.

Sapsford, F., 'The "Epic" of Martial', Ph.D thesis, Birmingham University (2012).

Swann, B., *Martial's Catullus: The Reception of an Epigrammatic Rival* (Hildesheim: Georg Olms, 1994).

Veyne, P., *Roman Erotic Elegy: Love, Poetry, and the West* (Chicago: University of Chicago Press, 1988).

Wyke, M., 'Mistress and Metaphor in Augustan Elegy', *Helios*, 16 (1989), 25–47.

Martial and his World

Edwards, C., *Writing Rome: Textual Approaches to the City* (Cambridge: Cambridge University Press, 1996).

Fitzgerald, W., *Martial: The World of the Epigram* (Chicago: Chicago University Press, 2007).

Gold, B. K. (ed.), *Literary and Artistic Patronage in Ancient Rome* (Austin, Tex.: University of Texas Press, 2003).

Larmour, D. H. J., and Spencer, D. (eds.), *The Sites of Rome: Time, Space, Memory* (Oxford: Oxford University Press, 2007).

Laurence, R., 'Literature and the Spatial Turn: Movement and Space in Martial's Epigrams', in R. Laurence and D. J. Newsome (eds.), *Rome, Ostia, Pompeii: Movement and Space* (Oxford: Oxford University Press, 2011), 81–99.

Nauta, R. R., *Poetry for Patrons: Literary Communication in the Age of Domitian* (Leiden: Brill, 2002).

Newlands, C., *Statius' Silvae and the Poetics of Empire* (Cambridge: Cambridge University Press, 2010).

Spencer, D., *Roman Landscape: Culture and Identity* (Cambridge: Cambridge University Press, 2010).

Woolf, G., 'The City of Letters', in C. Edwards and G. Woolf (eds.), *Rome the Cosmopolis* (Cambridge: Cambridge University Press, 2003), 203–21.

Ancient Epigram

Bing, P., and Bruss, J. S. (eds.), *Brill's Companion to Hellenistic Epigram: Down to Philip* (Leiden: Brill, 2007).

Fantuzzi, M., and Hunter, R., *Tradition and Innovation in Hellenistic Poetry* (Cambridge: Cambridge University Press, 2004).

Gutzwiller, K., *Poetic Garlands: Hellenistic Epigrams in Context* (Berkeley: University of California Press, 1998).

Livingstone, N., and Nisbet, G., *Epigram* (Cambridge: Cambridge University Press, 2010).

Food and Sex

Adams, J. N., *The Latin Sexual Vocabulary* (London: Duckworth, 1982).

Dalby, A., *Empire of Pleasures: Luxury and Indulgence in the Roman World* (London and New York: Routledge, 2000).

—— and Grainger, S., *The Classical Cookbook* (London: British Museum Press, 1996).

Diggle, J., and Goodyear, F. R. D. (eds.), *The Classical Papers of A. E. Housman. Volume II: 1897–1914* (Cambridge: Cambridge University Press, 1972).

Gowers, E., *The Loaded Table: Representations of Food in Roman Literature* (Oxford: Oxford University Press, 1993).

Grant, M., *Roman Cookery: Ancient Recipes for Modern Kitchens* (London: Serif, 1999).

Housman, A. E., 'Corrections and Explanations of Martial', *Journal of Philology*, 30 (1907), 229–65; repr. in Diggle and Goodyear (eds.) (1972), 711–39.

Richlin, A., *The Garden of Priapus: Sexuality and Aggression in Roman Humor* (New Haven: Yale University Press, 1983).

Martial in Reception

de Beer, S., Enenkel, K. A. E., and Rijser, D. (eds.), *The Neo-Latin Epigram: A Learned and Witty Genre* (Leuven: Leuven University Press, 2009).

Crane, M. T., and Goodrich, J., 'Martial', in A. Grafton, G. W. Most, and S. Settis (eds.), *The Classical Tradition* (Cambridge, Mass.: Harvard University Press, 2010), 565–6.

Harrison, S., and Stray, C. (eds.), *Expurgating the Classics: Editing Out in Greek and Latin* (London: Duckworth, 2012).

Hopkins, D., 'Roman Satire and Epigram', in S. Gillespie and D. Hopkins (eds.), *The Oxford History of Literary Translation in English*. Volume 3: *1660–1790* (Oxford: Oxford University Press, 2005), 218–40.

Nisbet, G., 'Revoicing Imperial Satire', in S. Braund and J. Osgood (eds.), *A Companion to Persius and Juvenal* (Malden, Mass.: Blackwell, 2013), 486–512.

Nisbet, G., *Greek Epigram in Reception: J. A. Symonds, Oscar Wilde, and the Invention of Desire, 1805–1929* (Oxford: Oxford University Press, 2013).

Sullivan, J., *Martial: The Unexpected Classic* (Cambridge: Cambridge University Press, 1991).

Sullivan, J. P., and Boyle, A. J. (eds.), *Martial in English* (Harmondsworth: Penguin, 1991).

Talbot. J., 'Latin Poetry', in P. France and K. Haynes (eds.), *The Oxford History of Literary Translation in English*. Volume 4: *1790–1900* (Oxford: Oxford University Press, 2006), 188–99.

Further Reading in Oxford World's Classics

Catullus, *The Complete Poems*, trans. and ed. Guy Lee.

Horace, *Satires and Epistles*, trans. John Davie, ed. Robert Cowan.

Juvenal, *The Satires*, trans. Niall Rudd, ed. William Barr.

Ovid, *The Love Poems*, trans. A. D. Melville, ed. E. J. Kenney.

Ovid, *Metamorphoses*, trans. A. D. Melville, ed. E. J. Kenney.

CHRONOLOGY

Epigrams of related interest are given in brackets. All dates are AD.

38–41	Birth of Martial in Bilbilis, Spain.
41	Assassination of Caligula; succeeded as emperor by Claudius.
43	Invasion of Britain (11.3, 53).
54	Death of Claudius; succeeded by Nero.
50s–60s	Lucillius and Nicarchus, epigrams.
early 60s	Persius, *Satires* (4.29).
mid-60s	Martial arrives in Rome.
64	Great Fire of Rome, raging for six days and causing wide-scale damage.
65	Pisonian conspiracy against Nero. Seneca and Lucan commit suicide (4.40).
66–74	First Jewish Revolt against Roman rule in Judaea, put down by Vespasian and his son Titus.
68	Revolt of Galba; Nero commits suicide and Galba declares himself emperor.
69	Civil war: 'Year of the Four Emperors'—Galba, Otha, Vitellius, and Vespasian.
79	Death of Vespasian; succeeded by Titus. Eruption of Vesuvius (4.44).
80	*Liber Spectaculorum* (*Book of Shows*). Opening of the Colosseum; fire in Rome (5.7).
81	Death of Titus, succeeded by Domitian.
83	Domitian takes the title 'Germanicus' (8. Preface; Martial frequently compliments Domitian throughout his reign, e.g. 6.4, 75, 8.32, 8.36, 9.66).
84–5	*Xenia* (*Party Favours*) and *Apophoreta* (*Doggy-bags*).
85	Domitian appointed Censor for life (1.4).
85–6	First phase of the Dacian conflict, between Rome and the Dacian kingdom; death of the Roman general Fuscus (6.76).
86	*Epigrams*, Book 1. Domitian revives the Capitoline Games (4.1, 9.40).

86–7   *Epigrams*, Book 2.

87   *Epigrams*, Book 3.

88   Domitian celebrates the Secular Games, involving sacrifices
            and theatrical performances (4.1).

89   *Epigrams*, Book 4. Second phase of the Dacian conflict;
            Domitian granted title 'Dacicus' (7.5-8). Statius begins the
            Silvae.

89–90   *Epigrams*, Book 5.

90–2   *Epigrams*, Book 6.

92   *Epigrams*, Book 7. Third phase of the Dacian conflict; Domitian
            defeats Dacia and its Suebian and Sarmatian allies (7.6).

94   *Epigrams*, Book 8.

94–5   *Epigrams*, Book 9.

95   *Epigrams*, Book 10 (first edition).

96   *Epigrams*, Book 11. Domitian assassinated; *damnatio memoriae*
            decreed by the Senate, to erase Domitian from the records.
            Nerva succeeds as emperor.

98   *Epigrams*, Book 10 (second edition). Martial retires to Bilbilis.
            Death of Nerva; succeeded by Trajan. Silius Italicus publishes
            Punica (4.14).

100–10   Juvenal begins his *Satires*.

101–2   *Epigrams*, Book 12.

101–5   Death of Martial.

EPIGRAMS

LIBER SPECTACULORUM

1

Barbara pyramidum sileat miracula Memphis,
    Assyrius iactet nec Babylona labor;
nec Triuiae templo molles laudentur Iones,
    dissimulet Delon cornibus ara frequens,
aere nec uacuo pendentia Mausolea
    laudibus immodicis Cares in astra ferant.
omnis Caesareo cedit labor Amphitheatro,
    unum pro cunctis fama loquetur opus.

2

Hic ubi sidereus propius uidet astra Colossus
    et crescunt media pegmata celsa uia,
inuidiosa feri radiabant atria regis
    unaque iam tota stabat in urbe domus.
hic ubi conspicui uenerabilis Amphitheatri
    erigitur moles, stagna Neronis erant.
hic ubi miramur uelocia munera thermas,
    abstulerat miseris tecta superbus ager.
Claudia diffusas ubi porticus explicat umbras,
    ultima pars aulae deficientis erat.
reddita Roma sibi est et sunt te praeside, Caesar,
    deliciae populi, quae fuerant domini.

3

Quae tam seposita est, quae gens tam barbara, Caesar,
    ex qua spectator non sit in urbe tua?
uenit ab Orpheo cultor Rhodopeius Haemo,
    uenit et epoto Sarmata pastus equo,
et qui prima bibit deprensi flumina Nili,
    et quem supremae Tethyos unda ferit;
festinauit Arabs, festinauere Sabaei,

BOOK OF SHOWS

I

Let savage Memphis speak not of the Wonders* that are her Pyramids; let Assyrian labour glory not in its Babylon; let the soft Ionians win no praise for their Temple of the Crossroads Goddess;* let the close-packed altar of antlers lure no crowds to Delos;* let not the Carians' immoderate praises elevate their Mausoleum, swaying in empty air, unto the stars. Each labour resigns its title in favour of the Amphitheatre of the Caesars, and Fame shall speak of one marvel in place of all.

2

Here, where the Colossus of the Sun* views the stars close at hand and towering cranes rise up in mid-street, the hateful halls of a bestial king once dazzled, when in all Rome stood just one house. Here, where the spectacular Amphitheatre's hallowed bulk is being raised up, was Nero's lake. Here, where we marvel at the baths—gifts to the people,* swift in coming—a regal estate had robbed the poor of their homes. Where the Claudian Portico spreads out generous shade, ended the palace's most distant wing. Rome is given back to herself, Caesar, and under your guardianship her former master's pleasures belong to her people.

3

What tribe is so remote, so savage, Caesar, that it sends no sightseer to your city? A Rhodopean field-tiller has come, from Orpheus' Haemus;* a Sarmatian* has come, who subsists by quaffing horse-blood; one who drinks from the stream where the Nile is first discerned, and one on whom crashes the wave of farthest Tethys.* An Arab has rushed here, the Sabaeans too, and here Cilicians have been drenched in their native mists.* Sygambrians have come, with their hair curled

et Cilices nimbis hic maduere suis.
crinibus in nodum tortis uenere Sygambri,
    atque aliter tortis crinibus Aethiopes.
uox diuersa sonat populorum, tum tamen una est,
    cum uerus patriae diceris esse pater.

6 (5)

Iunctam Pasiphaen Dictaeo credite tauro:
    uidimus, accepit fabula prisca fidem.
nec se miretur, Caesar, longaeua uetustas:
    quidquid fama canit, praestat harena tibi.

8

Prostratum uasta Nemees in ualle leonem
    nobile et Herculeum fama canebat opus.
prisca fides taceat: nam post tua munera, Caesar,
    hoc iam feminea Marte fatemur agi.

9 (7)

Qualiter in Scythica religatus rupe Prometheus
    adsiduam nimio pectore pauit auem,
nuda Caledonia sic uiscera praebuit urso
    non falsa pendens in cruce Laureolus.
uiuebant laceri membris stillantibus artus
    inque omni nusquam corpore corpus erat.
denique supplicium <dignum tulit: ille parentis>
    uel domini iugulum foderat ense nocens,
templa uel arcano demens spoliauerat auro,
    subdiderat saeuas uel tibi, Roma, faces.
uicerat antiquae sceleratus crimina famae,
    in quo, quae fuerat fabula, poena fuit.

12 (10)

Laeserat ingrato leo perfidus ore magistrum,
    ausus tam notas contemerare manus;

into a knot, and Ethiopians with their hair curled differently. The voice of the peoples sounds diverse, and yet it speaks as one, when you are hailed true Father of the Fatherland.

6 (5)

Believe that Pasiphae was coupled with the Dictaean bull; we have seen it, the ancient tale* has now been proved. Nor, Caesar, should fusty antiquity give itself airs: whatever Fame sings of, the arena tenders to you.

8

Highborn Fame formerly sang of the lion brought down in Nemea's broad valley, a deed of Hercules. Let ancient proof fall silent: for after your shows, Caesar, we have now seen these things achieved at a woman's hand.*

9 (7)

Just as Prometheus, bound fast to the Scythian cliff, nourished the constant bird with a glut of his stomach, just so did Laureolus, hanging from a cross that was no stage-prop, offer up his uncovered entrails to a Caledonian bear.* His torn joints carried on living as his limbs dripped, and in all his flesh, no flesh remained. At long last he met the punishment he deserved: he was a thug who'd thrust a sword through his father's or his master's throat, or a lunatic who'd stripped a temple of its hidden gold or set barbarous torches to you, O Rome. This wicked man had outstripped the crimes of ancient fame, and in him, what had been a tale became an expiation.

12 (10)

A malcontent lion had wounded its master with ungrateful mouth, and dared to defile the hands it knew so well; but it paid the penalty

sed dignas tanto persoluit crimine poenas,
et qui non tulerat uerbera, tela tulit.
quos decet esse hominum tali sub principe mores,
qui iubet ingenium mitius esse feris!

15 (13)

Icta graui telo confossaque uulnere mater
sus pariter uitam perdidit atque dedit.
o quam certa fuit librato dextera ferro!
hanc ego Lucinae credo fuisse manum.
experta est numen moriens utriusque Dianae,
quaque soluta parens quaque perempta fera est.

20 (17)

Quod pius et supplex elephas te, Caesar, adorat
hic modo qui tauro tam metuendus erat,
non facit hoc iussus, nulloque docente magistro,
crede mihi, nostrum sentit et ille deum.

24 (21)

Quidquid in Orpheo Rhodope spectasse theatro
dicitur, exhibuit, Caesar, harena tibi.
repserunt scopuli mirandaque silua cucurrit,
quale fuisse nemus creditur Hesperidum.
adfuit immixtum pecori genus omne ferarum
et supra uatem multa auis,
ipse sed ingrato iacuit laceratus ab urso.
haec tantum res est facta παρ' ἱστορίαν.

27 (24)

Si quis ades longis serus spectator ab oris,
cui lux prima sacri muneris ista fuit,
ne te decipiat ratibus naualis Enyo
et par unda fretis: hic modo terra fuit.
non credis? specta, dum lassant aequora Martem:
parua mora est, dices 'Hic modo pontus erat.'

it deserved for such a crime, and the beast that had not tolerated blows now bore javelins. What morals ought men adopt under such a leader,* at whose command wild beasts grow tamer?

15 (13)

Struck by a weighty javelin and pierced through by her wound, a mother boar gave up life and gave life in equal degree. How sure was the hand when it balanced the steel! This hand I believe belonged to Lucina. In death, she proved the power of both Dianas: by one brought to term as a mother, by the other brought down as a beast.

20 (17)

That the pious elephant* kneels and reveres you, Caesar, that of late filled the bull with dread—he does not do it under compulsion, nor at any trainer's coaching. Trust me, he is moved by the same divinity as are we.

24 (21)

Whatever sights Rhodope is said to have seen in Orpheus' theatre,* the arena, Caesar, has displayed for you. Rocky crags have skittered and a miraculous forest has galloped by, just like the legendary grove of the Hesperides. Every kind of wild beast was there, mingled with the tame, and above the poet-seer circled many a bird. But he himself lay dead, mangled by a malcontent bear. Only this one deed went against the script.*

27 (24)

If you have come here from far-off shores, a late-arriving sightseer, and this has been your first day at the sacred Games, let this sea-battle not fool you with its ships, nor the water churning like straits; lately this was dry land. You don't trust me? Keep watching, until the waters calm the God of War: a short delay, and you'll be saying: 'Lately this was sea.'

30 (26)

Lusit Nereidum docilis chorus aequore toto
     et uario faciles ordine pinxit aquas.
 fuscina dente minax recto fuit, ancora curuo:
     credidimus remum credidimusque ratem,
 et gratum nautis sidus fulgere Laconum
     lataque perspicuo uela tumere sinu.
 quis tantas liquidis artes inuenit in undis?
     aut docuit lusus hos Thetis aut didicit.

32 (28; 27)

Saecula Carpophorum, Caesar, si prisca tulissent,
     non Porthaoniam barbara terra feram,
 non Marathon taurum, Nemee frondosa leonem,
     Arcas Maenalium non timuisset aprum.
 hoc armante manus hydrae mors una fuisset,
     huic percussa foret tota Chimaera semel.
 igniferos possit sine Colchide iungere tauros,
     possit utramque feram uincere Pasiphaes.
 si uetus aequorei reuocetur fabula monstri,
     Hesionen soluet solus et Andromedan.
 Herculeae laudis numeretur gloria: plus est
     bis denas pariter perdomuisse feras.

34 (30; 28)

Augusti labor hic fuerat committere classes
     et freta nauali sollicitare tuba.
 Caesaris haec nostri pars est quota? uidit in undis
     et Thetis ignotas et Galatea feras;
 uidit in aequoreo feruentes puluere currus
     et domini Triton isse putauit equos:
 dumque parat saeuis ratibus fera proelia Nereus,
     horruit in liquidis ire pedestris aquis.
 quidquid et in Circo spectatur et Amphitheatro,
     id diues, Caesar, praestitit unda tibi.
 Fucinus et diri taceantur stagna Neronis:
     hanc norint unam saecula naumachiam.

30 (26)

A well-coached team of Nereids frisked across the calm surface, and their shifting formation gave colour to the waters. The trident* threatened us with straight tooth, the anchor with curved; a mast, a ship, we took for real; the star of the Spartan boys,* the sailors' friend, seemed really to shine, and sails to swell in a gauzy curve. Who devised such techniques amid the limpid waters? Either Thetis* taught him these ploys, or she was his pupil.

32 (28; 27)

If those primordial eons, Caesar, had brought forth a Carpophorus, the untamed Earth would not have feared Porthaon's beast,* nor Marathon her Bull, leafy Nemea her Lion, nor Arcadia the Macnalian Boar. If *he* had armed for the brawl, the Hydra would have died but once, and the whole Chimaera would have taken a single blow. *He* could yoke the fire-bearing bulls without the Colchian woman's aid, *he* could conquer both of Pasiphae's beasts.* If the old legend of sea-monsters were brought back to life, *he* would free Hesione and Andromeda* all by himself. Let the glory of Herculean honours be tallied: to have vanquished a score of beasts at once counts for more.

34 (30; 28)

It was once Augustus' labour to command the clash of fleets, and stir the straits with the trumpet of sea-battle.* Of our own Caesar, how small a part is this! Thetis, and Galatea too, saw in the waters beasts formerly unknown; Triton saw chariots seething in the water's dust and reckoned his own lord's horses had passed by; as Nereus plotted wild mêlées for ferocious ships, he was shocked to find himself walking on foot amid the limpid waters. Whatever sights are seen in the Circus and Amphitheatre alike, Caesar, the abundant water has displayed for you. Let Fucinus and dread Nero fall silent; let the eons know this sea-battle alone.

LIBER I

Spero me secutum in libellis meis tale temperamentum ut de illis
queri non possit quisquis de se bene senserit, cum salua infirmarum
quoque personarum reuerentia ludant; quae adeo antiquis auctori-
bus defuit ut nominibus non tantum ueris abusi sint, sed et magnis.
mihi fama uilius constet et probetur in me nouissimum ingenium.
absit a iocorum nostrorum simplicitate malignus interpres nec epi-
grammata mea inscribat: improbe facit qui in alieno libro ingeniosus
est. lasciuam uerborum ueritatem, id est epigrammaton linguam,
excusarem, si meum esset exemplum: sic scribit Catullus, sic Mar-
sus, sic Pedo, sic Gaetulicus, sic quicumque perlegitur. si quis tamen
tam ambitiose tristis est ut apud illum in nulla pagina latine loqui
fas sit, potest epistola uel potius titulo contentus esse. epigrammata
illis scribuntur qui solent spectare Florales. non intret Cato theatrum
meum, aut si intrauerit, spectet.

uideor mihi meo iure facturus si epistolam uersibus clusero:

> Nosses iocosae dulce cum sacrum Florae
> festosque lusus et licentiam uulgi,
> cur in theatrum, Cato seuere, uenisti?
> an ideo tantum ueneras, ut exires?

I

> Hic est quem legis ille, quem requiris,
> toto notus in orbe Martialis
> argutis epigrammaton libellis:
> cui, lector studiose, quod dedisti
> uiuenti decus atque sentienti,
> rari post cineres habent poetae.

BOOK 1

[*Epistolary Preface*] I hope the formula I've aimed at in my little books is such that no self-respecting person has grounds to complain about them. Even when they joke about the basest of characters, they never lose their sense of decorum—something so lacking in writers of old that they exploited not just real names, but great ones at that. I aim to hold fame cheap; when people praise me, the last thing they should say is, 'He's clever'. I hope the malignant critic keeps away from the artless candour of my jokes and doesn't assign headings* to my epigrams; it's criminal to parade your cleverness in someone else's book.

If it was up to me, I would dispense with naughty words that are true to life—that is to say, the natural idiom of epigrams; but that's how Catullus writes, and Marsus, and Pedo, and Gaetulicus, and everyone who gets read all the way through. However, if there's anyone with such a professionally long face that nobody's book is allowed to speak plain Latin when he's around, he may content himself with my letter, or even better, my title. Epigrams are written for people who enjoy being spectators at Flora's Games. Cato can stay out* of this theatre of mine—or he can come in and enjoy the show.

I think I'm within my rights if I close my letter with a poem:

Since you knew about the pleasurable rite of playful Flora, the holiday high-jinks when the crowd sheds its inhibitions, why did you come to the show, censorious Cato? Or did you only make an entrance so that you could storm out again?

I

The man you read, the man you want—here he is: *Martial*, famous all round the world for his gossipy little books of epigrams. While he still lives and breathes, Avid Fan, you have conferred on him distinction such as few poets achieve when dead and gone.

2

Qui tecum cupis esse meos ubicumque libellos
  et comites longae quaeris habere uiae,
hos eme, quos artat breuibus membrana tabellis:
  scrinia da magnis, me manus una capit.
ne tamen ignores ubi sim uenalis et erres
  urbe uagus tota, me duce certus eris:
libertum docti Lucensis quaere Secundum
  limina post Pacis Palladiumque forum.

4

Contigeris nostros, Caesar, si forte libellos,
  terrarum dominum pone supercilium.
consueuere iocos uestri quoque ferre triumphi,
  materiam dictis nec pudet esse ducem.
qua Thymelen spectas derisoremque Latinum,
  illa fronte precor carmina nostras legas.
innocuos censura potest permittere lusus:
  lasciua est nobis pagina, uita proba.

6

Aetherias aquila puerum portante per auras
  illaesum timidis unguibus haesit onus:
nunc sua Caesareos exorat praeda leones
  tutus et ingenti ludit in ore lepus.
quae maiora putas miracula? summus utrisque
  auctor adest: haec sunt Caesaris, illa Iouis.

7

Stellae delicium mei columba,
  Verona licet audiente dicam,
uicit, Maxime, passerem Catulli.
tanto Stella meus tuo Catullo
quanto passere maior est columba.

2

Want my little books with you all the time? Fancy them as travelling-companions on a long trip? Then purchase *these* ones: parchment binds them between narrow boards.* Boxed sets are for the Greats; me, you can hold in one hand. But to be sure you know where I'm to be found for sale and don't wander lost all over the city, I'll steer you right: seek out Secundus, freedman of erudite Lucensis, past the threshold of Peace and the Forum of Pallas.*

4

If you should happen to pick up my little books, Caesar, lay aside that stern look that masters the world. Taking a joke is the done thing at triumphs—your own included—and there's no shame in a Commander generating punch-lines. That face you wear when you're watching Thymele and Latinus* the stand-up comic? Wear it, please, as you read these poems of mine. As Censor,* you can exercise discretion: my jokes hurt no one; let them be. My page may be dirty, but my life is clean.*

6

Though the eagle carried the boy through the airy vault of the heavens,* the nervous grasp of its talons did not harm him; and now the entreaties of their prey persuade Caesar's lions to let the hare play safely in their huge maws. Which of these wonders do you think the greater? An almighty author inaugurates each: the latter is Caesar's work, the former, Jupiter's.

7

I tell you, Maximus—and I don't care if Verona hears it—my Stella's darling *Dove* sees off Catullus' *Sparrow*.* My Stella is as much better than that Catullus of yours as a dove is bigger than a sparrow.

16

Sunt bona, sunt quaedam mediocria, sunt mala plura
    quae legis hic: aliter non fit, Auite, liber.

22

Quid nunc saeua fugis placidi, lepus, ora leonis?
    frangere tam paruas non didicere feras.
seruantur magnis isti ceruicibus ungues
    nec gaudet tenui sanguine tanta sitis.
praeda canum lepus est, uastos non implet hiatus:
    non timeat Dacus Caesaris arma puer.

25

Ede tuos tandem populo, Faustine, libellos
    et cultum docto pectore profer opus,
quod nec Cecropiae damnent Pandionis arces
    nec sileant nostri praetereantque senes.
ante fores stantem dubitas admittere Famam
    teque piget curae praemia ferre tuae?
post te uicturae per te quoque uiuere chartae
    incipiant: cineri gloria sera uenit.

27

Hesterna tibi nocte dixeramus,
quincunces puto post decem peractos,
cenares hodie, Procille, mecum.
tu factam tibi rem statim putasti
et non sobria uerba subnotasti
exemplo nimium periculoso:
μισῶ μνάμονα συμπόταν, Procille.

30

Chirurgus fuerat, nunc est uispillo Diaulus:
    coepit quo poterat clinicus esse modo.

16

You're reading good poems here, Avitus—and a few that are so-so, and a lot that are bad; a book doesn't happen any other way.

22

Why, hare, do you now run away from the dire maws of the docile lions? They never learned to munch such tiny game. Those claws of theirs are kept for massive necks, nor can a mere trickle of blood sate a thirst as strong as theirs. A hare is dogs' prey, it does not make a mouthful for a monster; a Dacian boy would not fear Caesar's arms.*

25

Publish your little books at long last, Faustinus, and let the public see the masterpiece you've been mulling over so donnishly. Pandion's Cecropian citadel* would not cast it out, nor our own elders pass it over in silence. Do you hesitate to let Fame in when she's standing on your doorstep? Don't you want to collect the prize you've worked so hard for? Those pages that are destined to live on after you, should also begin living *through* you. The glory that comes when you are dead and gone, comes too late.*

27

Last night, Procillus, after the wine ladle had gone around I think fifty times, I said you should come for dinner at mine today. Right off the mark you decided it was a done deal, and you jotted down my less-than-sober words. A transcript is a very dangerous thing: I loathe, Procillus, a recollective guest.*

30

Diaulus used to be a surgeon, now he's a bargain-rate undertaker.* He's started making house-calls that put his skills to work.

34

Incustoditis et apertis, Lesbia, semper
 liminibus peccas nec tua furta tegis,
et plus spectator quam te delectat adulter
 nec sunt grata tibi gaudia si qua latent.
at meretrix abigit testem ueloque seraque
 raraque Submemmi fornice rima patet.
a Chione saltem uel ab Iade disce pudorem:
 abscondunt spurcas et monumenta lupas.
numquid dura tibi nimium censura uidetur?
 deprendi ueto te, Lesbia, non futui.

38

Quem recitas meus est, o Fidentine, libellus:
 sed male cum recitas, incipit esse tuus.

44

Lasciuos leporum cursus lususque leonum
 quod maior nobis charta minorque gerit
et bis idem facimus, nimium si, Stella, uidetur
 hoc tibi, bis leporem tu quoque pone mihi.

47

Nuper erat medicus, nunc est uispillo Diaulus:
 quod uispillo facit, fecerat et medicus.

52

Commendo tibi, Quintiane, nostros—
 nostros dicere si tamen libellos
possum, quos recitat tuus poeta:
 si de seruitio graui queruntur,
adsertor uenias satisque praestes,
 et, cum se dominum uocabit ille,
dicas esse meos manuque missos.
 hoc si terque quaterque clamitaris,
impones plagiario pudorem.

34

Always with the doors open and no lookout posted, Lesbia:* that's
how you sin. You don't hide your stolen pleasures; you enjoy an audi-
ence more than you do an illicit lover, and your orgasms are incom-
plete unless they're attracting attention. A real whore uses a curtain
and a bolt to shoo off the voyeurs; Summemmius' brothel doesn't
have many peepholes. If you've nothing else to learn from Chione*
and Ias, learn discretion; for *professional* cock-sucking bitches,* even
tombs can lend privacy. Do you feel my ruling is too harsh? I'm ban-
ning you from getting caught, Lesbia, not getting fucked.

38

That little book you're reciting is one of mine, Fidentinus; but you're
reciting it so badly, it's turning into one of yours.

44

My page, both large and small,* brings you frolicking hares and play-
ful lions.* If it's too much for you that I do the same thing twice,
Stella, you can always dish up hare for me twice at dinner.

47

Until recently Diaulus was a doctor, now he's a bargain-rate under-
taker; what he does as an undertaker, he used to do as a doctor.

52

I entrust my little books to your care,* Quintianus—if I can still
call them mine, that your pet poet keeps reciting. If they wail about
their intolerable servitude, please be their public defender and stand
bail for them; and, when he declares himself their master, please
testify that they were mine and I have set them free. Proclaim this
loudly three or four times and you'll shame the plagiarist* into keep-
ing quiet.

53

Vna est in nostris tua, Fidentine, libellis
pagina, sed certa domini signata figura,
quae tua traducit manifesto carmina furto.
sic interpositus uillo contaminat uncto
urbica Lingonicus Tyrianthina bardocucullus,
sic Arrentinae uiolant crystallina testae,
sic niger in ripis errat cum forte Caystri,
inter Ledaeos ridetur coruus olores,
sic ubi multisona feruet sacer Atthide lucus,
improba Cecropias offendit pica querelas.
indice non opus est nostris nec iudice libris:
stat contra dicitque tibi tua pagina, 'Fur es'.

61

Verona docti syllabas amat uatis,
    Marone felix Mantua est,
censetur Aponi Liuio suo tellus
    Stellaque nec Flacco minus,
Apollodoro plaudit imbrifer Nilus,
    Nasone Paeligni sonant,
duosque Senecas unicumque Lucanum
    facunda loquitur Corduba,
gaudent iocosae Canio suo Gades,
    Emerita Deciano meo:
te, Liciniane, gloriabitur nostra
    nec me tacebit Bilbilis.

70

Vade salutatum pro me, liber: ire iuberis
    ad Proculi nitidos, officiose, lares.
quaeris iter? dicam. uicinum Castora canae
    transibis Vestae uirgineamque domum;
inde sacro ueneranda petes Palatia cliuo,
    plurima qua summi fulget imago ducis.
nec te detineat miri radiata colossi
    quae Rhodium moles uincere gaudet opus.

53

In my little books, Fidentinus, there's just one page that's your own—
but one that's branded with the unmistakable style of its master, which
exposes your poems to public disgrace as blatant plagiarism. A Lin-
gonian kaftan* hung alongside double-dyed city purples dirties them
with its greasy tufts—just like this; if a black raven promenades along
the banks of the Cayster amidst Leda's swans it attracts mockery—
just like this; when a sacred grove swarms with Philomela's birds,*
the harmonious nightingales, the dastardly magpie clashes with their
Cecropian lullabies—just like this. My books have no need of an in-
former or a judge: your own page takes the stand against you and tells
you, 'You're a thief'.

61

Verona loves its learned poet's hendecasyllables; Mantua is blessed
with Maro;* Aponus' land is rated for its Livy—and no less for
Stella* and Flaccus; the brimming Nile applauds Apollodorus; the
Paelignians* chant Naso's name; the two Senecas and the one and
only Lucan are the talk of eloquent Cordoba; gay Cadiz* rejoices in
its Canius, and Emerita in my Decianus; and our own Bilbilis will
preen itself on you, Licinianus. Nor will it be silent about me.

70

Go stand in for me at the morning greeting, book: that's an order.
Head for the gleaming house of Proculus and fulfil my obligations as
his client. You want to know the way, I'll tell you. Go past the temple
of Castor that's next door to grey-haired Vesta and the house of the
Virgins; from there, make for the holy Palatine by way of the Sacred
Way, where glistens many a portrait of our Commander-in-Chief.
And please don't linger at the sun-rayed Colossus, that gigantic won-
der which delights in surpassing the masterwork at Rhodes. Veer off

flecte uias hac qua madidi sunt tecta Lyaei
et Cybeles picto stat Corybante tholus.
protinus a laeua clari tibi fronte Penates
atriaque excelsae sunt adeunda domus.
hanc pete: ne metuas fastus limenque superbum:
nulla magis toto ianua poste patet,
nec propior quam Phoebus amat doctaeque sorores.
si dicet 'Quare non tamen ipse uenit?',
sic licet excuses: 'Quia qualiacumque leguntur
ista, salutator scribere non potuit.'

72

Nostris uersibus esse te poetam,
Fidentine, putas cupisque credi?
sic dentata sibi uidetur Aegle
emptis ossibus Indicoque cornu;
sic quae nigrior est cadente moro,
cerussata sibi placet Lycoris.
hac et tu ratione qua poeta es,
caluus cum fueris, eris comatus.

77

Pulchre ualet Charinus et tamen pallet.
parce bibit Charinus et tamen pallet.
bene concoquit Charinus et tamen pallet.
sole utitur Charinus et tamen pallet.
tingit cutem Charinus et tamen pallet.
cunnum Charinus lingit et tamen pallet.

101

Illa manus quondam studiorum fida meorum
et felix domino notaque Caesaribus,
destituit primos uiridis Demetrius annos:
quarta tribus lustris addita messis erat.
ne tamen ad Stygias famulus descenderet umbras,
ureret implicitum cum scelerata lues,

at the spot where that old soak Bacchus has his dwelling, and where
Cybele's rotunda stands with its painted Corybant.*

Immediately on the left is a house with a noble frontage: the recep-
tion halls of this exalted home are where you're bound. Make for this
house, and you needn't fear arrogance and a scornful threshold; no
other door throws itself more widely open, nor is there another that
Phoebus and the learned sisters* love better. If it asks, 'But why doesn't
he come in person?', you may justify my absence as follows: 'Because
no matter how readable or unreadable these poems may be, a client
who showed up for you in the morning could never have written them.'

72

Do you tell yourself you're a poet, Fidentinus? Do you want people
to think it's true, when the lines you're using are mine? Just so does
Aegle reckon she has teeth, because she's bought ones made of bone
and Indian ivory; and Lycoris, who's blacker than a windfall mulberry,*
loves how she looks in white lead. Just so, and by the same rationale that
makes you a poet, you'll have a full head of hair when you go bald.

77

Charinus is in great shape—and still he's pale.
Charinus watches his drinking—and still he's pale.
Charinus's digestion is good—and still he's pale.
Charinus gets enough sun—and he's still pale.
Charinus wears a fake tan—and still he's pale.
Charinus licks cunt—and still he's pale.*

101

In times past the trusted agent of my studies, a blessing to his owner
and familiar to the Caesars, Demetrius was young when he forsook
his salad days; a fourth harvest had just been added to three five-year
spans. But I didn't want him to go down to the darkness of Styx still
a servant. As the vicious plague held him in its burning grasp, I took
care of it: I remitted all right of ownership. He should have got better.

cauimus et domini ius omne remisimus aegro:
   munere dignus erat conualuisse meo.
sensit deficiens sua praemia meque patronum
   dixit ad infernas liber iturus aquas.

104

Picto quod iuga deligata collo
pardus sustinet improbaeque tigres
indulgent patientiam flagello,
mordent aurea quod lupata cerui,
quod frenis Libyci domantur ursi
et, quantum Calydon tulisse fertur,
paret purpureis aper capistris,
turpes esseda quod trahunt uisontes
et molles dare iussa quod choreas
nigro belua non negat magistro:
quis spectacula non putet deorum?
haec transit tamen, ut minora, quisquis
uenatus humiles uidet leonum,
quos uelox leporum timor fatigat.
dimittunt, repetunt, amantque captos,
et securior est in ore praeda,
laxos cui dare peruiosque rictus
gaudent et timidos tenere dentes,
mollem frangere dum pudet rapinam,
stratis cum modo uenerint iuuencis.
haec clementia non paratur arte,
sed norunt cui seruiant leones.

107

Saepe mihi dicis, Luci carissime Iuli,
   'Scribe aliquid magnum: desidiosus homo es.'
otia da nobis, sed qualia fecerat olim
   Maecenas Flacco Vergilioque suo:
condere uicturas temptem per saecula curas
   et nomen flammis eripuisse meum.
in steriles nolunt campos iuga ferre iuuenci:
   pingue solum lassat, sed iuuat ipse labor.

He deserved to enjoy my gift to him. As he faded, he knew what he had earned: he called me 'patron'. He was free. And then he was gone, down to the river of the dead.

104

That the leopard endures a yoke hitched to its spotted neck, and monstrous tigers concede submission to the whip; that stags bite on toothed bits, fashioned in gold; that Libyan bears are broken to the reins, and a boar, big as Calydon's in legend,* yields to a purple halter; that ugly bison haul war-chariots, and that the behemoth, commanded to show off his graceful dancing, does not disappoint his black trainer: who would not think these are the gods' own shows?

But whoever sees the lions humbled in their hunting, worn out by the swift skittishness of the hares, skims those other sights and reckons them sideshows. They let them go, they chase them down again, and dote upon them once caught; their prey is safer in their mouths than out. The lions enjoy holding their jaws agape, anxiously restraining their bite so the hares can hop in and out. To munch such thin pickings would embarrass them, since they have just come from bringing down bullocks. This forbearance is not a trick they have been taught; the lions know whom they serve.

107

You often tell me, my dearest Lucius Julius: 'Write something big; you're such a slacker.' Well, give me leisure—the kind that Maecenas used to lay on for his Flaccus and his Virgil*—and I'll try to compose works that will live on through the centuries, and to rescue my name from the bonfire. Oxen won't wear the yoke on barren fields; a rich soil wearies them, but that toil brings joy.

109

Issa est passere nequior Catulli,
Issa est purior osculo columbae,
Issa est blandior omnibus puellis,
Issa est carior Indicis lapillis,
Issa est deliciae catella Publi.
hanc tu, si queritur, loqui putabis;
sentit tristitiamque gaudiumque.
collo nixa cubat capitque somnos,
ut suspiria nulla sentiantur;
et desiderio coacta uentris
gutta pallia non fefellit ulla,
sed blando pede suscitat toroque
deponi monet et rogat leuari.
castae tantus inest pudor catellae,
ignorat Venerem; nec inuenimus
dignum tam tenera uirum puella.
hanc ne lux rapiat suprema totam,
picta Publius exprimit tabella,
in qua tam similem uidebis Issam,
ut sit tam similis sibi nec ipsa.
Issam denique pone cum tabella:
aut utramque putabis esse ueram,
aut utramque putabis esse pictam.

110

Scribere me quereris, Velox, epigrammata longa.
ipse nihil scribis: tu breuiora facis?

113

Quaecumque lusi iuuenis et puer quondam
apinasque nostras, quas nec ipse iam noui,
male collocare si bonas uoles horas
et inuidebis otio tuo, lector,
a Valeriano Pollio petes Quinto,
per quem perire non licet meis nugis.

109

Issa is saucier than Catullus's *Sparrow*,
Issa is purer than a *Dove*'s kiss,
Issa is smoother-tongued than all the girls,
Issa is dearer than pearls from India,
Issa is Publius' darling . . . puppy.

If she whimpers, you'd think she was talking; she can tell when people
are sad or happy. She stretches with her head on his neck and has her
nap, and you can't feel her sighing little breaths; and when she needs
to give in to her tummy's demands not a single dribble dismays the
bedsheets—instead she pokes him awake with a winsome paw, lets
him know to set her down, and asks to be picked up when she's done.
This chaste puppy is so naturally modest, she knows not the Goddess
of Love, and we can find no husband worthy of such a tender maid.
That the end of her days may not rob him of her completely, Publius
is painting her portrait in miniature;* in it you will see a likeness of
Issa more like to her than she is herself. Indeed, put Issa next to the
picture and either:

1. you'll think them both real, or
2. you'll think them both paintings.

110

Swifty,* you moan that I write long epigrams. You aren't writing any-
thing yourself; is that you making shorter ones?

113

All the poems I used to scribble as a young man, a boy even—the hick
stuff,* the junk, the ones I don't even recognize these days—if you're
set on turning good hours into a bad investment and carry a grudge
against your own leisure time, reader, you can get them from Valeri-
anus Pollius Quintus, who simply will not let my juvenilia die.

114

Hos tibi uicinos, Faustine, Telesphorus hortos
Faenius et breue rus udaque prata tenet.
condidit hic natae cineres nomenque sacrauit
quod legis, Antullae; dignior ipse legi.
ad Stygias aequum fuerat pater isset ut umbras:
quod quia non licuit, uiuat, ut ossa colat.

117

Occurris quotiens, Luperce, nobis,
'Vis mittam puerum' subinde dicis,
'cui tradas epigrammaton libellum,
lectum quem tibi protinus remittam?'
non est quod puerum, Luperce, uexes.
longum est, si uelit ad Pirum uenire,
et scalis habito tribus, sed altis.
quod quaeris propius petas licebit.
Argi nempe soles subire Letum:
contra Caesaris est forum taberna
scriptis postibus hinc et inde totis,
omnis ut cito perlegas poetas:
illinc me pete. †nec† roges Atrectum—
hoc nomen dominus gerit tabernae—
de primo dabit alteroue nido
rasum pumice purpuraque cultum
denaris tibi quinque Martialem.
'Tanti non es' ais? sapis, Luperce.

118

Cui legisse satis non est epigrammata centum,
nil illi satis est, Caediciane, mali.

114

The suburban villa next door to you, Faustinus, with its little farm and water-meadows, is Faenius Telesphorus' place. Here he interred the ashes of his daughter and declared sacred the name you read,* Antulla's. He deserved that his own name should be there in her stead. It would have been natural justice if the father had gone to the ghosts along the Styx; since that was not permitted him, may he live, to revere her bones.

117

Every time you run into me, Lupercus, you immediately say: 'How about I send a boy over to pick up one of your little books of epigrams? I'll get it straight back to you once I've read it.' Lupercus, you've no cause to trouble the lad. It's a long way, if he's wanting the Pear Tree,* and I live up three flights of stairs—tall ones. It's alright to look closer to home for what you're after. I'm sure you're always popping down to the Argiletum;* opposite Caesar's Forum there's a shop with its doorposts entirely covered in writing, front and back, so you can quickly skim through all the poets. Look for me there. If you ask for Atrectus*—that's the name the shop's owner bears—then for five denarii, out of the first or second book-case, smoothed down with pumice* and elegant in purple, he'll give you: *Martial.* 'You're not worth that,' you say? Lupercus, you're wising up.

118

The person who reads a hundred epigrams and still wants more, Caedicianus—now *that's* a glutton for punishment.

LIBER II

I

Ter centena quidem poteras epigrammata ferre,
    sed quis te ferret perlegeretque, liber?
at nunc succincti quae sint bona disce libelli.
    hoc primum est, breuior quod mihi charta perit;
deinde, quod haec una peragit librarius hora,
    nec tantum nugis seruiet ille meis;
tertia res haec est, quod si cui forte legeris,
    sis licet usque malus, non odiosus eris.
te conuiua leget mixto quincunce, sed ante
    incipiat positus quam tepuisse calix.
esse tibi tanta cautus breuitate uideris?
    ei mihi, quam multis sic quoque longus eris!

5

Ne ualeam, si non totis, Deciane, diebus
    et tecum totis noctibus esse uelim.
sed duo sunt quae nos disiungunt milia passum:
    quattuor haec fiunt, cum rediturus eam.
saepe domi non es; cum sis quoque, saepe negaris:
    uel tantum causis uel tibi saepe uacas.
te tamen ut uideam, duo milia non piget ire;
    ut te non uideam, quattuor ire piget.

12

Esse quid hoc dicam quod olent tua basia murram
    quodque tibi est numquam non alienus odor?
hoc mihi suspectum est, quod oles bene, Postume, semper.
    Postume, non bene olet qui bene semper olet.

BOOK 2

I

Sure, you could have borne three hundred epigrams, but then who would bear *you*, book-roll,* and read you from start to finish? It's time you learned what's good about a concise little book. First: I waste less paper. Second: the copyist is done with it in just an hour, so he doesn't have to slave for ages over my trashy poems. The third thing: if you happen to get read to someone, you can be as bad as you like and still won't outstay your welcome. The party-goer will read you when his fifth ladle of wine has been mixed, but before the cup he's put down has started going lukewarm.* Do you think being so short makes you safe? Alas, how many readers will find you long even as you are!

5

I swear on my health, Decianus, that given the choice I'd spend all day and night in your company. But there are two miles keeping us apart; and they become four, when I go only to come back again. Often you're not in—and when you are, your people often tell me you're out; or else you only have time for your cases, or for yourself. I have no problem going two miles to see you, mind; I *do* have a problem going four miles *not* to see you.

12

How am I supposed to call it when your kisses smell of myrrh and you never have an odour that's not splashed on? That you smell good all the time, Postumus,* strikes me as suspect. Postumus, a man who smells good all the time, smells fishy.

23

Non dicam, licet usque me rogetis,
qui sit Postumus in meo libello.
non dicam: quid enim mihi necesse est
has offendere basiationes,
quae se tam bene uindicare possunt?

29

Rufe, uides illum subsellia prima terentem,
    cuius et hinc lucet sardonychata manus
quaeque Tyron totiens epotauere lacernae
    et toga non tactas uincere iussa niues,
cuius olet toto pinguis coma Marcellano
    et splendent uolso bracchia trita pilo,
non hesterna sedet lunata lingula planta,
    coccina non laesum pingit aluta pedem,
et numerosa linunt stellantem splenia frontem.
    ignoras quid sit? splenia tolle, leges.

32

Lis mihi cum Balbo est, tu Balbum offendere non uis,
    Pontice. cum Licino est: hic quoque magnus homo est.
uexat saepe meum Patrobas confinis agellum:
    contra libertum Caesaris ire times.
abnegat et retinet nostrum Laronia seruum:
    respondes 'Orba est, diues, anus, uidua'.
non bene, crede mihi, seruo seruitur amico:
    sit liber, dominus qui uolet esse meus.

37

Quidquid ponitur hinc et inde uerris,
mammas suminis imbricemque porci
communemque duobus attagenam,
mullum dimidium lupumque totum
muraenaeque latus femurque pulli

23

I'm not going to say, no matter how many times you all ask, who 'Postumus' is in my little book. I'm not going to say. What would make me provoke kisses* that can wreak such effective vengeance?

29

Rufus, do you see that man who always gets a front-row seat, whose sardonyx-studded hand sparkles even from here? See his cloaks,* that time and again have drunk vats of Tyrian purple dry; and his toga, which he has commanded must surpass virgin snows? You can smell his pomaded hair right across the Theatre of Marcellus. His exfoliated arms gleam—he's had them plucked—and his shoe with its half-moon badge has a new strap today; his foot gets no blisters, though the carmine kid-leather is staining it with cochineal, and numerous beauty-spots are plastered on his glittering brow. Do you not know what he is? Peel off those plasters and you can read the answer.*

32

I'm suing Balbus, but you don't want to get on Balbus' bad side, Ponticus. I'm suing Licinus too; no, he's an important man as well. My neighbour Patrobas keeps encroaching on my little patch of farm, but you're nervous about proceeding against a freedman of Caesar's. Laronia hangs onto my slave and won't give him back, but 'she's childless, she's rich, she's elderly, she's a widow'.* Believe me, no good comes from offering service to a friend who's servile; the man who wants to be my master, let him first be free.

37

Every dish that comes to table, you sweep them all up, left and right: teats from a sow's udder, pig's ear, a heath-cock meant for two to share, half a mullet and a whole pike, a lamprey fillet, a chicken leg, a wood-pigeon oozing into the couscous it came with. When you've folded them away in a soggy napkin, you pass them to your boy to

stillantemque alica sua palumbum.
haec cum condita sunt madente mappa,
traduntur puero domum ferenda:
nos accumbimus otiosa turba.
ullus si pudor est, repone cenam:
cras te, Caeciliane, non uocaui.

38

Quid mihi reddat ager quaeris, Line, Nomentanus?
    hoc mihi reddit ager: te, Line, non uideo.

48

Coponem laniumque balneumque,
tonsorem tabulamque calculosque
et paucos, sed ut eligam, libellos:
unum non nimium rudem sodalem
et grandem puerum diuque leuem
et caram puero meo puellam:
haec praesta mihi, Rufe, uel Butuntis,
et thermas tibi habe Neronianas.

51

Vnus saepe tibi tota denarius arca
    cum sit et hic culo tritior, Hylle, tuo,
non tamen hunc pistor, non auferet hunc tibi copo,
    sed si quis nimio pene superbus erit.
infelix uenter spectat conuiuia culi,
    et semper miser hic esurit, ille uorat.

53

Vis fieri liber? mentiris, Maxime, non uis:
    sed fieri si uis, hac ratione potes.
liber eris, cenare foris si, Maxime, nolis,
    Veientana tuam si domat uua sitim,

take home;* and all the rest of us just lie there twiddling our thumbs.
If you have any sense of shame, put our dinner back: Caecilianus,
I didn't invite you for tomorrow.

38

You're wondering what the yield is from my farm at Nomentum,
Linus? Here's the yield from my farm: Linus, I don't have to look
at *you*.

48

An innkeeper, a butcher, and a bathhouse; a barber, and a board and
pieces for draughts; just a few books—provided I get to pick them;
a solitary friend who's not a complete bumpkin; a well-hung boy
who'll stay beardless a long while, and a girl dear to that boy of mine.
Set me up with these, Rufus, even in Butuntum,* and you can keep
your Baths of Nero.

51

Although you often have just one denarius in your big strongbox,
Hyllus, and one rubbed smoother than your arse at that, the baker
won't rob you of it and nor will your innkeeper; instead you'll lose it
to whoever has an oversized hard-on. Your poor belly looks on as your
arse feasts; the one is sick with hunger, the other swallows whole.

53

You want to become a free man? You're lying, Maximus, you don't;
but if you really want to, this is how. You'll be a free man if, Maximus,
you have no desire to dine out; if Veii's grape subdues your thirst; if
you can laugh at poor Cinna's gold-inlaid dinner service;* if you can

si ridere potes miseri chrydendeta Cinnae,
contentus nostra si potes esse toga,
si plebeia Venus gemino tibi iungitur asse,
si tua non rectus tecta subire potes.
haec tibi si uis est, si mentis tanta potestas,
liberior Partho uiuere rege potes.

57

Hic quem uidetis gressibus uagis lentum,
amethystinatus media qui secat Saepta,
quem non lacernis Publius meus uincit,
non ipse Cordus alpha paenulatorum,
quem grex togatus sequitur et capillatus
recensque sella linteisque lorisque,
oppignerauit modo modo ad Cladi mensam
uix octo nummis anulum, unde cenaret.

58

Pexatus pulchre rides mea, Zoile, trita.
sunt haec trita quidem, Zoile, sed mea sunt.

65

Cur tristiorem cernimus Saleianum?
'An causa leuis est?' inquis, 'Extuli uxorem.'
o grande fati crimen! o grauem casum!
illa, illa diues mortua est Secundilla,
centena decies quae tibi dedit dotis?
nollem accidisset hoc tibi, Saleiane.

71

Candidius nihil est te, Caeciliane. notaui,
si quando ex nostris disticha pauca lego,
protinus aut Marsi recitas aut scripta Catulli.
hoc mihi das, tamquam deteriora legas,
ut collata magis placeant mea? credimus istud:
malo tamen recites, Caeciliane, tua.

be content to wear one of *my* togas; if the Lower Pleasures* will go with you for two copper pennies; if you can't get into your lodgings standing upright. If you can cope with all that, if you've got what it takes, you can live freer than the king of Parthia.*

57

That man you see ambling nowhere in particular, cutting across the middle of the Saepta,* his hand studded with amethysts;* whom my own Publius doesn't outdo in cloaks, nor Cordus himself, who's *numero uno* in woollen mantles; trailed by a flock in togas and long hair,* and a sedan-chair newly fitted with curtains and strapping: only just now at Cladus' stall he pawned a ring for scarcely eight pennies, to pay for his dinner.

58

Dressed in fine new wool, Zoilus, you poke fun at my worn old clothes. They may be worn, Zoilus, but at least I own them.

65

Why is Saleianus looking a bit down? Nothing serious, we hope? 'I've buried my wife.' What a cruel blow of fate! What an awful thing to happen! She is dead, that same Secundilla who had all that money and who came with a million in dowry?* I wish this hadn't happened to *you*, Saleianus.

71

No one has a disposition sunnier than yours, Caecilianus. I've noticed that, if ever I read out a few of my own couplets, you immediately recite some Marsus or Catullus. Are you doing this to humour me, as though what you're reading isn't as good, so people like my stuff more in comparison? I'm sure you are; all the same, I'd rather you recited work *you'd* written.*

75

Verbera securi solitus leo ferre magistri
    insertamque pati blandus in ora manum
dedidicit pacem subito feritate reuersa,
    quanta nec in Libycis debuit esse iugis.
nam duo de tenera puerilia corpora turba,
    sanguineam rastris quae renouabat humum,
saeuos et infelix furiali dente peremit:
    Martia non uidit maius harena nefas.
exclamare libet: 'Crudelis, perfide, praedo,
    a nostra pueris parcere disce lupa!'

77

Cosconi, qui longa putas epigrammata nostra,
    utilis unguendis axibus esse potes.
hac tu credideris longum ratione colosson
    et puerum Bruti dixeris esse breuem.
disce quod ignoras: Marsi doctique Pedonis
    saepe duplex unum pagina tractat opus.
non sunt longa quibus nihil est quod demere possis,
    sed tu, Cosconi, disticha longa facis.

87

Dicis amore tui bellas ardere puellas,
    qui faciem sub aqua, Sexte, natantis habes.

88

Nil recitas et uis, Mamerce, poeta uideri.
    quidquid uis esto, dummodo nil recites.

89

Quod nimio gaudes noctem producere uino
    ignosco: uitium, Gaure, Catonis habes.
carmina quod scribis Musis et Apolline nullo

75

A lion that had always put up with the blows of his unworried trainer, and patiently allowed a hand to be put in his mouth,* unlearned his peaceful ways, suddenly reverting to a savagery that his Libyan mountain ranges ought never to have known. Out of the gang of young lads who were refreshing the bloody sand with rakes, this furious bane snatched two boyish forms in his frenzied fangs. The martial sand* has seen no act more monstrous. I want to shout: 'You cruel and treacherous predator! Learn from our she-wolf* to spare the lives of boys!'

77

Cosconius, you think my epigrams are 'too long'. You're so thick they could use you for axle-grease. By the same reckoning you'd decide the Colossus was 'too tall', and call Brutus' *Boy** 'too short'. Do your homework: a single poem by Marsus or scholarly Pedo often takes up two columns. Things aren't 'too long' if there's no fat you can trim from them. But you, Cosconius? You write two-liners that are 'too long'.

87

Sextus, you say their passion for you sets the pretty girls on fire—you who have the face of a man swimming under water.

88

You don't read out any of your work, Mamercus, and still you want people to think you're a poet. Please be whatever you like, just as long as you don't read out any of your work.

89

That you love to prolong the night with too much wine, this I can forgive, Gaurus: this vice of yours was Cato's. That you write poems that Apollo and the Muses disown, entitles you to praise: this vice was

laudari debes: hoc Ciceronis habes.
quod uomis, Antoni: quod luxuriaris, Apici.
quod fellas, uitium dic mihi cuius habes?

90

Quintiliane, uagae moderator summe iuuentae,
    gloria Romanae, Quintiliane, togae,
uiuere quod propero pauper nec inutilis annis,
    da ueniam: properat uiuere nemo satis.
differat hoc patrios optat qui uincere census
    atriaque immodicis artat imaginibus:
me focus et nigros non indignantia fumos
    tecta iuuant et fons uiuus et herba rudis.
sit mihi uerna satur, sit non doctissima coniunx,
    sit nox cum somno, sit sine lite dies.

91

Rerum certa salus, terrarum gloria, Caesar,
    sospite quo magnos credimus esse deos,
si festinatis totiens tibi lecta libellis
    detinuere oculos carmina nostra tuos,
quod fortuna uetat fieri permitte uideri,
    natorum genitor credar ut esse trium.
haec, si displicui, fuerint solacia nobis;
    haec fuerint nobis praemia, si placui.

92

Natorum mihi ius trium roganti
Musarum pretium dedit mearum
solus qui poterat. ualebis, uxor:
non debet domini perire munus.

93

'Primus ubi est,' inquis, 'cum sit liber iste secundus?'
    quid faciam, si plus ille pudoris habet?
tu tamen hunc fieri si mauis, Regule, primum,
    unum de titulo tollere iota potes.

Cicero's.* That you throw up: Antony's;* that you indulge to excess:
Apicius'. That you suck cock, though: tell me, whose vice is that?

90

Quintilian, unequalled teacher* of the feckless young; Quintilian,
glory of Rome's civic affairs: although a poor man and not incapaci-
tated by old age, I'm keen to live to the full. Don't judge me harshly;
no one can be keen enough on life. The man who schemes to outdo
his father's fortune, and jams his reception rooms with an overload of
artworks—he can put it off if he likes. But what *I* like is a seat by the
fire, a roof that doesn't mind dark smoke, a freshly flowing spring, and
unmown grass. Give me a plump, home-grown slave; a wife who's not
too smart; a good night's sleep, and a day without squabbles.

91

Caesar, sure salvation of our fortunes and glory of the earth, we be-
lieve the gods to be great so long as they keep you safe and well. I've
bombarded you with my little books; if you've read them over and
over, if my poems have held your attention, then allow me the form of
what fate does not permit in reality, and let me be rated as the father
of three children. If I have caused offence, let *them* be my consolation;
if I have found favour, let *them* be my reward.

92

At my request* he granted me the Right of Three Children, recom-
pense for my Muses—he, the only one who could. So long, wife! My
master's* gift should not go to waste.

93

'So where's Book One,' you ask, 'if this one is Book Two?' What can
I do about it if that one's shyer? But if you'd like this to be Book One,
Regulus, you can always take one 'i' off the title.*

LIBER III

I

Hoc tibi, quidquid id est, longinquis mittit ab oris
    Gallia Romanae nomine dicta togae.
hunc legis, et laudas librum fortasse priorem:
    illa uel haec mea sunt, quae meliora putas.
plus sane placeat domina qui natus in urbe est:
    debet enim Gallum uincere uerna liber.

2

Cuius uis fieri, libelle, munus?
festina tibi uindicem parare,
ne nigram cito raptus in culinam
cordylas madida tegas papyro
uel turis piperisue sis cucullus.
Faustini fugis in sinum? sapisti.
cedro nunc licet ambules perunctus
et frontis gemino decens honore
pictis luxurieris umbilicis,
et te purpura delicata uelet,
et cocco rubeat superbus index.
illo uindice nec Probum timeto.

5

Vis commendari sine me cursurus in urbem,
    parue liber, multis? an satis unus erit?
unus erit, mihi crede, satis, cui non eris hospes,
    Iulius, adsiduum nomen in ore meo.
protinus hunc primae quaeres in limine Tectae;
    quos tenuit Daphnis, nunc tenet ille lares.
est illi coniunx, quae te manibusque sinuque
    excipiet, tu uel puluerulentus eas.
hos tu seu pariter siue hanc illumue priorem

BOOK 3

1

This book—such as it is—from far-off shores does Gaul send you, that is named for the Roman toga.* Perhaps you are reading it and already preferring my last one; whichever set of poems you think is better, that's the one that's mine. Well may the book please that had its birth in the Empress of Cities; a home-raised book ought to see off a Gaul.

2

Whose present, little book, do you wish to be? Sort yourself out with an owner quickly, or you might be snatched off to some soot-blackened kitchen,* to clothe whitebait in your soggy papyrus or make a conical wrap for frankincense or pepper. Are you making a run for Faustinus' lap? Smart move. Now you'll be at liberty to stroll about, slicked back with cedar-oil; nicely turned out with both borders prettified, you will exult in your painted finials, and voluptuous purple will clothe you, and your haughty title will blush with carmine. With him as your owner, you need not fear even Probus.

5

You're all set to run off to the city without me, little book.* Would you prefer to be commended to the care of many, or will one do? One *will* do, believe me, and you won't be a stranger to him: Julius,* a name that's constantly on my lips. Search for him right away just where the Covered Way begins; the house where Daphnis used to live is where he lives now. He has a wife, who'll take you in her hands and into her lap, even if you're dusty from the journey. Whether you see them both at once, or her first, or him, just say 'Marcus says hi' and it's done. Let a letter commend others to a guardian's care;

uideris, hoc dices, 'Marcus hauere iubet',
et satis est. alios commendet epistula: peccat
qui commendandum se putat esse suis.

8

Thaida Quintus amat. quam Thaida? Thaida luscam.
unum oculum Thais non habet, ille duos.

9

Versiculos in me narratur scribere Cinna.
non scribit, cuius carmina nemo legit.

10

Constituit, Philomuse, pater tibi milia bina
    menstrua perque omnis praestitit illa dies,
luxuriam premeret cum crastina semper egestas
    et uitiis essent danda diurna tuis.
idem te moriens heredem ex asse reliquit.
    exheredauit te, Philomuse, pater.

11

Si tua Thais nec lusca est, Quinte, puella,
    cur in te factum distichon esse putas?
'Sed simile est aliquid.' pro Laide Thaida dixi?
    dic mihi, quid simile est Thais et Hermione?
tu tamen es Quintus: mutemus nomen amantis:
    si non uult Quintus, Thaida Sextus amet.

12

Vnguentum, fateor, bonum dedisti
conuiuis here, sed nihil scidisti.
res salsa est bene olere et esurire.
qui non cenat et unguitur, Fabulle,
hic uere mihi mortuus uidetur.

he causes offence who reckons he needs commending to his own family.

8

Quintus loves Thais. Which Thais? Thais the half-blind. Thais is missing one eye; he's missing both.

9

They say Cinna* is writing epigrams and I'm his target. He's not 'writing' if no one's reading him.

10

Philomusus, your father gave you an allowance of two thousand a month and paid it all his days. Bankruptcy was never more than a day away, nipping at the heels of your party lifestyle, and your vices depended on daily handouts. He's dead now, and he's left you every penny. Philomusus, your father has left you penniless.*

11

If your girl isn't called Thais and isn't half-blind, Quintus, why do you think my two-liner was targeted at you? 'But there's a certain resemblance.' Did I say Thais when I meant Lais? Tell me, how are Thais and Hermione alike? But you *are* Quintus, all the same, so let's change the lover's name: if Quintus doesn't want her, let's have Sextus* be Thais' boyfriend.

12

The perfume you gave your guests last night was good, I admit it, but you didn't carve us any meat. How chic, to smell lovely and be starving. The man who gets no food but gets anointed, Fabullus, it seems to me he's really stiffed.*

19

Proxima centenis ostenditur ursa columnis,
  exornant fictae qua platanona ferae.
huius dum patulos adludens temptat hiatus
  pulcher Hylas, teneram mersit in ora manum:
uipera sed caeco scelerata latebat in aere
  uiuebatque anima dereriore fera.
non sensit puer esse dolos, nisi dente recepto
  dum perit. o facinus, falsa quod ursa fuit!

20

Dic, Musa, quid agat Canius meus Rufus:
  utrumque chartis tradit ille uicturis
legenda temporum acta Claudianorum,
  an quae Neroni falsus adstruit scriptor?
an aemulatur improbi iocos Phaedri?
  lasciuus elegis an seuerus herois?
an in cothurnis horridus Sophocleis?
  an otiosus in schola poetarum
lepore tinctos Attico sales narrat?
  hinc si recessit, porticum terit templi
an spatia carpit lentus Argonautarum?
  an delicatae sole rursus Europae
inter tepentes post meridiem buxos
  sedet ambulatue liber acribus curis?
Titine thermis an lauatur Agrippae
  an impudici balneo Tigillini?
an rure Tulli fruitur atque Lucani?
  an Pollionis dulce currit ad quartum?
an aestuantis iam profectus ad Baias
  piger Lucrino nauculatur in stagno?
'Vis scire quid agat Canius tuus? Ridet.'

22

Dederas, Apici, bis trecenties uentri,
  sed adhuc supererat centies tibi laxum.

19

A *Bear* is being exhibited near the Hundred Columns, where moulded beasts adorn the grove of planes. As pretty Hylas* played at teasing its gaping jaws, he plunged his delicate hand into its mouth. But a vicious viper lurked within the hollow bronze, animating the beast with a soul more wicked than its own. The boy did not notice its treachery until he had been bitten and was dying. What an outrage, that the bear was not true!*

20

Say, Muse, what is my Canius Rufus* up to? Is he immortalizing on paper the noteworthy deeds of Claudian history? Or is he matching himself against the works a lying author has ascribed to Nero, or the *Fables* of that reprobate Phaedrus?* Is he being saucy in elegiacs, rugged in hexameters, hair-raising in Sophoclean buskins? Or does he take his ease in the School of the Poets and tell witty stories tinged with Attic charm? If he's taken his leave of there, is he pacing the temple portico or ambling along the colonnaded walks of the Argonauts? Or maybe he sits or strolls among box-trees warmed by delightful Europa's* afternoon sun, free from stinging cares? Or is he washing in the Baths of Titus, Agrippa, or shameless Tigellinus?* Or partying at the country villa of Tullus and Lucanus? Or rushing off to that sweet place of Pollio's at the fourth milestone? Or has he already made it to sweltering Baiae, and is now rowing his little boat on Lake Lucrinus?* 'You want to know what your Canius is up to? He's laughing at you.'

22

You had sacrificed twice-three million to your stomach, Apicius,* and there was still an ample million left over for *you*. You found this

hoc tu grauatus ut famem et sitim ferre,
summa uenenum potione perduxti.
nihil est, Apici, tibi gulosius factum.

23

Omnia cum retro pueris obsonia tradas,
cur non mensa tibi ponitur a pedibus?

26

Praedia solus habes et solus, Candide, nummos,
aurea solus habes, murrina solus habes,
Massica solus habes et Opimi Caecuba solus,
et cor solus habes, solus et ingenium.
omnia solus habes—nec me puta uelle negare—
uxorem sed habes, Candide, cum populo.

27

Numquam me reuocas, uenias cum saepe uocatus:
ignosco, nullum si modo, Galle, uocas.
inuitas alios: uitium est utriusque. 'Quod?' inquis.
et mihi cor non est et tibi, Galle, pudor.

28

Auriculam Mario grauiter miraris olere.
tu facis hoc: garris, Nestor, in auriculam.

29

Has cum gemina compede dedicat catenas,
Saturne, tibi Zoilus, anulos priores.

a burden as heavy as hunger and thirst, and threw it off: you knocked
back poison as your final cocktail. Never, Apicius, had you lived
higher than that.

23

Seeing as you're passing all the savouries to your slaves behind you,
why isn't the table set next to your feet?*

26

You're the only man who has estates, Candidus,* the only
    man with money;
the only man with gold plate, the only man with murrine-
    ware;*
the only man with Massic, the only man with Opimius'
    Caecuban;*
the only man with a brain, the only man who has talent.
You're the only man who has everything—don't think I'm
    saying you aren't;
but, Candidus, the whole city has your wife.

27

I often invite you to dinner, and you come, but you never return the
invitation. I can forgive you, Gallus, provided you're not inviting any-
body. But you are. We're both at fault. 'What fault?' you say. I have no
sense, Gallus, and you have no shame.

28

You wonder why Marius' ear smells bad. You're making it smell,
Nestor:* you keep talking shit into it.

29

These chains with twin leg-irons, Saturn, does Zoilus dedicate to
you; they're his old set of rings.*

30

Sportula nulla datur; gratis conuiua recumbis:
    dic mihi, quid Romae, Gargiliane, facis?
unde tibi togula est et fuscae pensio cellae?
    unde datur quadrans? unde uir es Chiones?
cum ratione licet dicas te uiuere summa,
    quod uiuis, nulla cum ratione facis.

32

An possim uetulam quaeris, Matrinia? possum
    et uetulam, sed tu mortua, non uetula es.
possum Hecubam, possum Niobam, Matrinia, sed si
    nondum erit illa canis, nondum erit illa lapis.

36

Quod nouus et nuper factus tibi praestat amicus,
    hoc praestare iubes me, Fabiane, tibi:
horridus ut primo semper te mane salutem
    per mediumque trahat me tua sella lutum,
lassus ut in thermas decima uel serius hora
    te sequar Agrippae, cum lauer ipse Titi.
hoc per triginta merui, Fabiane, Decembres,
    ut sim tiro tuae semper amicitiae?
hoc merui, Fabiane, toga tritaque meaque,
    ut nondum credas me meruisse rudem?

38

Quae te causa trahit uel quae fiducia Romam,
    Sexte? quid aut speras aut petis inde? refer.
'Causas' inquis 'agam Cicerone disertior ipso
    atque erit in triplici par mihi nemo foro.'
egit Atestinus causas et Ciuis utrumque
    noras; sed neutri pensio tota fuit.
'Si nihil hinc ueniet, pangentur carmina nobis:
    audieris, dices esse Maronis opus.'

30

The dole is cancelled; you're attending dinners out of kindness. Tell me, Gargilianus, what are you doing in Rome? How can you afford your wretched toga, and the rent on your gloomy bedsit? How can you afford a quarter for the baths? How can you afford to be Chione's boyfriend? You say you live by careful accounting; but there's no accounting for you being alive.

32

Can I do a granny, Matrinia? You want to know? Well, I can; but you're not a granny, you're a corpse. I can do Hecuba, I can do Niobe,* Matrinia, but only if Hecuba's not yet a bitch and Niobe's not yet a stone.

36

The services a new and freshly-minted friend performs for you, Fabianus, are the ones you demand of me: that I come and pay my respects first thing every morning, shivering with cold; that I trail after your sedan-chair through the deep mud; that at the tenth hour or even later I follow you into the Baths of Agrippa, although I myself scrub up at Titus'. Is this what I have earned, Fabianus, by my thirty Decembers? Must I always be an entry-level friend? Is this what I deserve, Fabianus, with my worn old toga that I paid for myself, that you don't yet think I've earned my wooden sword?*

38

What opportunity brings you to Rome, Sextus? What's making you so confident? What do you expect here, what are you after? Give us the details. 'Cases!' you say. 'I'll argue them better than Cicero himself, and no one in the three Fora will be my equal.' Atestinus used to argue cases, so did Civis—you knew them both—but it didn't cover their rent. 'If that doesn't go anywhere, we shall write poems. When you hear them, you'll say it's Maro's work.' Lunatic. See that lot in the ice-matted overcoats? Every last man of them is a Naso* or

insanis: omnes gelidis quicumque lacernis
    sunt tibi, Nasones Vergiliosque uides.
'Atria magna colam.' uix tres aut quattuor ista
    res aluit; pallet cetera turba fame.
'Quid faciam suade: nam certum est uiuere Romae.'
    si bonus es, casu uiuere, Sexte, potes.

39

Iliaco similem puerum, Faustine, ministro
    lusca Lycoris amat. quam bene lusca uidet!

43

Mentiris iuuenem tinctis, Laetine, capillis,
    tam subito coruus, qui modo cycnus eras.
non omnes fallis; scit te Proserpina canum:
    personam capiti detrahet illa tuo.

46

Exigis a nobis operam sine fine togatam:
    non eo, libertum sed tibi mitto meum.
'Non est' inquis 'idem'. multo plus esse probabo:
    uix ego lecticam subsequar, ille feret.
in turbam incideris, cunctos umbone repellet:
    inualidum est nobis ingenuumque latus.
quidlibet in causa narraueris, ipse tacebo:
    at tibi tergeminum mugiet ille sophos.
lis erit, ingenti faciet conuicia uoce:
    esse pudor uetuit fortia uerba mihi.
'Ergo nihil nobis' inquis 'praestabis amicus?'
    quidquid libertus, Candide, non poterit.

47

Capena grandi porta qua pluit gutta
Phrygiumque Matris Almo qua lauat ferrum,
Horatiorum qua uiret sacer campus

a Virgil. 'I shall cultivate the halls of the great.' That old trick used to feed three or four at most; the rest of the gang goes pale with hunger. 'So tell me what I should be doing, because I'm living in Rome and that's that.' If you're a good man, Sextus, you can live here—live hand to mouth.

39

Faustinus, that half-blind Lycoris'* boyfriend is the spitting image of the Trojan cup-bearer.* What a good eye she has!

43

You counterfeit youth with hair-dye, Laetinus: all of a sudden you're a raven, when just now you were a swan. You don't fool everyone: Proserpina* knows you are grey; she will drag the mask from your head.

46

You extort from me no end of toga-work;* well, I'm not going. I'm sending my freedman instead. 'It's not the same thing,' you say. It's actually much better, and I'll prove it. I can hardly keep up with your litter; he'll carry it. If you run into a crowd, he'll elbow them aside (I have the weak ribs of a freeborn man). Spinning some story in court? I won't say a thing, but he'll bellow three rounds of 'Hear, hear!' Suing someone? He'll hurl abuse at the top of his voice; my sense of shame has forbidden me strong language. 'Are you saying you'll do nothing for me as a friend?' you ask. Candidus, what I'll do for you is what a freedman never could.

47

Where the Capena Gate rains with swollen drips, where the Almo washes the Phrygian steel of the Mother Goddess, where the hallowed field of the Horatii sprouts green and where the shrine of the Small

qua pusilli feruet Herculis fanum,
Faustine, plena Bassus ibat in raeda,
omnis beati copias trahens ruris.
illic uideres frutice nobili caules
et utrumque porrum sessilesque lactucas
pigroque uentri non inutiles betas;
illic coronam pinguibus grauem turdis
leporemque laesum Gallici canis dente
nondumque uicta lacteum faba porcum;
nec feriatus ibat ante carrucam,
sed tuta faeno cursor oua portabat.
urbem petebat Bassus? immo rus ibat.

50

Haec tibi, non alia, est ad cenam causa uocandi,
    uersiculos recites ut, Ligurine, tuos.
deposui soleas, adfertur protinus ingens
    inter lactucas oxygarumque liber:
alter perlegitur, dum fercula prima morantur:
    tertius est, nec adhuc mensa secunda uenit:
et quartum recitas et quintum denique librum.
    putidus est, totiens si mihi ponis aprum.
quod si non scombris scelerata poemata donas,
    cenabis solus iam, Ligurine, domi.

52

Empta domus fuerat tibi, Tongiliane, ducentis:
    abstulit hanc nimium casus in urbe frequens.
collatum est deciens. rogo, non potes ipse uideri
    incendisse tuam, Tongiliane, domum?

57

Callidus imposuit nuper mihi copo Rauennae:
    cum peterem mixtum, uendidit ille merum.

Hercules* swarms with visitors: there, Faustinus, was Bassus on his way in a fully loaded wagon, lugging all the bounty of a fruitful farm. There you'd have seen brassicas with splendid sprouts on them, both kinds of leek, spreading lettuces, and beets—just the thing for a lazy bowel; there, too, a hoop heavy with fat thrushes, a hare bearing the tooth-marks of a Gaulish hound, and a suckling-pig that had not yet munched a bean. The runner in front of the carriage wasn't getting a holiday either; he was carrying eggs* swaddled in hay. Was Bassus on his way into town? Quite the opposite:* he was heading for his place in the country.

50

You have just one reason for inviting people to dinner, Ligurinus: so you can recite your little poems. As soon as I've taken my sandals off, we're served lettuce* with fish vinaigrette and an enormous . . . book; a second gets read from start to finish while the main course plays for time; a third, and no sign of the dessert; and then you recite a fourth book, and finally a fifth. If it had been that many helpings of boar you'd served up, it'd still be a rotten business. But if you don't donate your wretched poems to the mackerel,* Ligurinus, you'll be eating at home alone from now on.

52

You'd arranged to buy a house, Tongilianus, for two-hundred thousand; but an accident, all too common in the city, robbed you of it. The payout's a million. I ask you, Tongilianus: mightn't people think you've torched your own house?

57

A sneaky innkeeper pulled a fast one on me at Ravenna recently. I asked for my wine watered; he served it neat.*

58

Baiana nostri uilla, Basse, Faustini
non otiosis ordinata myrtetis
uiduaque platano tonsilique buxeto
ingrata lati spatia detinet campi,
sed rure uero barbaroque laetatur.
hic farta premitur angulo Ceres omni
et multa fragrat testa senibus autumnis;
hic post Nouembres imminente iam bruma
seras putator horridus refert uuas.
truces in alta ualle mugiunt tauri
uitulusque inermi fronte prurit in pugnam.
uagatur omnis turba sordidae chortis,
argutus anser gemmeique pauones
nomenque debet quae rubentibus pinnis
et picta perdix Numidicaeque guttatae
et impiorum phasiana Colchorum;
Rhodias superbi feminas premunt galli;
sonantque turres plausibus columbarum,
gemit hinc palumbus, inde cereus turtur.
auidi secuntur uilicae sinum porci
matremque plenam mollis agnus expectat.
cingunt serenum lactei focum uernae
et larga festos lucet ad lares silua.
non segnis albo pallet otio caupo,
nec perdit oleum lubricus palaestrita,
sed tendit auidis rete subdolum turdis
tremulaue captum linea trahit piscem
aut impeditam cassibus refert dammam.
exercet hilares facilis hortus urbanus,
et paedagogo non iubente lasciui
parere gaudent uilico capillati,
et delicatus opere fruitur eunuchus.
nec uenit inanis rusticus salutator:
fert ille ceris cana cum suis mella
metamque lactis Sassinate de silua;
somniculosos ille porrigit glires,
hic uagientem matris hispidae fetum,

58

Our Faustinus' villa at Baiae, Bassus, does not hog tracts of the wide plain with plantations of useless myrtle, sterile plane-trees, and box topiary; it's a proper, scruffy farm,* and a prosperous one. Here close-packed grain is squeezed into every corner, and many a clay jug carries the odour of ancient harvests; here with November gone and winter looming the unkempt pruner brings in the late grapes. Fierce bulls bellow in the deep valley, and the bull-calf with his weaponless brow itches for battle. The whole flock forages in the kitchengarden—the shrill goose, the jewelled peacocks, the one that owes its name to its red plumage, the painted partridge, the speckled Numidians, and the pheasant of the depraved Colchians;* proud cockerels mount their Rhodian females, and the dovecotes echo with the wingbeats of fowl: here a wood-pigeon coos, there a pale turtle-dove. The greedy pigs follow the apron of the overseer's wife and the tender lamb waits for its plump mother. The unweaned slave-children form a circle round the cheery hearth and plenty of wood blazes up to the merry household gods. The lazy barkeep does not turn sallow with pale inactivity, the slippery wrestling-coach wastes no oil; instead he stretches a crafty net for the greedy thrushes or draws in a hooked fish on a quivering line or brings home a doe caught in a snare. The fruitful kitchen-garden gives these cheerful townies a workout, and the effete eunuch is happy to get stuck in.

Nor does the country client come to pay his respects emptyhanded. This one brings pale honey with its comb, and a pyramidshaped cheese of milk from the woods of Sassina; this one passes you dozy dormice; that one, the bleating kid of a shaggy mother; another, capons, constrained to be celibate; and the big-boned daughters of honest tenant farmers present their mothers' gifts in wicker baskets. When work is over a delighted neighbour is asked to dinner, and the table's no miser, keeping back a banquet for the next day; everyone eats their fill, and it never occurs to the stuffed servant to envy the tipsy diner.

You, though, in your suburban villa, are lord and master of an elegant famine: from your high tower you look out over a sea of laurel, without a care (your Priapus* fears no scrumper). You feed your vinedresser on grits from town and, with nothing better to do, you ship to your frescoed villa greens, eggs, chicks, apples, cheese, and new-made

alius coactos non amare capones;
et dona matrum uimine offerunt texto
grandes proborum uirgines colonorum.
facto uocatur laetus opere uicinus;
nec auara seruat crastinas dapes mensa:
uescuntur omnes ebrioque non nouit
satur minister inuidere conuiuae.
at tu sub urbe possides famem mundam
et turre ab alta prospicis meras laurus,
furem Priapo non timente securus;
et uinitorem farre pascis urbano
pictamque portas otiosus ad uillam
holus, oua, pullos, poma, caseum, mustum.
rus hoc uocari debet, an domus longe?

59

Sutor Cerdo dedit tibi, culta Bononia, munus,
 fullo dedit Mutinae: nunc ubi copo dabit?

65

Quod spirat tenera malum mordente puella,
 quod de Corycio quae uenit aura croco;
uinea quod primis cum floret cana racemis,
 gramina quod redolent, quae modo carpsit ouis;
quod myrtus, quod messor Arabs, quod sucina trita,
 pallidus Eoo ture quod ignis olet;
gleba quod aestiuo leuiter cum spargitur imbre,
 quod madidas nardo passa corona comas:
hoc tua, saeue puer Diadumene, basia fragrant.
 quid si tota dares illa sine inuidia?

68

Huc est usque tibi scriptus, matrona, libellus.
 cui sint scripta rogas interiora? mihi.
gymnasium, thermas, stadium est hac parte: recede.
 exuimur: nudos parce uidere uiros.

wine. Should this be called a place in the country, or a town-house far
from town?

59

The cobbler Cerdo* threw games for you, fertile Bologna; a fuller
funded games in Modena; where will a barkeep throw the next ones?

65

The scent of an apple as a young girl bites into it; the aroma that
comes from Corycian saffron;* the bloom from a dewy vineyard as it
begins to fruit; the way grass smells when a sheep has just grazed it;
the smell of myrtle, an Arabian reaper,* buffed amber, a fire yellow-
green with Eastern incense; cut turf with a light sprinkling of sum-
mer rain, or a garland resting on hair slick with spikenard.* That,
Diadumenus,* is how your kisses smell, you cruel boy. What if you
gave me all of them, without holding back?

68

Up to this point, Madam,* this little book has been written for you.
You want to know for whom the bits further in were written? For me.
The gym, baths, and running-track are in this district: take your leave,
I'm stripping for action; spare yourself the sight of men in the buff.

hinc iam deposito post uina rosasque pudore,
quid dicat nescit saucia Terpsichore:
schemate nec dubio, sed aperte nominat illam
quam recipit sexto mense superba Venus,
custodem medio statuit quam uilicus horto,
opposita spectat quam proba uirgo manu.
si bene te noui, longum iam lassa libellum
ponebas, totum nunc studiosa leges.

76

Arrigis ad uetulas, fastidis, Basse, puellas,
nec formosa tibi, sed moritura placet.
hic, rogo, non furor est, non haec est mentula demens,
cum possis Hecaben, non potes Andromachen?

80

De nullo quereris, nulli maledicis, Apici:
rumor ait linguae te tamen esse malae.

82

Conuiua quisquis Zoili potest esse,
Summemmianas cenet inter uxores
curtaque Ledae sobrius bibat testa:
hoc esse leuius puriusque contendo.
iacet occupato galbinatus in lecto
cubitisque trudit hinc et inde conuiuas
effultus ostro Sericisque puluillis.
stat exoletus suggeritque ructanti
pinnas rubentes cuspidesque lentisci,
et aestuanti tenue uentilat frigus
supina prasino concubina flabello,
fugatque muscas myrtea puer uirga.
percurrit agili corpus arte tractatrix
manumque doctam spargit omnibus membris;
digiti crepantis signa nouit eunuchus
et delicatae sciscitator urinae

From here on in, with her modesty set aside after the wine and roses,
Terpsichore gets wobbly and doesn't know what she's saying; with no
vague figures of speech, she frankly calls by name that thing* which
proud Venus accepts in the sixth month, which the farm steward sets
up as a guardian in the middle of the kitchen-garden, and which a well-
brought-up girl looks at with her hand in front of her eyes. If I know
you well, you were tired of this too-long little book by now and were just
putting it down—but now you'll read the whole of it avidly.*

76

You get it up for old women, Bassus, but are turned off by girls;
a pretty woman isn't your type, you want one who's knocking on
death's door. I ask you—isn't this madness? Is your cock out of its
mind? You can do Hecabe, but not Andromache?

80

You don't whine about anyone, don't speak ill of anyone; all the same,
Apicius,* rumour has it you're bad-mouthing.

82

Up for an evening with Zoilus? Why not try dining among Summem-
mius' 'brides', or drinking (but not too much) from Leda's broken
wine-jug? You'll have a nicer time, guaranteed, and you won't come
away feeling as dirty. He flops in his green suit* on a crowded couch,
elbowing his neighbours on each side, and props himself up on pur-
ple coverlets and little silk cushions. A strapping young fellow stands
at attention and passes him red feathers and mastic-wood toothpicks
when he belches, and a jumped-up concubine wafts a cool breeze at
him with a leek-green fan when he starts sweating; a boy shoos the
flies away with a switch of myrtle. A masseuse works him over with
quick, skilled moves, pattering her trained hands over every part of
his body; a eunuch notes when he snaps his fingers and teases out
the shy urine, steering his tipsy penis even as their master continues
drinking.

　　He himself, meanwhile, twists round towards the crowd at his feet;
surrounded by lapdogs that are licking at goose-livers, he portions

domini bibentis ebrium regit penem.
at ipse retro flexus ad pedum turbam
inter catellas anserum exta lambentis
partitur apri glandulas palaestritis
et concubino turturum natis donat;
Ligurumque nobis saxa cum ministrentur
uel cocta fumis musta Massilitanis,
Opimianum morionibus nectar
crystallinisque murrinisque propinat;
et Cosmianis ipse fusus ampullis
non erubescit murice aureo nobis
diuidere moechae pauperis capillare.
septunce multo deinde perditus stertit:
non accubamus et silentium rhonchis
praestare iussi nutibus propinamus.
hoc malchionis patimur improbi fastus,
nec uindicari, Rufe, possumus: fellat.

83

Vt faciam breuiora mones epigrammata, Corde.
'Fac mihi quod Chione': non potui breuius.

86

Ne legeres partem lasciui, casta, libelli,
praedixi et monui: tu tamen, ecce, legis.
sed si Panniculum spectas et, casta, Latinum,
non sunt haec mimis improbiora: lege.

87

Narrat te rumor, Chione, numquam esse fututam
atque nihil cunno purius esse tuo.
tecta tamen non hac, qua debes, parte lauaris:
si pudor est, transfer subligar in faciem.

98

Sit culus tibi quam macer, requiris?
pedicare potes, Sabelle, culo.

out goujons of boar to his wrestling-coaches and treats his boy-toy
to the rumps of turtle-doves. While *we* are served up the rocks of
Liguria or unaged wines scorched in the smoke-rooms of Marseilles,*
he toasts his home-born slaves with Opimian nectar served in crystal
and murrine glasses. His own complexion is darkened out of Cosmus'
little bottles,* but he doesn't blush as he issues us—from a gilded
murex-shell!—the hair-oil of a slutty pauper. Then, wasted from all
those half-pints of wine, he starts snoring; and we lie there on our
couches, under orders to hush when he snorts, and toast each other
with nods of the head. That's the kind of ill-treatment we put up with
from the vicious bastard, and we can't pay him back, Rufus: he *likes*
the taste of cock.

83

You urge me to make my epigrams more concise, Cordus. 'Do me like
Chione does':* I can't get more concise than that.

86

I warned you in advance, bashful lady. I told you: there's part of my
naughty little book you shouldn't read. But look, you're reading it.
But if you watch Panniculus and Latinus, bashful lady—well, my
poems are no wickeder than the mimes.* So, carry on reading.

87

The gossip says, Chione, you've never been fucked, that there's noth-
ing squeakier-clean than your cunt. But when you go to the baths,
you don't cover the part you should. If you've any shame, put your
knickers on your face.

98

Want to know how skinny your arse is, Sabellus? It's so skinny you can
fuck people in the arse with it.

99

Irasci nostro non debes, Cerdo, libello:
    ars tua, non uita, est carmine laesa meo.
innocuos permitte sales. cur ludere nobis
    non liceat, licuit si iugulare tibi?

100

Cursorem sexta tibi, Rufe, remisimus hora
    carmina quem madidum nostra tulisse reor:
imbribus immodicis caelum nam forte ruebat.
    non aliter mitti debuit iste liber.

99

You oughtn't to get angry with my little book, Cerdo. Your trade has taken a hit from my poem, but not your life. Allow some harmless teasing. Why shouldn't I get away with a joke, when you got away with murder?*

100

I sent your courier back to you at midday, Rufus, and I bet he was soaked through when he delivered you my poems; the sky was falling* on us just then, the rain was unbelievable. It was exactly the reception that book deserved.

LIBER IV

I

Caesaris alma dies et luce sacratior illa
  conscia Dictaeum qua tulit Ida Iouem,
longa, precor, Pylioque ueni numerosior aeuo
  semper et hoc uultu uel meliore nite.
hic colat Albano Tritonida multus in auro
  perque manus tantas plurima quercus eat;
hic colat ingenti redeuntia saecula lustro
  et quae Romuleus sacra Tarentos habet.
magna quidem, superi, petimus, sed debita terris:
  pro tanto quae sunt improba uota deo?

4

Quod siccae redolet palus lacunae,
crudarum nebulae quod Albularum,
piscinae uetus aura quod marinae,
quod pressa piger hircus in capella,
lassi uardaicus quod euocati,
quod bis murice uellus inquinatum,
quod ieiunia sabbatariarum,
maestorum quod anhelitus reorum,
quod spurcae moriens lucerna Ledae,
quod ceromata faece de Sabina,
quod uulpis fuga, uiperae cubile,
mallem quam quod oles olere, Bassa.

5

Vir bonus et pauper linguaque et pectore uerus,
  quid tibi uis urbem qui, Fabiane, petis?
qui nec leno potes nec comissator haberi,
  nec pauidos tristi uoce citare reos,
nec potes uxores cari corrumpere amici,
  nec potes algentes arrigere ad uetulas,

BOOK 4

I

Life-giving day of Caesar,* a day more holy than that dawn when
Ida conspired to bear Dictaean Jupiter: I pray you, come. Last long;
outdo the span of Nestor's years. Beam on us always, with your cur-
rent face or an even better one. May *he* honour Minerva many a time
in Alban gold, and may countless oak-wreaths* pass through his
mighty hands; may *he* honour the ages, as the centuries complete
their cycle, and honour the rites that Romulus' own Tarentos* keeps.
We ask no small favours of you, gods above, but the earth is owed
them; for on behalf of a divinity so great as *he*, what prayer counts as
more than is due?

4

The stench of a marsh when its pond dries up;
The fumes that rise from the polluted Tiber;*
The stale whiff of a salt-water fish-farm;
A lazy he-goat mounting its nanny;
A weary veteran's boot;
A fleece twice dyed with murex;
The fast-days of Jewish women keeping the Sabbath;
The exhalations of wretched defendants;
. The guttering lamp of Leda the slut;
Wrestlers out of the scum of the Sabines;
A fox on the run, a viper's den:
I'd rather smell any of them, Bassa, than what you smell of.*

5

A good man (a poor man), true in word and heart: Fabianus, what are
you thinking, relocating to Rome? You can't cut it as a pimp or party
animal, or put on a scary voice to subpoena terrified defendants, or
ruin your best friend's wife, or get it up for frosty old biddies, or
tout vapourware* around the Palace, or clap for Canus, or clap for
Glaphyrus; you poor man, how will you make a living? 'A staunch

uendere nec uanos circa Palatia fumos,
plaudere nec Cano, plaudere nec Glaphyro:
unde miser uiues? — 'Homo certus, fidus amicus . . .'
hoc nihil est: numquam sic Philomelus eris.

7

Cur, here quod dederas, hodie, puer Hylle, negasti,
durus tam subito qui modo mitis eras?
sed iam causaris barbamque annosque pilosque.
o nox quam longa es, quae facis una senem!
quid nos derides? here qui puer, Hylle, fuisti,
dic nobis, hodie qua ratione uir es?

8

Prima salutantes atque altera conterit hora,
exercet raucos tertia causidicos,
in quintam uarios extendit Roma labores,
sexta quies lassis, septima finis erit,
sufficit in nonam nitidis octaua palaestris,
imperat extructos frangere nona toros:
hora libellorum decuma est, Eupheme, meorum,
temperat ambrosias cum tua cura dapes
et bonus aetherio laxatur nectare Caesar
ingentique tenet pocula parca manu.
tunc admitte iocos: gressu timet ire licenti
ad matutinum nostra Thalia Iouem.

9

Sotae filia clinici, Labulla,
deserto sequeris Clytum marito,
et donas et amas: ἔχεις ἀσώτως.

10

Dum nouus est nec adhuc rasa mihi fronte libellus,
pagina dum tangi non bene sicca timet,
i, puer, et caro perfer leue munus amico
qui meruit nugas primus habere meas.

fellow, a steadfast friend . . .'—that counts for nothing: you'll never
be a Philomelus* talking like that.

7

What yesterday you gave me, today you refuse: Hyllus, my boy,* why?
Why are you suddenly stony-faced, when lately you were soft and
yielding? But now you plead your beard, your age, your hair.* Last
night was such a long one—all by itself, it has turned me into an old
man.* Why are you making fun of me? Yesterday, Hyllus, you were
a boy; explain to me how come you're a man today.

8

The first hour and the second* grind down the clients paying their
respects; the third keeps hoarse-voiced barristers on their toes; Rome
stretches out her various jobs into the fifth; the sixth will bring siesta
to the weary, the seventh will end it; the eighth running into the ninth
does for the oil-slicked wrestling-schools; the ninth commands us to
hit the dining-couches piled with cushions. The tenth, Euphemus,* is
the hour for my little books, when your diligence makes the ambrosial
feast run smoothly, and good Caesar unwinds with heavenly nectar,
a little cup clutched in his mighty hand. Then, let in my jokes: my
Muse is frightened to saunter saucily up to our Jupiter before the sun
is over the yardarm.

9

Labulla, daughter of Dr Saver,* you've dumped your husband to
chase after Clytus—showering him with presents, constantly on heat.
You're quite unsavoury.

10

While my little book is brand new and its ends not yet trimmed,*
while its page is still not quite dry and fears to be touched, go, boy,
and fetch it as a token gift to my dear friend. He deserves to get my
trashy poems before anyone else. Hurry, but take everything you

curre, sed instructus: comitetur Punica librum
spongea: muneribus conuenit illa meis.
non possunt nostros multae, Faustine, liturae
emendare iocos: una litura potest.

13

Claudia, Rufe, meo nubit Peregrina Pudenti:
macte esto taedis, o Hymenaee, tuis.
tam bene rara suo miscentur cinnama nardo,
Massica Theseis tam bene uina fauis;
nec melius teneris iunguntur uitibus ulmi,
nec plus lotos aquas, litora myrtus amat.
candida perpetuo reside, Concordia, lecto,
tamque pari semper sit Venus aequa iugo:
diligat illa senem quondam, sed et ipsa marito
tum quoque, cum fuerit, non uideatur anus.

14

Sili, Castalidum decus sororum,
qui periuria barbari furoris
ingenti premis ore perfidosque
astus Hannibalis leuisque Poenos
magnis cedere cogis Africanis:
paulum seposita seueritate,
dum blanda uagus alea December
incertis sonat hinc et hinc fritillis
et ludit tropa nequiore talo,
nostris otia commoda Camenis;
nec torua lege fronte, sed remissa
lasciuis madidos iocis libellos.
sic forsan tener ausus est Catullus
magno mittere Passerem Maroni.

17

Facere in Lyciscam, Paule, me iubes uersus,
quibus illa lectis rubeat et sit irata.
o Paule, malus es: irrumare uis solus.

need: a Punic sponge* should go with the book—it's the ideal accompaniment to gifts from me. Many erasures can't fix my jokes,* Faustinus; but one erasure can.

13

Rufus, you know Claudia? Claudia Peregrina? She's marrying my friend Pudens.* Their union brings honour on the God of Weddings: a union as perfect as when a handful of cinnamon-twigs is blended with just the right nard-oil, or Massic wines with Theseus' honeycombs.* No more aptly are elms paired with young vine-shoots; no more does the lotus love water, or the myrtle the sea-coast. Fair Harmony, dwell ever in their bed, and may Venus always look kindly on such a partnership of equals. May she love him even when he's old; and may he, though she be old as well, not find her so.

14

Silius, pride of the Castalian sisterhood,* your mighty voice harries the broken oaths of the ravening barbarian and Hannibal's deceitful strategies; you make fickle Carthaginians yield to the mighty Scipios.* Yet put aside your gravity for a moment. While December does his rounds, tempting us to gamble and making the dice-boxes rattle with anticipation at every turn, and taking his turn to roll a loaded knucklebone,* lend your leisure hours to my own Muses. And don't frown but smooth your brow as you read my little books, sauced as they are with naughty jokes. Just so, perhaps, did tender Catullus dare send his *Sparrow* to great Maro.*

17

You urge me, Paulus, to write poems with Lycisca* as their target: poems she'll blush to read, that'll make her angry. Paulus, you bastard—you want her blow-jobs all to yourself.

18

Qua uicina pluit Vipsanis porta columnis
   et madet adsiduo lubricus imbre lapis,
in iugulum pueri, qui roscida tecta subibat,
   decidit hiberno praegrauis unda gelu:
cumque peregisset miseri crudelia fata,
   tabuit in calido uolnere mucro tener.
quid non saeua sibi uoluit Fortuna licere?
   aut ubi non mors est, si iugulatis aquae?

22

Primos passa toros et adhuc placanda marito
   merserat in nitidos se Cleopatra lacus,
dum fugit amplexus. sed prodidit unda latentem;
   lucebat, totis cum tegeretur aquis:
condita sic puro numerantur lilia uitro,
   sic prohibet tenuis gemma latere rosas.
insilui mersusque uadis luctantia carpsi
   basia: perspicuae plus uetuistis aquae.

23

Dum tu lenta nimis diuque quaeris
quis primus tibi quisue sit secundus,
Graium quos epigramma conparauit,
palmam Callimachus, Thalia, de se
facundo dedit ipse Bruttiano.
qui si Cecropio satur lepore
Romanae sale luserit Mineruae,
ille me facias, precor, secundum.

24

Omnes quas habuit, Fabiane, Lycoris amicas
   extulit: uxori fiat amica meae.

18

Where the gate drips with rain next to Agrippa's portico and the
stone is slippery-wet* from the constant runoff, a water-flow heavy
with winter ice fell upon the neck of a boy who was passing under the
dripping roofs; and when it had performed its brutal execution on the
poor child, the fragile dagger melted away in the still-warm wound.
Does Fortune place no limit on her own cruelty? What place is safe
from Death, when waters turn cutthroat?

22

She'd made it through her first night with her husband, but had yet
to give him what he *really* wanted; and now Cleopatra had sunk her-
self deep in the glittering waters,* hiding from his embraces. But the
water gave up its fugitive: though quite submerged, still she caught
the light. Just so can lilies in a clear vase still be counted; just so
does thin crystal forbid roses to lie unseen. I leapt in, dived deep,
and snatched squirming kisses: the waters were too clear to allow me
more.

23

You've been spending far too long trying to decide which of the
Greeks in epigram's muster-roll you'd rank in first or second place.
Meanwhile, Muse, Callimachus* has taken the initiative: he has per-
sonally awarded first prize to Bruttianus.* But if *he* ever loses his
appetite for Attic charm and tries his hand at the wit of Roman Min-
erva, please let me be runner-up to *him*.

24

Every girlfriend she's had, Fabianus: Lycoris has buried them all.
I hope she makes friends with my wife.

25

Aemula Baianis Altini litora uillis
    et Phaethontei conscia silua rogi,
quaeque Antenoreo Dryadum pulcherrima Fauno
    nupsit ad Euganeos Sola puella lacus,
et tu Ledaeo felix Aquileia Timauo,
    hic ubi septenas Cyllarus hausit aquas:
uos eritis nostrae requies portusque senectae,
    si iuris fuerint otia nostra sui.

26

Quod te mane domi toto non uidimus anno,
    uis dicam quantum, Postume, perdiderim?
tricenos, puto, bis, uicenos ter, puto, nummos.
    ignosces: togulam, Postume, pluris emo.

27

Saepe meos laudare soles, Auguste, libellos.
    inuidus ecce negat: num minus ergo soles?
quid quod honorato non sola uoce dedisti
    non alius poterat quae dare dona mihi?
ecce iterum nigros conrodit liuidus ungues:
    da, Caesar, tanto tu magis, ut doleat.

29

Obstat, care Pudens, nostris sua turba libellis
    lectoremque frequens lassat et implet opus.
rara iuuant: primis sic maior gratia pomis,
    hibernae pretium sic meruere rosae;
sic spoliatricem commendat fastus amicam,
    ianua nec iuuenem semper aperta tenet.
saepius in libro numeratur Persius uno
    quam leuis in tota Marsus Amazonide.
tu quoque de nostris releges quemcumque libellis,
    esse puta solum: sic tibi pluris erit.

25

You coast at Altinum,* that rival the villas of Baiae; you woods, that witnessed Phaethon's pyre; you maiden Sola, most beautiful of the Dryads, who married Antenor's Faunus beside the lakes of Euganus; and you, Aquileia, who delight in Leda's Timavus, here where Cyllarus drank sevenfold waters: you will be the quiet harbour of my old age, if my free time is free then to decide.

26

I haven't caught you at home of a morning all year, Postumus.* Do you want to know how much it has cost me? Sixty, I guess, or maybe thirty. Sorry, Postumus, but I pay more than that for my stupid toga.

27

You keep saying nice things about my little books, Augustus; but look, some envious type is saying you don't. Does that make you say them any less? And what about this: you didn't just honour me in words; the presents you gave me,* no one else could. Look, he's jealous; he's biting his dirty nails again. Give me more next time, Caesar. Let's make him squirm.

29

What gets in the way of my little books, dear Pudens, is my little books: they crowd each other out. They're published so often, they wear my Reader out. He's glutted. People like what they can't get much of. The earliest apples are the most delicious; roses command a premium in winter; the fact she's finicky makes a gold-digging mistress irresistible (young men won't linger by a door that's always open). Same with literature: Persius gets more hits with just one book than silly Marsus* in his whole *Amazonid*. So if you're rereading one of those little books of mine, tell yourself it's the only one there is: it'll mean more to you that way.

32

Et latet et lucet Phaethontide condita gutta,
    ut uideatur apis nectare clusa suo.
dignum tantorum pretium tulit illa laborum:
    credibile est ipsam sic uoluisse mori.

38

Galla, nega: satiatur amor nisi gaudia torquent:
    sed noli nimium, Galla, negare diu.

40

Atria Pisonum stabant cum stemmate toto
    et docti Senecae ter numeranda domus,
praetulimus tantis solum te, Postume, regnis:
    pauper eras et eques, sed mihi consul eras.
tecum ter denas numeraui, Postume, brumas:
    communis nobis lectus et unus erat.
iam donare potes, iam perdere, plenus honorum,
    largus opum: expecto, Postume, quid facias.
nil facis et serum est alium mihi quaerere regem.
    hoc, Fortuna, placet? 'Postumus imposuit.'

42

Si quis forte mihi possit praestare roganti,
    audi, quem puerum, Flacce, rogare uelim.
Niliacis primum puer hic nascatur in oris:
    nequitias tellus scit dare nulla magis.
sit niue candidior: namque in Mareotide fusca
    pulchrior est quanto rarior iste color.
lumina sideribus certent mollesque flagellent
    colla comae: tortas non amo, Flacce, comas.
frons breuis atque modus leuiter sit naribus uncis,
    Paestanis rubeant aemula labra rosis.
saepe et nolentem cogat nolitque uolentem;

32

Vased in Phaethon's drop* is a bee. She lies unseen, yet catches the
light, as though casked in her own nectar.* This bee has won a prize
worthy of her tireless labours; one may believe she chose this death
herself.

38

Galla, tell me 'No': love stales unless its joys bring pain. But, Galla,
don't say 'No' for very long.

40

When the mansion of the Pisos still stood, and visitors saw a fam-
ily tree as-yet undocked; and the house of learned Seneca as well,
a house thrice noteworthy:* *then*, there was one man more important
to me than lords and masters so exalted, and one alone. Postumus, it
was you. You were a poor man, a knight, but to me you were a consul.
With you I counted thirty winters, Postumus; we had just the one
couch, and we shared it. *Now*, you can afford to give it away, to throw
it away; you're loaded with honours, rolling in wealth: and there's me
waiting, Postumus, to see what you do. But you do nothing—and I've
left it too late to line up another patron. How do you like that, For-
tune? 'Postumus is an imposter.'

42

If some friend of mine happened to be in a position to fulfil a re-
quest—Flaccus, are you taking notes? I'd like a boy, as follows. First,
let this boy have been born on the banks of the Nile: no nation knows
better how to put out, in really dirty ways. Let him be whiter than
snow, because in dusky Mareotis that colour is all the more beautiful
for being so rare. Let his eyes rival the stars, and let his long, soft hair
whip against his neck (I don't like curly hair, Flaccus). Let his fore-
head be low, and his nose just a little bit hooked. Let his lips blush as
red as Paestum's roses. May he often make me do it when I'm saying
'No',* and say 'No' himself when it's my turn to want it—let him
take greater liberties than his master half the time. Let him beware of

liberior domino saepe sit ille suo;
et timeat pueros, excludat saepe puellas:
uir reliquis, uni sit puer ille mihi.
'Iam scio, nec fallis: nam me quoque iudice uerum est.
talis erat' dices 'noster Amazonicus.'

44

Hic est pampineis uiridis modo Vesbius umbris,
  presserat hic madidos nobilis uua lacus:
haec iuga quam Nysae colles plus Bacchus amauit;
  hoc nuper Satyri monte dedere choros;
haec Veneris sedes, Lacedaemone gratior illi;
  hic locus Herculeo nomine clarus erat.
cuncta iacent flammis et tristi mersa fauilla:
  nec superi uellent hoc licuisse sibi.

46

Saturnalia diuitem Sabellum
fecerunt: merito tumet Sabellus,
nec quemquam putat esse praedicatque
inter causidicos beatiorem.
hos fastus animosque dat Sabello
farris semodius fabaeque fresae,
et turis piperisque tres selibrae,
et Lucanica uentre cum Falisco,
et nigri Syra defruti lagona,
et ficus Libyca gelata testa
cum bulbis cocleisque caseoque.
Piceno quoque uenit a cliente
parcae cistula non capax oliuae,
et crasso figuli polita caelo
septenaria synthesis Sagunti,
Hispanae luteum rotae toreuma,
et lato uariata mappa clauo.
Saturnalia fructuosiora
annis non habuit decem Sabellus.

the boys,* let him often spurn the girls' attentions: he can be a man
to the rest, if he's a boy to me (and me alone). 'I get it now, you're not
fooling me—that's the real deal you're describing, and I should know.
That', you say, 'was an exact description of my own boy Amazonicus.'

44

Here is Vesuvius, that till recently was green with shady vines. Here
did the noble grape load the vats with juice; here was the ridge that
Bacchus loved more than the hills of Nysa; on this peak, not long ago,
Satyrs held their dances. Here was Venus' seat, that she favoured over
Sparta; this spot was famous for its Herculean name.* All lie sunk in
flames and dismal ash. The gods themselves must have wished this
was not in their power.

46

Saturnalia has made Sabellus rich. He can swell with self-importance
and tell himself, and the rest of us, that no fellow barrister is doing
better for himself. And what gives Sabellus such self-regarding
airs? Half a peck of emmer and bean-meal, and three half-pounds
of incense and pepper, and Lucanian sausages and a Faliscan hag-
gis,* and a flask of black grape-syrup from Syria, and a sticky fig
out of a jar from Libya—and don't forget the onions and the snails
and the cheese. What's more, a client at Picenum has sent a little box
that couldn't hold a handful of olives, and a seven-piece table set-
ting smoothed by the crude graving-tool of a Saguntine potter; some
cheap-and-nasty earthenware thrown on a wheel in Spain; and a nap-
kin titivated with a broad stripe.* Saturnalia hasn't paid off so well for
Sabellus in ten years.

48

Percidi gaudes, percisus, Papyle, ploras:
    cur, quae uis fieri, Papyle, facta doles?
paenitet obscenae pruriginis? an magis illud
    fles, quod percidi, Papyle, desieris?

49

Nescit, crede mihi, quid sint epigrammata, Flacce,
    qui tantum lusus illa iocosque uocat.
ille magis ludit qui scribit prandia saeui
    Tereos aut cenam, crude Thyesta, tuam,
aut puero liquidas aptantem Daedalon alas,
    pascentem Siculas aut Polyphemon ouis.
a nostris procul est omnis uesica libellis,
    Musa nec insano syrmate nostra tumet.
'Illa tamen laudant omnes, mirantur, adorant.'
    confiteor: laudant illa, sed ista legunt.

56

Munera quod senibus uiduisque ingentia mittis,
    uis te munificum, Gargiliane, uocem?
sordidius nihil est, nihil est te spurcius uno,
    qui potes insidias dona uocare tuas:
sic auidis fallax indulget piscibus hamus,
    callida sic stultas decipit esca feras.
quid sit largiri, quid sit donare docebo,
    si nescis: dona, Gargiliane, mihi.

62

Tibur in Herculeum migrauit nigra Lycoris,
    omnia dum fieri candida credit ibi.

64

Iuli iugera pauca Martialis
hortis Hesperidum beatiora

48

You love taking it in the arse, Papylus, but when it's over, you cry.
You want it to happen, Papylus, so why are you upset once it's done?
You're sorry you're turned on by something dirty? Or do you cry *be-cause* it's over, Papylus?

49

Trust me, Flaccus, anyone who says it's just 'ditties' and 'jokes'*
doesn't know what epigram is. The real joker is the poet who describes
the feast of cruel Tereus, or the dinner that gave Thyestes indigestion,
or Daedalus strapping melting wings to his son, or Polyphemus pas-
turing his Sicilian sheep. No puffery gets near *my* little books; *my*
Muse doesn't swell and strut in the trailing robe of Tragedy.* 'But
that stuff gets all the applause, the awe, the worship.' I can't deny it:
that stuff does get the applause. But *my* stuff gets read.

56

You send presents to old folks and widows, Gargilianus, and for that
you want me to call you a big benefactor? They don't come grub-
bier or cheaper than you: no one but you could set a snare and call
it a 'gift'. This is how the deceitful hook lures in the hungry fishes;
this is how the cleverly laid bait fools the dumb beasts. If you don't
know what it is to be generous, what it is to really *give*, I can teach you.
Gargilianus, give your presents to me.

62

Dusky Lycoris* has moved to Herculean Tivoli. She thinks every-
thing turns white there.*

64

The few acres of Julius Martial, more blissful than the gardens of the
Hesperides, sit on the long escarpment of the Janiculan. His eyrie

longo Ianiculi iugo recumbunt.
lati collibus eminent recessus,
et planus modico tumore uertex
caelo perfruitur sereniore,
et curuas nebula tegente ualles
solus luce nitet peculiari;
puris leniter admouentur astris
celsae culmina delicata uillae.
hinc septem dominos uidere montis
et totam licet aestimare Romam,
Albanos quoque Tusculosque colles
et quodcumque iacet sub urbe frigus,
Fidenas ueteres breuesque Rubras,
et quod uirgineo cruore gaudet
Annae pomiferum nemus Perennae.
illinc Flaminiae Salariaeque
gestator patet essedo tacente,
ne blando rota sit molesta somno,
quem nec rumpere nauticum celeuma
nec clamor ualet helciariorum,
cum sit tam prope Muluius sacrumque
lapsae per Tiberim uolent carinae.
hoc rus, seu potius domus uocanda est,
commendat dominus: tuam putabis,
tam non inuida tamque liberalis,
tam comi patet hospitalitate:
credas Alcinoi pios Penates
aut facti modo diuitis Molorchi.
uos nunc omnia parua qui putatis,
centeno gelidum ligone Tibur
uel Praeneste domate pendulamque
uni dedite Setiam colono,
dum me iudice praeferantur istis
Iuli iugera pauca Martialis.

66

Egisti uitam semper, Line, municipalem,
qua nihil omnino uilius esse potest.

looms above the hills, and its flat summit, set on a low mound, enjoys a serener sky. When mist veils the winding valleys, it gleams by itself in its own private sunshine; on clear nights, the dainty finials of its lofty villa reach toward the stars. From here, on the one side, you can see the seven imperious hills and take in all of Rome—the Alban hills too, and the Tusculans, and every cool spot* in the city's orbit; and ancient Fidenae, and little Rubrae, and the fruitful orchard of Anna Perenna that delights in virgins' blood.* On the other side, the driver on the Flaminian and Salarian Way lies in plain sight, although his car is hushed, so its wheels don't disturb a sleep so tranquil that bosuns' calls and shouting barge-haulers could not rouse you from it—no matter that the Milvian Bridge is so close by, and the shipping that scuds down holy Tiber.

What makes this country seat stand out—or perhaps we should call it a townhouse instead?—is its owner. You will think the place is yours, he's so unstinting, so open-handed, so free with his taste-ful hospitality. You'd believe you were in Alcinous' god-fearing home, or Molorchus'*—a Molorchus who'd just come into money. You modern types for whom nothing is expensive enough can farm chilly Tivoli or Praeneste into submission with a hundred mattocks and make over lofty Setia* to a single tenant, so long as they rank higher in *my* esteem—those few acres of Julius Martial.

66

The life you've led, Linus, has always been small-town: as cheap as it gets. You've dusted off your piddling toga for the Ides and occasional

Idibus et raris togula est excussa Kalendis,
   duxit et aestates synthesis una decem.
saltus aprum, campus leporem tibi misit inemptum,
   silua grauis turdos exagitata dedit;
raptus flumineo uenit de gurgite piscis,
   uina ruber fudit non peregrina cadus.
nec tener Argolica missus de gente minister,
   sed stetit inculti rustica turba foci.
uilica uel duri conpressa est nupta coloni,
   incaluit quotiens saucia uena mero.
nec nocuit tectis ignis nec Sirius agris,
   nec mersa est pelago nec fuit ulla ratis.
supposita est blando numquam tibi tessera talo,
   alea sed parcae sola fuere nuces.
dic ubi sit decies, mater quod auara reliquit.
   nusquam est: fecisti rem, Line, difficilem.

71

Quaero diu totam, Safroni Rufe, per urbem,
   si qua puella neget: nulla puella negat.
tamquam fas non sit, tamquam sit turpe negare,
   tamquam non liceat, nulla puella negat.
casta igitur nulla est? castae sunt mille. quid ergo
   casta facit? non dat, non tamen illa negat.

72

Exigis ut donem nostros tibi, Quinte, libellos.
   non habeo, sed habet bibliopola Tryphon.
'Aes dabo pro nugis et emam tua carmina sanus?
   non' inquis 'faciam tam fatue.' nec ego.

81

Epigramma nostrum cum Fabulla legisset,
   negare nullam quo queror puellarum,
semel rogata bisque terque neglexit
   preces amantis. iam, Fabulla, promitte:
negare iussi, pernegare non iussi.

Kalends, and a single set of party clothes has lasted you ten sum-
mers. The wooded hills have sent you boar, and the plains, hare, and
not a penny spent; the beaten forest has gifted you plump thrushes.
A fish has come, hooked from the river rapids; an earthenware jug
has poured out untravelled wine. Nor did some slip of a pageboy sent
from the Argive race stand duty, but the homespun gang of a rug-
ged hearth. The wife of your estate-manager or of some rough tenant
took your weight, whenever strong wine got your man-parts tipsy and
excited. Fire did not damage your house, nor the dog-star your fields;
you lost no ship at sea—you had none to lose. In your world the die
was never substituted for the alluring knucklebone; *your* only dice
were a handful of nuts. Tell me where the million is, that your penny-
pinching mother's left you. It's gone. It wasn't easy, Linus, but you
pulled it off.*

71

I've looked and looked, Safronius Rufus, all over town, for a girl who
says 'No'; but not one girl says 'No'. It's as if it was a sin, as if it was
disgraceful to say it, as if it was against the law—not one girl says
'No'. Are virgins extinct? There are a thousand virgins. What does
a virgin *do*, then? She doesn't put out—but she doesn't say 'No'.

72

You keep pestering me to give you my little books, Quintus. I don't
have them, but Tryphon the bookseller has them in stock. 'You ex-
pect me to *pay* for that trash? To *buy* your poetry, and me in my right
mind? I'm not doing something so stupid', you say. Me neither.

81

Fabulla had read my epigram where I complain that none of the girls
say 'No'. Her lover asked her once, twice, three times, and she ig-
nored his begging. Now though, Fabulla, tell him you will. I said to
say 'No', not to *keep* saying 'No'.

87

Infantem secum semper tua Bassa, Fabulle,
conlocat et lusus deliciasque uocat,
et, quo mireris magis, infantaria non est.
ergo quid in causa est? pedere Bassa solet.

87

That Bassa of yours, Fabullus, always has a baby beside her on the couch, and calls it 'her darling' and 'her pet'. What makes you all the more surprised is, she's not one of those women who's into babies. So what's her deal? Bassa can't stop farting.

LIBER V

2

Matronae puerique uirginesque,
uobis pagina nostra dedicatur.
tu, quem nequitiae procaciores
delectant nimius salesque nudi,
lasciuos lege quattuor libellos:
quintus cum domino liber iocatur;
quem Germanicus ore non rubenti
coram Cecropia legat puella.

3

Accola iam nostrae Degis, Germanice, ripae,
    a famulis Histri qui tibi uenit aquis,
laetus et attonitus uiso modo praeside mundi,
    adfatus comites dicitur esse suos:
'Sors mea quam fratris melior, cui tam prope fas est
    cernere, tam longe quem colit ille deum.'

5

Sexte, Palatinae cultor facunde Mineruae,
    ingenio frueris qui propiore dei —
nam tibi nascentes domini cognoscere curas
    et secreta ducis pectora nosse licet —
sit locus et nostris aliqua tibi parte libellis,
    qua Pedo, qua Marsus quaque Catullus erit.
ad Capitolini caelestia carmina belli
    grande cothurnati pone Maronis opus.

7

Qualiter Assyrios renouant incendia nidos,
    una decem quotiens saecula uixit auis,
taliter exuta est ueterem noua Roma senectam

BOOK 5

2

Housewives, boys, and maidens: to you is my page dedicated. As for *you*, that take immoderate pleasure in edgier naughtiness and in jokes stripped bare, read my four sexy little books; the fifth book shares its jokes with our Lord. Germanicus may read it without blushing, in company with his girl.*

3

Degis, dweller on a riverbank* that now belongs to us, who has come to you from the servile waters of the lower Danube, glad and astonished after having just seen the world's ruler, is said to have made this speech to his companions: 'How much better is my luck than my brother's, since I was allowed to see so close at hand the one he worships as a god.'

5

Sextus, eloquent worshipper of Palatine Minerva, you enjoy our God's genius closer at hand—you have the opportunity to spot our Lord's concerns as they emerge, and to know the secrets of our Master's heart. Please find room for my little books on whatever shelf Pedo, Marsus, and Catullus share. Next to the heavenly poem of the Capitoline War* place the masterpiece of tragic Maro.

7

Just as fires renew the Assyrian nests, each time the immortal Phoenix has lived ten aeons—just so has new Rome sloughed her former skin,* and assumed the very face of her ruler. And now I pray you,

et sumpsit uultus praesidis ipsa sui.
　iam, precor, oblitus notae, Vulcane, querelae,
　　parce: sumus Martis turba, sed et Veneris;
　parce, pater: sic Lemniacis lasciua catenis
　　ignoscat coniunx et patienter amet.

8

Edictum domini deique nostri,
quo subsellia certiora fiunt
et puros eques ordines recepit,
dum laudat modo Phasis in theatro,
Phasis purpureis rubens lacernis,
et iactat tumido superbus ore:
'Tandem commodius licet sedere,
nunc est reddita dignitas equestris;
turba non premimur, nec inquinamur'—
haec et talia dum refert supinus,
illas purpureas et arrogantes
iussit surgere Leitus lacernas.

10

'Esse quid hoc dicam uiuis quod fama negatur
　et sua quod rarus tempora lector amat?'
hi sunt inuidiae nimirum, Regule, mores,
　praeferat antiquos semper ut illa nouis.
sic ueterem ingrati Pompei quaerimus umbram,
　sic laudant Catuli uilia templa senes;
Ennius est lectus saluo tibi, Roma, Marone,
　et sua riserunt saecula Maeoniden;
rara coronato plausere theatra Menandro;
　norat Nasonem sola Corinna suum.
uos tamen o nostri ne festinate libelli;
　si post fata uenit gloria, non propero.

11

Sardonychas, zmaragdos, adamantas, iaspidas uno
uersat in articulo Stella, Seuere, meus.

forget your well-known grudge,* Vulcan: spare us; we are Mars' tribe,
but Venus' too; spare us, father: and may your sexy wife forgive your
Lemnian chains and love you patiently.

8

The edict of our Lord and God makes the seating clearer and ensures
the knights get their rows to themselves. Just the other day, Phasis*
was in the theatre and praising it—Phasis, ablush in his purple cloak.
With a self-confident look, he disdainfully boasted: '*Finally* one is
seated properly; we equestrians have our dignity back; we're not
hemmed in and dirtied by the mob.' As he slouched there, holding
forth in terms like these, Leitus* ordered that arrogant purple cloak
to vacate its seat.

10

'Fame is denied to the living, and it's a rare reader loves his own
times—what's that about?' There's no doubt these are Envy's habits,
Regulus: she always ranks classics above moderns. Just so do we
ingrates seek out Pompey's ancient portico for shade; just so do the
elderly praise Catulus' excuse for a temple.* While Maro was alive,
Rome, you read Ennius; Homer himself, they laughed at in his time;
not many audiences clapped Menander or saw him win prizes; none
but Corinna* recognized her Ovid. You though, you little books of
mine, don't be impatient. If glory follows death—I'm in no rush.*

11

Sardonyxes, emeralds, diamonds, jaspers:* Severus, my friend Stella
twiddles them all on just one finger-joint. You'll find many gems on

multas in digitis, plures in carmine gemmas
inuenies: inde est haec, puto, culta manus.

12

Quod nutantia fronte perticata
gestat pondera Masclion superbus,
aut grandis Ninus omnibus lacertis
septem quod pueros leuat uel octo,
res non difficilis mihi uidetur,
uno cum digito uel hoc uel illo
portet Stella meus decem puellas.

13

Sum, fateor, semperque fui, Callistrate, pauper,
   sed non obscurus nec male notus eques,
sed toto legor orbe frequens et dicitur 'Hic est',
   quodque cinis paucis, hoc mihi uita dedit.
at tua centenis incumbunt tecta columnis
   et libertinas arca flagellat opes,
magnaque Niliacae seruit tibi gleba Syenes,
   tondet et innumeros Gallica Parma greges.
hoc ego tuque sumus: sed quod sum, non potes esse;
   tu quod es, e populo quilibet esse potest.

18

Quod tibi Decembri mense, quo uolant mappae
gracilesque ligulae cereique chartaeque
et acuta senibus testa cum Damascenis,
praeter libellos uernulas nihil misi,
fortasse auarus uidear aut inhumanus.
odi dolosas munerum et malas artes;
imitantur hamos dona: namque quis nescit
auidum uorata decipi scarum musca?
quotiens amico diuiti nihil donat,
o Quintiane, liberalis est pauper.

his digits, but more in his poetry: *that*, I reckon, is what makes his
hand sparkle.

12

That proud Masclion can balance tottering weights on a pole on his
forehead; that hefty Ninus can flex his pecs and lift seven or even
eight boys: that doesn't strike me as hard to pull off,* when with just
one finger—this one, or that—my friend Stella can carry ten girls.*

13

Yes, I'm poor, Callistratus,* and I don't deny it. I always have been;
but I'm not a nobody. I'm a knight, of no mean reputation; indeed,
I'm widely read all round the world.* 'Here he is,' people say. What
the pyre has given to few, my lifetime has given me. *Your* roof squats
atop a hundred columns, and your strongbox whisks up a freedman's
wealth, and a huge chunk of Syene on the Nile is slaving for your
benefit, and Gaulish Parma* shears your numberless flocks. That's
what we are, you and I: but what I am, you're not capable of being;
what you are, any fool could be.

18

It's December, when gifts speed to and fro—napkins, slender spoons,
wax tapers, writing-paper, a tapering jar of wrinkly damsons;* and
I've sent nothing but my little home-grown books. So perhaps I seem
mean; devoid of human feeling. I *hate* the sly and wicked ploys of
present-giving. Gifts are like hooks: everyone knows the greedy
parrot-wrasse* is duped by the fly he's swallowed. Any time a poor
man *doesn't* give a present to his rich friend, Quintianus, he's being
generous.

20

Si tecum mihi, care Martialis,
securis liceat frui diebus,
si disponere tempus otiosum
et uerae pariter uacare uitae,
nec nos atria nec domos potentum
nec litis tetricas forumque triste
nossemus nec imagines superbas;
sed gestatio, fabulae, libelli,
campus, porticus, umbra, Virgo, thermae,
haec essent loca semper, hi labores.
nunc uiuit necuter sibi, bonosque
soles effugere atque abire sentit,
qui nobis pereunt et imputantur.
quisquam, uiuere cum sciat, moratur?

22

Mane domi nisi te uolui meruitque uidere,
    sint mihi, Paule, tuae longius Esquiliae.
sed Tiburtinae sum proximus accola pilae,
    qua uidet anticum rustica Flora Iouem:
alta Suburani uincenda est semita cliui   .
    et numquam sicco sordida saxa gradu,
uixque datur longas mulorum rumpere mandras
    quaeque trahi multo marmora fune uides.
illud adhuc grauius quod te post mille labores,
    Paule, negat lasso ianitor esse domi.
exitus hic operis uani togulaeque madentis:
    uix tanti Paulum mane uidere fuit.
semper inhumanos habet officiosus amicos:
    rex, nisi dormieris, non potes esse meus.

24

Hermes Martia saeculi uoluptas,
Hermes omnibus eruditus armis,
Hermes et gladiator et magister,

20

If I could spend my days with you, dear Martial,* days free from care;
if we could arrange our leisure as we wished and free up both our time
for really living, we'd know nothing of the entrance-halls and man-
sions of powerful men, of frowning lawsuits and the gloomy Forum,
of haughty ancestor-masks.* Instead—going out for a drive, some
plays, some little books, the Campus, the portico, a bit of shade, the
Virgo, the baths. That's where we'd be, that's what we'd work at. As it
is now, neither of us lives for his own benefit; each of us can feel his
best days slipping away and leaving us behind. They're gone, they've
been debited from our account.* What kind of person knows how to
live, but keeps putting it off?

22

If I wasn't keen to catch you at home this morning, and if I hadn't
earned it—well, Paulus, then let your place on the Esquiline be even
farther from mine than now. As it is, I live right next door to the
Tiburtine Column, where rustic Flora looks on ancient Jupiter,* so
I have to scale the steep stair of the road up from the Subura. The
cobbles are dirty, the steps are never dry; it's next to impossible to
cut past the long mule-trains, and the marble blocks you see being
dragged with lots of ropes. But there's something even worse, Paulus:
after these thousand labours, your doorman tells me you're not at
home. And I'm exhausted! This is what I get for my wasted effort
and my drenched toga. It'd hardly have been worth all that if I *had*
caught you in. The dutiful, respectful man always gets friends with
no human feeling;* you can't be my patron unless you sleep in.

24

Hermes, martial darling of the age;
Hermes, learned in all arms;
Hermes, gladiator and trainer in one;

Hermes turbo sui tremorque ludi,
Hermes, quem timet Helius, sed unum,
Hermes, cui cadit Aduolans, sed uni,
Hermes uincere nec ferire doctus,
Hermes subpositicius sibi ipse,
Hermes diuitiae locariorum,
Hermes cura laborque ludiarum,
Hermes belligera superbus hasta,
Hermes aequoreo minax tridente,
Hermes casside languida timendus,
Hermes gloria Martis uniuersi,
Hermes omnia solus et ter unus.

29

Si quando leporem mittis mihi, Gellia, dicis:
'Formosus septem, Marce, diebus eris.'
si non derides, si uerum, lux mea, narras,
edisti numquam, Gellia, tu leporem.

34

Hanc tibi, Fronto pater, genetrix Flaccilla, puellam
oscula commendo deliciasque meas,
paruula ne nigras horrescat Erotion umbras
oraque Tartarei prodigiosa canis.
impletura fuit sextae modo frigora brumae,
uixisset totidem ni minus illa dies.
inter iam ueteres ludat lasciua patronos
et nomen blaeso garriat ore meum.
mollia non rigidus caespes tegat ossa nec illi,
terra, grauis fueris: non fuit illa tibi.

35

Dum sibi redire de Patrensibus fundis
ducena clamat coccinatus Euclides
Corinthioque plura de suburbano

Hermes, storm and earthquake of his school;
Hermes, whom alone Helius fears;
Hermes, to whom alone Advolans falls;
Hermes, skilled in winning without wounding;
Hermes, stand-in to his own self;
Hermes, who makes the ticket-touts rich;
Hermes, whom the fan-girls love and fret for;
Hermes, standing proud with the battle-spear;
Hermes, looming with the sea-trident;
Hermes, casting terror in his drooping helmet;
Hermes, glory of Mars in all his aspects;
Hermes, all things in one and thrice unique.

29

Whenever you send me a hare, Gellia, you say: 'Marcus, you'll be
handsome for seven days.' If you're not poking fun, if you're telling
the truth: Gellia, darling, you've never eaten hare.*

34

This girl, father Fronto and mother Flaccilla,* I commit to your care,
so that little Erotion, my pet and darling, may not tremble at the dark
shades and at the monstrous mouths of the hound of Tartarus. She
would have just seen out the frosts of her sixth midwinter, had her life
not fallen that many days short. I hope she plays and skips now* in
her former patrons' keeping; I hope her hare-lip mumbles my name.
Please let the turf that covers her bones not be hard, and, earth, be not
heavy upon her; she was no weight on you.

35

As scarlet-dyed Euclides was braying about how he gets two-hun-
dred thousand from his farms at Patras—more, from his place in the
Corinth suburbs—and can trace his family tree all the way back to

longumque pulchra stemma repetit a Leda
et suscitanti Leito reluctatur,
equiti superbo, nobili, lucupleti
cecidit repente magna de sinu clauis.
numquam, Fabulle, nequior fuit clauis.

36

Laudatus nostro quidam, Faustine, libello
dissimulat, quasi nil debeat: imposuit.

37

Puella senibus dulcior mihi cycnis,
agno Galaesi mollior Phalantini,
concha Lucrini delicatior stagni,
cui nec lapillos praeferas Erythraeos
nec modo politum pecudis Indicae dentem
niuesque primas liliumque non tactum;
quae crine uicit Baetici gregis uellus
Rhenique nodos aureamque nitelam;
fragrauit ore quod rosarium Paesti,
quod Atticarum prima mella cerarum,
quod sucinorum rapta de manu gleba;
cui conparatus indecens erat pauo,
inamabilis sciurus et frequens phoenix,
adhuc recenti tepet Erotion busto,
quam pessimorum lex amara fatorum
sexta peregit hieme, nec tamen tota,
nostros amores gaudiumque lususque.
et esse tristem me meus uetat Paetus,
pectusque pulsans pariter et comam uellens:
'Deflere non te uernulae pudet mortem?
ego coniugem' inquit 'extuli et tamen uiuo,
notam, superbam, nobilem, lucupletem.'
quid esse nostro fortius potest Paeto?
ducentiens accepit et tamen uiuit.

beautiful Leda . . . all while struggling with Leitus, who was *ejecting him from his seat* . . . Well, from out of the folded toga of this haughty, noble, wealthy knight there fell a big key. Fabullus, there's never been a naughtier key.*

36

A certain fellow who was praised in my little book is turning a deaf ear, Faustinus, as if he doesn't owe me anything; he's a fraud.*

37

A girl more sweetly voiced than ageing swans,* softer than a lamb of Phalantine Galaesus,* and more delicate than a shell from Lake Lucrinus; a girl you'd pick over Erythraean pearls, new-polished Indian ivory, the first snowfall, and the untouched lily; a girl whose hair outdid fleeces of Baetica, and braids of the Rhine,* and the golden dormouse; a girl who breathed as sweet as Paestum's rose-beds, or Attic combs' first honey, or a nugget of amber snatched from the hand; a girl who made the peacock look ugly, the squirrel unlovable, and the Phoenix commonplace: Erotion lies still warm, her pyre still fresh. The bitter law of the vile Fates killed her in her sixth winter; she didn't even get to see it through. She was my love, my joy. The games we played! And Paetus tells me* I'm not allowed to grieve. He beats his breast and tears his hair: 'Aren't you ashamed to be sobbing over the death of some little slave? I have buried my wife!' he says, 'And still I carry on; and she was somebody! She had pride! Good breeding! Wealth!'

Stiff upper lip? You've nothing on our Paetus: comes into twenty million, and somehow he *makes himself go on.*

42

Callidus effracta nummos fur auferet arca,
    prosternet patrios impia flamma lares;
debitor usuram pariter sortemque negabit,
    non reddet sterilis semina iacta seges;
dispensatorem fallax spoliabit amica,
    mercibus extructas obruet unda rates.
extra fortunam est quidquid donatur amicis:
    quas dederis solas semper habebis opes.

43

Thais habet nigros, niueos Laecania dentes.
    quae ratio est? emptos haec habet, illa suos.

46

Basia dum nolo nisi quae luctantia carpsi,
    et placet ira mihi plus tua quam facies,
ut te saepe rogem, caedo, Diadumene, saepe:
    consequor hoc, ut me nec timeas nec ames.

56

Cui tradas, Lupe, filium magistro
quaeris sollicitus diu rogasque.
omnes grammaticosque rhetorasque
deuites moneo: nihil sit illi
cum libris Ciceronis aut Maronis,
famae Tutilium suae relinquat;
si uersus facit, abdices poetam.
artes discere uult pecuniosas?
fac discat citharoedus aut choraules;
si duri puer ingeni uidetur,
praeconem facias uel architectum.

57

Cum uoco te dominum, noli tibi, Cinna, placere:
    saepe etiam seruum sic resaluto tuum.

42

Savings—the cunning thief will crack your safe and steal them; ancestral home—the fires don't care, they'll trash it; the guy who owes you money—won't pay the interest, won't pay at all. Your field—it's barren, sow seed and you'll get no return; your girlfriend—she'll con your accountant and leave you penniless; your shipping line—the waves will swamp your stacks of cargo. But whatever you give to friends is out of fortune's reach. The wealth you give away is the only wealth you'll never lose.

43

Thais' teeth are black; Laecania's, snowy-white. How come? Laecania bought hers; Thais' are her own.*

46

I only want struggling kisses*—kisses I've seized; I get more of a kick out of your bad temper than your good looks. I want to beg you often, Diadumenus, so I beat you often. Result: you're not afraid of me *or* in love with me.

56

You've been worried for ages, Lupus, and you keep asking—begging me, really—to tell you where to send your son to school. My advice is, steer clear of all the teachers of literature and rhetoric: let him have nothing to do with the books of Cicero and Maro, let him leave Tutilius* to enjoy his fame in peace; and if he starts writing poetry, write him out of your will. Want him to learn a trade that pays? Get him trained as a guitarist* or a flautist; or if you think he's thick, turn him into an auctioneer. Or an architect.

57

When I call you 'Boss', Cinna, don't be so pleased with yourself; I often reply that way when your slave says hello, even.

58

Cras te uicturum, cras dicis, Postume, semper:
   dic mihi, cras istud, Postume, quando uenit?
quam longe cras istud! ubi est? aut unde petendum?
   numquid apud Parthos Armeniosque latet?
iam cras istud habet Priami uel Nestoris annos.
   cras istud quanti, dic mihi, possit emi?
cras uiues? hodie iam uiuere, Postume, tardum est:
   ille sapit quisquis, Postume, uixit heri.

65

Astra polumque dedit quamuis obstante nouerca
   Alcidae Nemees terror et Arcas aper
et castigatum Libycae ceroma palaestrae
   et grauis in Siculo puluere fusus Eryx,
siluarumque tremor, tacita qui fraude solebat
   ducere non rectas Cacus in antra boues.
ista tuae, Caesar, quota pars spectatur harenae?
   dat maiora nouus proelia mane dies.
quot grauiora cadunt Nemeaeo pondera monstro!
   quot tua Maenalios collocat hasta sues!
reddatur si pugna triplex pastoris Hiberi,
   est tibi qui possit uincere Geryonen.
saepe licet Graiae numeretur belua Lernae,
   improba Niliacis quid facit Hydra feris?
pro meritis caelum tantis, Auguste, dederunt
   Alcidae cito di, sed tibi sero dabunt.

69

Antoni Phario nihil obiecture Pothino
   et leuius tabula quam Cicerone nocens,
quid gladium demens Romana stringis in ora?
   hoc admisisset nec Catilina nefas.
impius infando miles corrumpitur auro,
   et tantis opibus uox tacet una tibi.
quid prosunt sacrae pretiosa silentia linguae?
   incipient omnes pro Cicerone loqui.

58

'Tomorrow I'll start living', you say, Postumus: always tomorrow.
Tell me, that 'tomorrow', Postumus, when's it coming? How far off
is that 'tomorrow'? Where is it? Where should we look for it? Is it
under cover among the Parthians and Armenians? That 'tomorrow'
is already as old as Priam or Nestor. That 'tomorrow'—tell me, how
much would it cost to buy? You'll 'start living tomorrow'? Start living
today already, Postumus, you're running out of time.* Anyone with
sense started living yesterday.

65

His stepmother tried to stop him, but the stars and sky were Her-
cules' reward for the Terror of Nemea and the Arcadian boar; the
pummelled dirt of the Libyan wrestling-ring;* massive Eryx, laid
out flat in the dust of Sicily; and Cacus, the forests' bogeyman, the
underhanded rustler who stocked his cave with stolen cattle. But what
fraction is this of the show in *your* arena, Caesar? Each new morning
brings us mightier battles. How many behemoths topple, weightier
than the Nemean prodigy! How many Maenalian swine* does your
spear lay low! If the threefold duel of the Spanish herdsman were to
recur—well, you have a man who could defeat Geryon.* The monster
of Grecian Lerna has an impressive head-count, sure, but what can
the vicious Hydra achieve against the wildlife of the Nile? As his due
for deeds as great as these, Augustus, the gods gave Hercules heaven.
They gave it swiftly; but may they be late in giving it to you.

69

Antony, you can cast no aspersions on Alexandrian Pothinus; your
list* makes you a murderer, and Cicero compounds your guilt. Lu-
natic, why do you draw your sword against the mouthpiece of Rome?
This crime, even Catiline* would never have committed. The thug-
gish soldier is bribed with monstrous gold, and all that loot buys you
one silenced voice. A holy tongue, stilled so expensively—and what's
the use? All will begin to speak in Cicero's stead.

74

Pompeios iuuenes Asia atque Europa, sed ipsum
   terra tegit Libyes, si tamen ulla tegit.
quid mirum toto si spargitur orbe? iacere
   uno non poterat tanta ruina loco.

76

Profecit poto Mithridates saepe ueneno
   toxica ne possent saeua nocere sibi.
tu quoque cauisti cenando tam male semper
   ne posses umquam, Cinna, perire fame.

78

Si tristi domicenio laboras,
Torani, potes esurire mecum.
non derunt tibi, si soles προπίνειν,
uiles Cappadocae grauesque porri,
diuisis cybium latebit ouis.
ponetur digitus tenendus unctis
nigra coliculus uirens patella,
algentem modo qui reliquit hortum,
et pultem niueam premens botellus,
et pallens faba cum rubente lardo.
mensae munera si uoles secundae,
marcentes tibi porrigentur uuae
et nomen pira quae ferunt Syrorum,
et quas docta Neapolis creauit,
lento castaneae uapore tostae:
uinum tu facies bonum bibendo.
post haec omnia forte si mouebit
Bacchus quam solet esuritionem,
succurrent tibi nobiles oliuae,
Piceni modo quas tulere rami,
et feruens cicer et tepens lupinus.
parua est cenula—quis potest negare?—
sed finges nihil audiesue fictum

74

Pompey's sons lie beneath Asia and Europe, but he, beneath the soil
of Libya—if at all. And if he's strewn around the world,* what of it?
So great a wreck could not lie in just one spot.

76

By taking regular draughts of poison, King Mithridates built up
immunity against deadly toxins. You too have taken precautions: by
always dining so wretchedly, Cinna, you've made yourself immune
against ever starving to death.

78

If single-serving meals at home* are getting you down, Toranius, you
can come be hungry with me. If you tend towards an *aperitivo*, you
won't be short of cheap Cappadocian lettuces and stinky leeks; pot-
ted tunny will lurk in halved eggs.* Green broccoli that's just come
from the icy kitchen-garden will be served up on a black plate—grab
it with oily fingers—and a small sausage resting on snowy-white por-
ridge, and pale beans with red pancetta. If you're up for an ample des-
sert, you'll be offered shrivelling grapes and pears that bear the name
of Syrians, and a dish clever Naples invented: chestnuts, roasted over
a slow fire. The wine, you'll make good by drinking it. After all this,
if Bacchus happens to provoke an appetite—he often does—noble
olives will rush to your aid (branches at Picenum* recently bore
them), and simmering chickpeas and warm lupins.

It's a poor little dinner—no one could say otherwise—but you
won't have to fake anything, or listen to fakes: you can kick back,
relax, and wear your own face. There'll be no patron reading out his
big stupid book, no endlessly horny girls from sinful Gades shaking
their frisky loins in a deft wiggle. Instead, little Condylus' flute will
play something light and sensitive. That's our little dinner. You'll go
next to Claudia. What girl do you want to go next to me?*

et uultu placidus tuo recumbes;
nec crassum dominus leget uolumen,
nec de Gadibus improbis puellae
uibrabunt sine fine prurientes
lasciuos docili tremore lumbos;
sed quod nec graue sit nec infacetum,
parui tibia Condyli sonabit.
haec est cenula. Claudiam sequeris.
quam nobis cupis esse tu priorem?

81

Semper pauper eris, si pauper es, Aemiliane:
    dantur opes nullis nunc nisi diuitibus.

83

Insequeris, fugio; fugis, insequor; haec mihi mens est:
    uelle tuum nolo, Dindyme, nolle uolo.

84

Iam tristis nucibus puer relictis
clamoso reuocatur a magistro,
et blando male proditus fritillo,
arcana modo raptus e popina,
aedilem rogat udus aleator.
Saturnalia transiere tota,
nec munuscula parua nec minora
misisti mihi, Galla, quam solebas.
sane sic abeat meus December:
scis certe, puto, uestra iam uenire
Saturnalia, Martias Kalendas;
tunc reddam tibi, Galla, quod dedisti.

81

You'll always be poor, if you're poor, Aemilianus. Only rich people get handouts these days.

83

You chase me, I run; you run, I chase: that's how I'm wired. I don't want you to want me, Dindymus; I want you not to.

84

Now the gloomy schoolboy leaves his nuts, summoned back by his yelling teacher, and the gambler, shabbily betrayed by the lure of his dice-box, has just been dragged drunk out of some shady tavern and is pleading with the aedile.* Saturnalia is utterly over, and you've not sent me any little presents, Galla; not even littler ones than you used to. So much for *my* December. But I'm sure you know your own Saturnalia's coming, the first of March:* then, Galla, I'll repay your generosity.

LIBER VI

1

Sextus mittitur hic tibi libellus,
in primis mihi care Martialis:
quem si terseris aure diligenti,
audebit minus anxius tremensque
magnas Caesaris in manus uenire.

2

Lusus erat sacrae conubia taedae,
   lusus et immeritos exsecuisse mares;
ultraque tu prohibes, Caesar, populisque futuris
   succurris, nasci quos sine fraude iubes.
nec spado iam nec moechus erit te praeside quisquam:
   at prius—o mores!—et spado moechus erat.

3

Nascere Dardanio promissum nomen Iulo,
   uera deum suboles; nascere, magne puer,
cui pater aeternas post saecula tradat habenas,
   quique regas orbem cum seniore senex.
ipsa tibi niueo trahet aurea pollice fila
   et totam Phrixi Iulia nebit ouem.

4

Censor maxime principumque princeps,
cum tot iam tibi debeat triumphos,
tot nascentia templa, tot renata,
tot spectacula, tot deos, tot urbes,
plus debet tibi Roma quod pudica est.

BOOK 6

I

This sixth book is dedicated to you, Martial, the man I love the most. You are my expert listener: buff it up, and it won't shake so much with stage-fright as it enters Caesar's mighty grasp.

2

Once it was 'sport' to betray the sanctity of marriage, 'sport' to castrate innocent males. You are putting a stop to both, Caesar, and safeguarding future generations; your law makes their births legitimate. There will be no eunuchs now, no adulterers—not on your watch. Before, we had sunk so low that even eunuchs committed adultery.*

3

Come to birth, you earnest pledged to Dardan Iulus,* of the true divine lineage; come to birth, great boy, that your father may after long ages pass on the reins of everlasting power; that you may rule the world as an old man alongside one older. With her snow-white finger, Julia herself will draw out golden threads for you,* spinning them from the whole of Phrixus' fleece.

4

Censor-in-Chief, Lord of Lords: Rome has you to thank for countless triumphs; countless temples newly founded or refounded; countless games, gods, cities—but most of all because her morals are clean.

5

Rustica mercatus multis sum praedia nummis;
    mutua des centum, Caeciliane, rogo.
nil mihi respondes? tacitum te dicere credo
    'Non reddes.' ideo, Caeciliane, rogo.

7

Iulia lex populis ex quo, Faustine, renata est
    atque intrare domos iussa Pudicitia est,
aut minus aut certe non plus tricesima lux est,
    et nubit decimo iam Telesilla uiro.
quae nubit totiens, non nubit: adultera lege est.
    offendor moecha simpliciore minus.

10

Pauca Iouem nuper cum milia forte rogarem,
    'Ille dabit' dixit 'qui mihi templa dedit.'
templa quidem dedit ille Ioui, sed milia nobis
    nulla dedit: pudet, ah, pauca rogasse Iouem.
at quam non tetricus, quam nulla nubilus ira,
    quam placido nostras legerat ore preces!
talis supplicibus tribuit diademata Dacis
    et Capitolinas itque reditque uias.
'Dic precor, o nostri dic conscia uirgo Tonantis,
    si negat hoc uultu, quo solet ergo dare?'
sic ego: sic breuiter posita mihi Gorgone Pallas:
    'Quae nondum data sunt, stulte, negata putas?'

11

Quod non sit Pylades hoc tempore, non sit Orestes
    miraris? Pylades, Marce, bibebat idem,
nec melior panis turdusue dabatur Orestae,
    sed par atque eadem cena duobus erat.
tu Lucrina uoras, me pascit aquosa peloris:
    non minus ingenua est et mihi, Marce, gula.

5

I've bought a country estate; a really expensive one.* 'Caecilianus,'
I'm asking, 'could you lend me a hundred thousand?' Silence in re-
turn. 'You won't pay it back,' I bet you're saying under your breath.
Caecilianus, that's exactly why I'm asking.

7

Less than thirty days have passed, Faustina—not more than that,
surely?—since the Julian Law was newly reinstated and Morality
ordered into our homes . . . and already Telesilla* is marrying her
tenth husband. A woman who gets married that often isn't getting
married—she's a state-licensed slut. Good old-fashioned adultery of-
fends me less.

10

I was recently asking Jupiter to send me a few thousand cash, and
he said: 'He will give, who has given me temples.' And yes, he had;
but he didn't give me my thousands. I'm so ashamed I asked Jupiter
for just a few! But he *so* didn't scowl, or cloud over with rage—he
looked *so* calm and peaceful as he read my petition, just like when he
granted crowns to those submissive Dacians,* or when he takes the
road to the Capitol and back.* 'Tell me, I beseech you, Virgin with
whom our Thunderer shares his secrets: if that's how he looks when
he says "No,"* how does he look when it's a "Yes"?' I ask, and Pallas,
her aegis set aside, keeps her answer short: 'Moron! Just because he
hasn't said "Yes" yet, you think it's a "No"?'

11

That this age boasts no Pylades, no Orestes*—Marcus, do you want
to know why? Pylades always got the same wine, and Orestes never
got served better bread or a bigger thrush; the pair of them shared the
same menu. But *you* gobble down Lucrine oysters while I get by on
big, soggy mussels, though my taste-buds are every bit as free-born as
your own. Cadmus' Tyre clothes you; me, shaggy Gaul. Marcus, do

te Cadmea Tyros, me pinguis Gallia uestit:
uis te purpureum, Marce, sagatus amem?
ut praestem Pyladen, aliquis mihi praestet Oresten.
Hoc non fit uerbis, Marce: ut ameris, ama.

12

Iurat capillos esse, quos emit, suos
Fabulla: numquid illa, Paule, peierat?

16

Tu qui pene uiros terres et falce cinaedos,
    iugera seposisiti pauca tuere soli.
sic tua non intrent uetuli pomaria fures,
    sed puer et longis pulchra puella comis.

17

Cinnam, Cinname, te iubes uocari:
non est hic, rogo, Cinna, barbarismus?
tu si Furius ante dictus esses,
Fur ista ratione dicereris.

19

Non de ui neque caede nec ueneno,
sed lis est mihi de tribus capellis:
uicini queror has abesse furto.
hoc iudex sibi postulat probari:
tu Cannas Mithridaticumque bellum
et periuria Punici furoris
et Sullas Mariosque Muciosque
magna uoce sonas manuque tota.
iam dic, Postume, de tribus capellis.

20

Mutua te centum sestertia, Phoebe, rogaui,
cum mihi dixisses 'Exigis ergo nihil?'

you expect me to be your 'best mate' when you're in purple and I'm in an itchy blanket? If I'm to be a proper Pylades, someone needs to make like Orestes. Saying it doesn't make it happen, Marcus. Want me to be your best mate? Start being mine.

12

Fabulla swears that hair is hers—the hair she bought; tell me, Paulus, is she lying?*

16

You who terrify men with your pruning-hook and queers with your cock, watch over my quiet little patch* of dirt. In return, may no old thieves enter your orchards, but a boy or a long-haired, pretty girl.

17

You tell us to call you 'Cinna', Cinnamus.* But, 'Cinna', isn't that a barbarous way with words?* If your name had been Furius before, by this reckoning you'd now be 'Fur'.*

19

It's not over assault or manslaughter or poisoning that I'm pressing charges, but my three little goats:* they're gone, and I'm charging my neighbour with stealing them. The judge demands proof—but you're holding forth on Carrhae and the Mithridatic War and the treacherous Punic Menace, and Sullas and Mariuses and Muciuses, at the top of your lungs and with all the gestures. Postumus, can we get to the bit about my three little goats?

20

I asked you for a loan of a hundred thousand,* Phoebus, when you'd already said to me, 'Well, is there anything you need?' And now you

inquiris, dubitas, cunctaris meque diebus
teque decem crucias: iam rogo, Phoebe, nega.

22

Quod nubis, Proculina, concubino
et, moechum modo, nunc facis maritum,
ne lex Iulia te notare possit:
non nubis, Proculina, sed fateris.

28

Libertus Melioris ille notus,
tota qui cecidit dolente Roma,
cari deliciae breues patroni,
hoc sub marmore Glaucias humatus
iuncto Flaminiae iacet sepulcro:
castus moribus, integer pudore,
uelox ingenio, decore felix.
bis senis modo messibus peractis
uix unum puer applicabat annum.
qui fles talia, nil fleas, uiator.

32

Cum dubitaret adhuc belli ciuilis Enyo
    forsitan et posset uincere mollis Otho,
damnauit multo staturum sanguine Martem
    et fodit certa pectora tota manu.
sit Cato, dum uiuit, sane uel Caesare maior:
    dum moritur, numquid maior Othone fuit?

33

Nil miserabilius, Matho, pedicone Sabello
    uidisti, quo nil laetius ante fuit.
furta, fugae, mortes seruorum, incendia, luctus
    affligunt hominem; iam miser et futuit.

query the details, you're 'not sure', you keep putting it off—you've
left me hanging for thirty days, and yourself too. Please, Phoebus,
just say no already.

22

The way you're marrying your toy-boy, and making your former
adulterer your husband, so the Julian Law can't make an example
of you—Proculina, you're not getting married; you're signing your
confession.

28

That well-known freedman of Melior's, whose death made all Rome
grieve, briefly the darling of his fond benefactor: Glaucias lies buried
here, beneath this marble tomb on the Flaminian Way. His behaviour
was chaste, his morals pure, his wit swift, his good looks a blessing.
To twice-six harvests not long completed was the boy just now adding
one more year. Weep for all this, wayfarer, that you may have nothing
to weep for.

32

Though the madness of civil war hung in the balance, and perhaps
he could have won, Otho* the 'sissy' passed sentence on a conflict
that only great bloodshed could otherwise resolve: he ran himself
through. His hand was steady. In how he lived, let Cato* by all means
be ranked greater than Caesar; tell me though, in how he died, was he
greater than Otho?

33

Matho, you have never seen anything more wretched than that poof
Sabellus, though once he was the happiest creature on earth. Burglar-
ies, slaves running or dying off, fires, deaths in the family—his life's
a mess. It's got so bad, he's even fucking girls.

34

Basia da nobis, Diadumene, pressa. 'Quot' inquis?
   Oceani fluctus me numerare iubes
et maris Aegaei sparsas per litora conchas
   et quae Cecropio monte uagantur apes,
quaeque sonant pleno uocesque manusque theatro
   cum populus subiti Caesaris ora uidet.
nolo quot arguto dedit exorata Catullo
   Lesbia: pauca cupit qui numerare potest.

53

Lotus nobiscum est, hilaris cenauit, et idem
   inuentus mane est mortuus Andragoras.
tam subitae mortis causam, Faustine, requiris?
   in somnis medicum uiderat Hermocraten.

65

'Hexametris epigramma facis' scio dicere Tuccam:
   Tucca, solet fieri, denique, Tucca, licet.
'Sed tamen hoc longum est.' Solet hoc quoque, Tucca, licetque:
   si breuiora probas, disticha sola legas.
conueniat nobis ut fas epigrammata longa
   sit transire tibi, scribere, Tucca, mihi.

67

Cur tantum eunuchos habeat tua Caelia, quaeris,
   Pannyche? uult futui Caelia nec parere.

68

Flete nefas uestrum, sed toto flete Lucrino,
   Naides, et luctus sentiat ipsa Thetis:
inter Baianas raptus puer occidit undas
   Eutychos ille, tuum, Castrice, dulce latus.
hic tibi curarum socius blandumque leuamen,

34

Give me kisses, Diadumenus,* kisses thick and fast. 'How many,' you ask? You're telling me to count the waves of Ocean, and the seashells scattered along the beaches of the Aegean, and every bee that waggles on the Cecropian mountain,* and every voice that cheers and hand that claps in the packed theatre when Caesar makes a surprise appearance. I don't want however many Lesbia gave tuneful Catullus, when he finally wore her down; he who can number his kisses wants only a few.

53

He came to the baths with us, he was a blast at dinner—and that same Andragoras turned up dead this morning. You wonder what could cause such a sudden death, Faustinus? In his dreams, he caught sight of Dr Hermocrates.*

65

'You're making an epigram out of hexameters.'* I know that's what Tucca's saying. Lots of people do that, Tucca, and you know what? It's not against the law. 'All the same, this one is long.' Lots of people do that *too*, Tucca, and it's not against the law either. If short ones are your thing, just read the two-liners. Tucca, let's make a deal: you can keep skipping the long epigrams, and I can keep writing them.

67

Don't you know why all Caelia's slaves are eunuchs, Pannychis?* Caelia wants to get screwed, not knocked up.

68

Weep, Naiads, at your crime; fill Lake Lucrinus with your tears, and let Thetis herself hear your lamentation. A boy is dead, pulled into the undertow at Baiae—sweet Eutychos, who, Castricus, was your inseparable friend.* He was your companion through bad times, your welcome distraction; he was your love; he was the Alexis of our bard.*

hic amor, hic nostri uatis Alexis erat.
numquid te uitreis nudum lasciua sub undis
    uidit et Alcidae nympha remisit Hylan?
an dea femineum iam neglegit Hermaphroditum
    amplexu teneri sollicita uiri?
quidquid id est, subitae quaecumque est causa rapinae,
    sit, precor, et tellus mitis et unda tibi.

71

Edere lasciuos ad Baetica crusmata gestus
    et Gaditanis ludere docta modis,
tendere quae tremulum Pelian Hecubaeque maritum
    posset ad Hectoreos sollicitare rogos,
urit et excruciat dominum Telethusa priorem:
    uendidit ancillam, nunc redimit dominam.

72

Fur notae nimium rapacitatis
compilare Cilix uolebat hortum,
ingenti sed erat, Fabulle, in horto
praeter marmoreum nihil Priapum.
dum non uult uacua manu redire,
ipsum surripuit Cilix Priapum.

76

Ille sacri lateris custos Martisque togati,
    credita cui summi castra fuere ducis,
hic situs est Fuscus. licet hoc, Fortuna, fateri:
    non timet hostilis iam lapis iste minas.
grande iugum domita Dacus ceruice recepit
    et famulum uictrix possidet umbra nemus.

82

Quidam me modo, Rufe, diligenter
inspectum, uelut emptor aut lanista,
cum uultu digitoque subnotasset,

Tell me, boy, did some lust-struck nymph see you unclothed beneath
the glassy waters, and send Hercules back his Hylas?* Or does the
goddess have no time for unmanly Hermaphroditus, now she melts in
the embrace of a youth who's all man? Whatever the truth, whatever
the reason you were taken so suddenly, I pray that the earth may rest
gently on you, and the water too.

71

Adept in sexy moves to an Andalusian soundtrack and writhing to
Cadiz* beats, Telethusa could tease a hard-on from decrepit old
Pelias, or from Hecuba's husband* at Hector's own funeral. Now she
inflames and tortures her former master. He sold her as his slave; he's
buying her back as his mistress.*

72

Cilix,* thief and notorious kleptomaniac, decided to burgle a garden.
The garden was huge, Fabullus, but all it had in it was a marble Pria-
pus.* Since he didn't want to come away empty-handed, Cilix made
off with that same Priapus.

76

That bodyguard of the sacred person, of Mars when he wears the
toga, to whom the barracks* of our Commander-in-Chief were en-
trusted: here Fuscus lies. This much, Fortune, we may affirm: that
his gravestone apprehends no threats from our enemies. The Dacian
is tamed;* his neck once more bows under our mighty yoke. A victori-
ous ghost holds the servile grove.

82

Some guy was checking me out recently, Rufus—really closely, as if
he was going to purchase me or train me as a gladiator. He was frown-
ing, twitching his fingers; taking mental notes. And then he said: 'Are

'Tune es, tune' ait 'ille Martialis,
cuius nequitias iocosque nouit
aurem qui modo non habet Batauam?'
subrisi modice, leuique nutu
me quem dixerat esse non negaui.
'Cur ergo' inquit 'habes malas lacernas?'
respondi: 'Quia sum malus poeta.'
hoc ne saepius accidat poetae,
mittas, Rufe, mihi bonas lacernas.

85

Editur en sextus sine te mihi, Rufe Camoni,
　　nec te lectorem sperat, amice, liber:
impia Cappadocum tellus et numine laeuo
　　uisa tibi cineres reddit et ossa patri.
funde tuo lacrimas orbata Bononia Rufo,
　　et resonet tota planctus in Aemilia:
heu qualis pietas, heu quam breuis occidit aetas!
　　uiderat Alphei praemia quinta modo.
pectore tu memori nostros euoluere lusus,
　　tu solitus totos, Rufe, tenere iocos,
accipe cum fletu maesti breue carmen amici
　　atque haec absentis tura fuisse puta.

you him? Are you that Martial, whose dirty jokes anyone knows who
doesn't have the ear of a Dutchman?' I flashed him a self-deprecating
smile and with a discreet nod of the head conceded that he'd got his
man. 'If that's so,' he asked, 'why do you wear such rotten coats?'*
'Because I'm a rotten poet,' I replied. This needn't happen to a poet,
Rufus, not so often: just send me some decent coats.

85

Look, my sixth book is out, Rufus Camonius; but you are not here to
see it,* my friend, and it cannot hope for you as its reader. Cappado-
cia, a cruel land you were unlucky to lay eyes on, returns your ashes
and bones to your father. Gush with tears, Bononia, at the loss of your
Rufus, and let lamentation resound along the whole Aemilian Way.
Alas! What a good son he was! Alas! How short a lifespan has fallen
into darkness! He had just now seen Alpheus' prizes* for the fifth
time. You used to recite my jokes from memory, Rufus; you had them
all by heart. Take now this short poem, and the tears of a sorrowful
friend. I was not there: reckon this the incense I should have burned.

5

Si desiderium, Caesar, populique patrumque
  respicis et Latiae gaudia uera togae,
redde deum uotis poscentibus. inuidet hosti
  Roma suo, ueniat laurea multa licet:
terrarum dominum propius uidet ille tuoque
  terretur uultu barbarus et fruitur.

6

Ecquid Hyperboreis ad nos conuersus ab oris
  Ausonias Caesar iam parat ire uias?
certus abest auctor, sed uox hoc nuntiat omnis:
  credo tibi, uerum dicere, Fama, soles.
publica uictrices testantur gaudia chartae,
  Martia laurigera cuspide pila uirent.
rursus, io, magnos clamat tibi Roma triumphos,
  inuictusque tua, Caesar, in urbe sonas.
sed iam laetitiae quo sit fiducia maior,
  Sarmaticae laurus nuntius ipse ueni.

8

Nunc hilares, si quando mihi, nunc ludite, Musae:
  uictor ab Odrysio redditur orbe deus.
certa facis populi tu primus uota, December:
  iam licet ingenti dicere uoce 'Venit!'
felix sorte tua! Poteras non cedere Iano,
  gaudia si nobis quae dabit ille dares.
festa coronatus ludet conuicia miles,
  inter laurigeros cum comes ibit equos.
fas audire iocos leuioraque carmina, Caesar,
  et tibi, si lusus ipse triumphus amat.

BOOK 7

5

If, Caesar, you are mindful of what the people and Senate miss, and what will make the citizens of Rome* truly happy, answer the prayers of your petitioners: give us back our god. Rome is jealous of her enemy, though many a laurel comes; he sees the Lord of the earth close at hand. Your face fills the savage with terror—and delight.

6

Has Caesar about-faced from Polar lands towards us? Is he now readying to travel Ausonian* roads? There is no sure witness, but every voice proclaims it. I believe in you: you tend, Rumour, to speak the truth. Letters reporting victory call forth public happiness; the spears of Mars are green, their points twined with laurel. Once again Rome shouts 'Hurrah!' at your mighty triumphs, Caesar, and you are hailed as 'the Invincible' in your own city. But now make our rejoicing all the more confident by coming in person to proclaim your own Sarmatian victory.

8

Now skip and be cheerful, my Muses, now if ever: our god is returned to us victorious from the land of Thrace. December, you bring first confirmation of the people's prayers: now we may shout at the top of our voice, 'He is coming!' Happy in your lot, you might not give way to Janus,* if you were giving us the happiness that he will give. The infantry, crowned with garlands, will enjoy their carnival banter as they mingle with the laurel-decked cavalry.* It's fine for you too, Caesar, to hear jokes and silly songs, if the Triumph itself loves fun.

13

Dum Tiburtinis albescere solibus audit
antiqui dentis fusca Lycoris ebur,
uenit in Herculeos colles. quid Tiburis alti
aura ualet! paruo tempore nigra redit.

16

Aera domi non sunt; superest hoc, Regule, solum
ut tua uendamus munera: numquid emis?

17

Ruris bibliotheca delicati,
uicinam uidet unde lector urbem,
inter carmina sanctiora si quis
lasciuae fuerit locus Thaliae,
hos nido licet inseras uel imo
septem quos tibi misimus libellos
auctoris calamo sui notatos:
haec illis pretium facit litura.
at tu munere delicata paruo
quae cantaberis orbe nota toto,
pignus pectoris hoc mei tuere,
Iuli bibliotheca Martialis.

23

Phoebe, ueni, sed quantus eras cum bella tonanti
ipse dares Latiae plectra secunda lyrae.
quid tanta pro luce precer? tu, Polla, maritum
saepe colas et se sentiat ille coli.

24

Cum Iuuenale meo quae me committere temptas,
quid non audebis, perfida lingua, loqui?

13

Hearing that the ivory of an antique tusk turns white in the sun at Tivoli, dark-skinned Lycoris journeyed to Hercules' hills. What power resides in the air of high Tivoli!* Not long after, she came home black.

16

I've not a penny in the house. There's nothing else for it, Regulus: I'm going to have to sell the presents you sent. I don't suppose you're buying?

17

You library of a gracious country villa, from where the reader can see the city close by: might you squeeze in my naughty Muse, between your more respectable poems? Those seven little books I've sent you, you're welcome to stick in a nook, even a really obscure one. They're annotated by their author's pen: these corrections add value. Graced by this little gift, your fame will be sung all round the world.* Watch over this token of my affection, you library of Julius Martial.

23

Come, Phoebus, but as you were when you presented the second plectrum of the Latin lyre to the one who thundered forth Wars.* What prayer should I offer for the coming of so great a light?* May you, Polla, always cherish your husband's memory, and may he know himself cherished.

24

You're trying to start a fight between me and my dear Juvenal;* traitorous tongue, what *don't* you have the brass cheek to say? The horrid

te fingente nefas Pyladen odisset Orestes,
   Thesea Pirithoi destituisset amor;
tu Siculos fratres et maius nomen Atridas
   et Ledae poteras dissociare genus.
hoc tibi pro meritis et talibus imprecor ausis,
   ut facias illud quod, puto, lingua, facis.

27

Tuscae glandis aper populator et ilice multa
   iam piger, Aetolae fama secunda ferae,
quem meus intrauit splendenti cuspide Dexter,
   praeda iacet nostris inuidiosa focis.
pinguescant madido laeti nidore penates
   flagret et exciso festa culina iugo.
sed cocus ingentem piperis consumet aceruum,
   addet et arcano mixta Falerna garo:
ad dominum redeas, noster te non capit ignis,
   conturbator aper: uilius esurio.

31

Raucae chortis aues et oua matrum
et flauas medio uapore Chias
et fetum querulae rudem capellae
nec iam frigoribus pares oliuas
et canum gelidis holus pruinis
de nostro tibi missa rure credis?
o quam, Regule, diligenter erras!
nil nostri, nisi me, ferunt agelli.
quidquid uilicus Vmber aut colonus
aut rus marmore tertio notatum
aut Tusci tibi Tusculiue mittunt,
id tota mihi nascitur Subura.

36

Cum pluuias madidumque Iouem perferre negaret
   et rudis hibernis uilla nataret aquis,

lies you spin would have made Orestes hate Pylades, made Pirithous forsake his love for Theseus; you could have broken up the Sicilian brothers and (a greater name) the Atreides and Leda's brood.* I call this curse upon you, tongue—your brazen deeds have earned it: may you do that thing* I'm pretty sure you do . . .

27

He had ravaged Tuscan acorns and grown sluggish from many holm-oaks, that boar; he ranked second in fame to the Beast of Aetolia.* My friend Dexter ran him through with his gleaming spear-point, and now he lies at my hearth. What enviable loot! May the gods of my household rejoice and grow fat on his juicy aroma, and may my kitchen strip the ridge-line to set a holiday blaze. But my cook will waste a huge heap of pepper, and Falernian mixed with his special stash of fish sauce*. . . Go back to your master, please, my oven won't take you. Boar? You're a white elephant. I'm better off going hungry.

31

Cackling kitchen-garden poultry, and eggs from their mothers; Chian figs tawny from middling heat; the young litter of a bleating nanny-goat; olives that are no longer a match for cold weather, and greens blanched by icy frosts:* do you really think they come from my 'country estate'? Oh, Regulus, you couldn't be more wrong! My little patch* yields nothing but myself. All that stuff you get sent by your Umbrian estate-manager, or your tenant-farmer, or the country estate you've got on your books at the third milestone, or that lot in Tuscany or Tusculum—for me its *terroir* is the broad Subura.*

36

When my tumbledown villa refused to see out the showers sent by rainy Jupiter* and was awash with winter downpours, a big shipment

plurima, quae posset subitos effundere nimbos,
  muneribus uenit tegula missa tuis.
horridus, ecce, sonat Boreae stridore December:
  Stella, tegis uillam, non tegis agricolam.

50

Fons dominae, regina loci quo gaudet Ianthis,
  gloria conspicuae deliciumque domus,
cum tua tot niueis ornetur ripa ministris
  et Ganymedeo luceat unda choro,
quid facit Alcides silua sacratus in ista?
  tam uicina tibi cur tenet antra deus?
numquid Nympharum notos obseruat amores,
  tam multi pariter ne rapiantur Hylae?

53

Omnia misisti mihi Saturnalibus, Vmber,
  munera, contulerant quae tibi quinque dies:
bis senos triplices et dentiscalpia septem;
  his comes accessit spongea, mappa, calix,
semodiusque fabae cum uimine Picenarum
  et Laletanae nigra lagona sapae;
paruaque cum canis uenerunt cottana prunis
  et Libycae fici pondere testa grauis.
uix puto triginta nummorum tota fuisse
  munera, quae grandes octo tulere Syri.
quanto commodius nullo mihi ferre labore
  argenti potuit pondera quinque puer!

61

Abstulerat totam temerarius institor urbem
  inque suo nullum limine limen erat.
iussisti tenuis, Germanice, crescere uicos,
  et modo quae fuerat semita, facta uia est.
nulla catenatis pila est praecincta lagonis

of roof-tiles arrived to shed sudden rainstorms—you'd sent them as a present. But listen! December bristles with thunder; the North Wind is howling. Stella, you clothe my farm, but not its farmer.*

50

The mistress' fountain, queen of the place in which Ianthis* delights, glory and indulgence of a distinguished house: since your margin is embellished with so many snowy-white serving-boys, and your water glows with a parade of Ganymedes, what is Hercules up to, receiving cult in yonder wood? Why does the god dwell in a grotto so near at hand? Is he on the watch for the loves he knows nymphs feel, to stop so many Hylases* being snatched away at once?

53

At the Saturnalia, Umber, you sent me all the presents* that five days had raked in: twelve three-leaved notepads, and seven toothpicks. Further, a complementary sponge; one napkin; one cup; a gallon of dry beans, with a basket of Picene olives and a smoke-blackened flagon of Laletanian grape syrup.* These came with a small Syrian fig, some wrinkly prunes, and a clay pot carrying a heavy load of Libyan figs. These presents I'd put at thirty sesterces the lot, tops— but eight giant Syrians carried them. How much more conveniently, with no bother, could one boy have popped round with five pounds of silverware!

61

The rude street vendor had taken our whole city away from us: no shop entrance stayed in its own doorway. Germanicus, you have com- manded the narrow lanes to widen, and what was recently an alley is now a street. No column is ringed with chained flagons; the praetor is not compelled to track through the mud; the razor is not drawn

nec praetor medio cogitur ire luto,
stringitur in densa nec caeca nouacula turba
occupat aut totas nigra popina uias.
tonsor, copo, cocus, lanius sua limina seruant.
nunc Roma est, nuper magna taberna fuit.

64

Qui tonsor fueras tota notissimus urbe
  et post hoc dominae munere factus eques,
Sicanias urbes Aetnaeaque regna petisti,
  Cinname, cum fugeres tristia iura fori.
qua nunc arte graues tolerabis inutilis annos?
  quid facit infelix et fugitiua quies?
non rhetor, non grammaticus ludiue magister,
  non Cynicus, non tu Stoicus esse potes,
uendere nec uocem Siculis plausumque theatris:
  quod superest, iterum, Cinname, tonsor eris.

67

Pedicat pueros tribas Philaenis
et tentigine saeuior mariti
undenas dolat in die puellas.
harpasto quoque subligata ludit
et flauescit haphe, grauesque draucis
halteras facili rotat lacerto,
et putri lutulenta de palaestra
uncti uerbere uapulat magistri:
nec cenat prius aut recumbit ante
quam septem uomuit meros deunces;
ad quos fas sibi tunc putat redire,
cum coloephia sedecim comedit.
post haec omnia cum libidinatur,
non fellat — putat hoc parum uirile —
sed plane medias uorat puellas.
di mentem tibi dent tuam, Philaeni,
cunnum lingere quae putas uirile.

indiscriminately amid a packed crowd, nor does the smoke-blackened cantina* take over whole streets. Barber, innkeeper, cook, and butcher keep to their own doorways. Now it is Rome; not long ago it was one huge stall.

64

You used to be a barber, the most famous in the whole city, until your mistress arranged for you to get a knighthood; and now you have headed for the cities of Sicily and estates near Etna, Cinnamus, a fugitive from the Forum's stern laws.* But how will you occupy yourself, you useless man, and endure the dragging years? What good is 'the quiet life' with no useful outlet, and warrants outstanding? You don't have the makings of a speaker, a scholar, a teacher, or a Cynic—and no way a Stoic; and you can't sell your voice and your applause in *Sicilian* theatres.* Only one thing for it, Cinnamus: you'll be a barber again.

67

Butch Philaenis* fucks boys in the arse. Rougher than a husband's hard-on, she sticks it to eleven girls a day. She tucks up her skirt and plays handball, gets covered in the wrestlers' yellow sand, and easily arm-curls weights that queer *guys* would find heavy. Smeared with the dust of the wrestling-ring, she gets worked over hard by her oiled-up trainer; and she won't eat dinner or recline at table before she's thrown up a good six pints* of unmixed wine—which she thinks it's alright to come back to, once she's wolfed down sixteen rib-eyes.* When she's done with all this, she sates her lust. She doesn't suck cock—that's not macho enough for her; instead she absolutely gobbles up girls' middles. May the gods bring you to your senses, Philaenis, for thinking it macho to lick cunt.

68

Commendare meas, Instanti Rufe, Camenas
    parce, precor, socero: seria forsan amat.
quod si lasciuos admittit et ille libellos,
    haec ego uel Curio Fabricioque legam.

69

Haec est illa tibi promissa Theophila, Cani,
    cuius Cecropia pectora dote madent.
hanc sibi iure petat magni senis Atticus hortus,
    nec minus esse suam Stoica turba uelit.
uiuet opus quodcumque per has emiseris aures;
    tam non femineum nec populare sapit.
non tua Pantaenis nimium se praeferat illi,
    quamuis Pierio sit bene nota choro.
carmina fingentem Sappho laudabat amatrix:
    castior haec et non doctior illa fuit.

81

'Triginta toto mala sunt epigrammata libro.'
    si totidem bona sunt, Lause, bonus liber est.

84

Dum mea Caecilio formatur imago Secundo
    spirat et arguta picta tabella manu,
i, liber, ad Geticam Peucen Histrumque iacentem:
    haec loca perdomitis gentibus ille tenet.
parua dabis caro, sed dulcia, dona sodali:
    certior in nostro carmine uultus erit;
casibus hic nullis, nullis delebilis annis
    uiuet, Apelleum cum morietur opus.

68

Please, Istantius Rufus, lay off recommending my Muses to your father-in-law; chances are he likes them serious. But if someone like him can find house-room for my naughty little books, I might even read them to Curius and Fabricius.*

69

This is the girl who was promised to you, Canius—Theophila, whose breast drips with a Cecropian* dowry. The Attic garden of wonderful old Epicurus might lawfully claim her for its own, and the hubbub of the Stoics would want her for themselves every bit as much. Whatever work you broadcast through these ears of hers will endure: she's such a scholar, not like a woman or the man in the street. Your own Pantaenis* would not rank herself too far ahead of her, however well known she herself is to the Pierian chorus. Sappho the woman-lover* would praise her versification: *this* girl is the purer of the two, and *that* one was not the more learned.

81

'There are thirty bad epigrams in this book.' If there are thirty good ones, Lausus, it's a good book.

84

While my portrait is being taken for Caecilius Secundus, and the painted board is coming to life under the artist's fast-moving hand, go, little book, to Getic Peucē* and the sluggish Danube: these regions and their vanquished tribes he rules. Small, but sweet, are the gifts you will give my dear and close friend: a more faithful likeness will be found in my verse.* This portrait fate and time can never erase; it still shall live when the work of Apelles* dies.

85

Quod non insulse scribis tetrasticha quaedam,
    disticha quod belle pauca, Sabelle, facis,
laudo nec admiror. facile est epigrammata belle
    scribere; sed librum scribere difficile est.

90

Iactat inaequalem Matho me fecisse libellum:
    si uerum est, laudat carmina nostra Matho.
aequales scribit libros Caluinus et Vmber:
    aequalis liber est, Cretice, qui malus est.

91

De nostro facunde tibi Iuuenalis agello
    Saturnalicias mittimus, ecce, nuces:
cetera lasciuis donauit poma puellis
    mentula custodis luxuriosa dei.

85

You can write a four-liner that shows promise, Sabellus, and you're coming up with a few neat couplets. I congratulate you; but I'm not impressed. Writing neat epigrams is easy. Writing a book is hard.

90

Matho is crowing that I've 'made an inconsistent book'. If he's right, he's actually praising my poems. Calvinus and Umber write 'consistent' books; if a book's 'consistent', Creticus,* it's consistently bad.

91

Eloquent Juvenal, see what I'm sending you from my little farm: nuts for Saturnalia. Horny girls possess its other crops, gifts from the lustful prick of its guardian god.

LIBER VIII

IMPERATORI DOMITIANO CAESARI AVGVSTO GERMANICO DACICO
VALERIVS MARTIALIS S.

Omnes quidem libelli mei, domine, quibus tu famam, id est uitam,
dedisti, tibi supplicant; et, puto, propter hoc legentur. hic tamen, qui
operis nostri octauus inscribitur, occasione pietatis frequentius frui-
tur. minus itaque ingenio laborandum fuit, in cuius locum materia
successerat: quam quidem subinde aliqua iocorum mixtura uariare
temptauimus, ne caelesti uerecundiae tuae laudes suas, quae facilius
te fatigare possint quam nos satiare, omnis uersus ingereret. quamuis
autem epigrammata a seuerissimis quoque et summae fortunae uiris
ita scripta sint ut mimicam uerborum licentiam adfectasse uidean-
tur, ego tamen illis non permisi tam lasciui loqui quam solent. cum
pars libri et maior et melior ad maiestatem sacri nominis tui alligata
sit, meminerit non nisi religiosa purificatione lustratos accedere ad
templa debere. quod ut custoditurum me lecturi sciant, in ipso libelli
huius limine profiteri breuissimo placuit epigrammate:

I

Laurigeros domini, liber, intrature penates
  disce uerecundo sanctius ore loqui.
nuda recede Venus; non est tuus iste libellus:
  tu mihi, tu, Pallas Caesariana, ueni.

4

Quantus, io, Latias mundi conuentus ad aras
  suscipit et soluit pro duce uota suo!

BOOK 8

TO THE EMPEROR DOMITIAN CAESAR AUGUSTUS GERMANICUS*
DACICUS, VALERIUS MARTIAL, GREETINGS.

[*Preface*] All my books, Lord, or all those to which you have given
fame—which is to say, life—are your humble petitioners; and, I think,
this has secured their readership in posterity. But this one, which is
enrolled as the eighth of my opus, takes more frequent advantage of
the opportunity to pay its respects. This meant there was less work
to be done in the line of clever ideas; real substance took their place.
Now and then, though, I have tried to lend variety to that substance
by adulterating it with a little humour, so that not every line gushes
its own praises for your heavenly modesty—praises which would be
more likely to wear you out than satisfy our enthusiasm. On the other
hand, and although men of the sternest morals and highest station
have written epigrams that make them look as though they are striv-
ing for the verbal licence accorded to stage-farce, I have not allowed
these poems to speak as naughtily as is their wont. Since the larger and
better part of the book is laid under obligation to the majesty of your
sacred name, let it remember that pilgrims should never approach the
shrine before they have been ritually cleansed. So that prospective
readers know I will be observing this rule, I have decided to declare
it frankly, right on the threshold of this little book, in an epigram of
extreme brevity:

I

Book, who are about to enter the laurel-decked home of our Lord,
learn to speak more chastely from a modest mouth. Nude Venus, re-
tire; this little book is not yours. But come you to me, come, Caesarian
Pallas.*

4

Hurrah! What a global convention enters upon and discharges
its oaths at Latin altars in its Leader's name!* Not only mortals,

non sunt haec hominum, Germanice, gaudia tantum,
   sed faciunt ipsi nunc, puto, sacra dei.

13

Morio dictus erat: uiginti milibus emi.
   redde mihi nummos, Gargiliane: sapit.

23

Esse tibi uideor saeuus nimiumque gulosus,
   qui propter cenam, Rustice, caedo cocum.
si leuis ista tibi flagrorum causa uidetur,
   ex qua uis causa uapulet ergo cocus?

24

Si quid forte petam timido gracilique libello,
   improba non fuerit si mea charta, dato.
et si non dederis, Caesar, permitte rogari:
   offendunt numquam tura precesque Iouem.
qui fingit sacros auro uel marmore uultus,
   non facit ille deos: qui rogat, ille facit.

27

Munera qui tibi dat locupleti, Gaure, senique,
   si sapis et sentis, hoc tibi ait: 'Morere.'

29

Disticha qui scribit, puto, uult breuitate placere.
   quid prodest breuitas, dic mihi, si liber est?

30

Qui nunc Caesareae lusus spectatur harenae,
   temporibus Bruti gloria summa fuit.
aspicis ut teneat flammas poenaque fruatur

Germanicus, share these joys; the gods themselves, I think, make sacrifice.

13

He was advertised as a fool; I paid twenty thousand for him. I want a refund, Gargilianus: he's got sense.

23

You think I'm a monster, Rusticus, that I'm obsessed with fine dining, because I'm beating my cook on account of that dinner. If you think that's a flimsy excuse for a whipping, what *ought* a cook to get a hiding for?

24

If I happen to ask for some boon in this poor, timid little book, and if my page has not been shameless, say 'Yes'; and even if you don't say 'Yes', Caesar, put up with me asking. Incense and prayers are never hateful to Jupiter. He who shapes sacred visages in gold or marble does not make gods; he makes them who entreats.

27

Whoever gives you presents, you being so old and rich—Gaurus, if you've your wits about you, you'll know they're saying: 'Die!'

29

Whoever writes couplets wants to please by concision, I suppose. But what's the good of concision when they're a book?*

30

What now is spectacle in Caesar's arena, in Brutus' times was utmost glory.* You see how the steadfast hand clutches the flames, revels in its punishment, and masters the astonished fire! Its owner stands there,

fortis, et attonito regnet in igne manus!
ipse sui spectator adest et nobile dextrae
funus amat: totis pascitur illa sacris;
quod nisi rapta foret nolenti poena, parabat
saeuior in lassos ire sinistra focos.
scire piget post tale decus quid fecerit ante:
quam uidi satis hanc est mihi nosse manum.

31

Nescio quid de te non belle, Dento, fateris,
coniuge qui ducta iura paterna petis.
sed iam supplicibus dominum lassare libellis
desine et in patriam serus ab urbe redi:
nam dum tu longe deserta uxore diuque
tres quaeris natos, quattuor inuenies.

32

Aera per tacitum delapsa sedentis in ipsos
fluxit Aretullae blanda columba sinus.
luserat hoc casus, nisi inobseruata maneret
permissaque sibi nollet abire fuga.
si meliora piae fas est sperare sorori
et dominum mundi flectere uota ualent,
haec a Sardois tibi forsitan exulis oris,
fratre reuersuro, nuntia uenit auis.

36

Regia pyramidum, Caesar, miracula ride;
iam tacet Eoum barbara Memphis opus:
pars quota Parrhasiae labor est Mareoticus aulae?
clarius in toto nil uidet orbe dies.
septenos pariter credas adsurgere montes,
Thessalicum breuior Pelion Ossa tulit;
aethera sic intrat nitidis ut conditus astris
inferiore tonet nube serenus apex

an audience to his own show; he delights in the noble end afforded to his right hand, which gluts itself on every stage of its funeral. Had the means of punishment not been snatched away against its victim's will, his raging left hand was readying to enter the exhausted pyre. After such an edifying display, I prefer not to know what that hand had done before; I am content to know it as I saw it.

31

You're admitting something about yourself, Dento, when you seek the perks of fatherhood,* having only just married; I'm not sure what, but it's not pretty. Stop pestering our Lord already with your wheedling petitions;* get out of town, finally, and go back where you came from. It's far away your wife is, and long neglected while you've sought your Three Children; you'll find you have four.

32

A cooing dove flew down through the silent air and settled right in Arctulla's lap. It could have been chance playing tricks—but, left to its own devices, there it stayed. It was free to go, but did not wish to fly. If it is lawful for a devoted sister to wish for better things, and if prayers have power to sway the Lord of Mankind, perhaps this bird came to you as a messenger from Sardinia's exile shore, and your brother is about to return.

36

Scoff, Caesar, at the kingly Wonders of the Pyramids;* barbarous Memphis no longer speaks of the works of Dawn.* What fraction of the Parrhasian palace does the labour of Mareotis* equal? The sun sees nothing more resplendent in the whole world. You would think the seven hills were rising as one; Ossa bore Thessalian Pelion* and was less tall. It so pierces the heavens that, hidden in the gleaming stars, its fair summit thunders above the clouds; and it takes its fill of Phoebus' mystic light before Circe sees her father's dawning face.

et prius arcano satietur numine Phoebi
    nascentis Circe quam uidet ora patris.
haec, Auguste, tamen, quae uertice sidera pulsat,
    par domus est caelo, sed minor est domino.

39

Qui Palatinae caperet conuiuia mensae
    ambrosiasque dapes, non erat ante locus:
hic haurire decet sacrum, Germanice, nectar
    et Ganymedea pocula mixta manu.
esse uelis, oro, serus conuiua Tonantis:
    at tu si properas, Iuppiter, ipse ueni.

40

Non horti neque palmitis beati
    sed rari nemoris, Priape, custos,
ex quo natus es et potes renasci,
    furaces moneo manus repellas
et siluam domini focis reserues:
    si defecerit haec, et ipse lignum es.

50 (51)

Quis labor in phiala? docti Myos anne Myronos?
    Mentoris haec manus est an, Polyclite, tua?
liuescit nulla caligine fusca nec odit
    exploratores nubila massa focos.
uera minus flauo radiant electra metallo
    et niueum felix pustula uincit ebur.
materiae non cedit opus: sic alligat orbem,
    plurima cum tota lampade luna nitet.
stat caper Aeolio Thebani uellere Phrixi
    cultus: ab hoc mallet uecta fuisse soror;
hunc nec Cinyphius tonsor uiolauerit et tu
    ipse tua pasci uite, Lyaee, uelis.
terga premit pecudis geminis Amor aureus alis;
    Palladius tenero lotos ab ore sonat:

And yet, Augustus, this House, this star-scraper, though equal to heaven, is unequal to its Lord.

39

Before, there was no venue that could accommodate the Palatine's guest dinners and ambrosial feasts; but here, Germanicus, you may properly quaff the sacred nectar and wine-cups mixed by Ganymede's hand. I pray you may choose long to postpone dining with the Thunderer; but if *you* are impatient, Jupiter, come yourself.

40

Guardian not of a garden or a prosperous vineyard, but of a scant woodland, from which, Priapus, you were born—and could be reborn: I caution you to fend off thieving hands, and keep the copse safe for its master's hearth. If it runs out, you too are made of wood . . .

50 (51)

Whose craft informs this cup? Clever Mys', or Myron's? Is this Mentor's hand—or yours, Polyclitus?* It bears no dark bruise from soot, nor has any cloudy mass rebuffed the furnace's prying flames; works of genuine electrum do not gleam so yellow-gold, and its stippled silver* exquisitely outshines snowy ivory. The workmanship does not take second place to the material: thus does the moon put a bracelet to her disc, when she shines brightest with her full splendour. A goat stands here, clothed in the Aeolian fleece of Theban Phrixus,* whose sister would have preferred him for her voyage; this goat no Cinyphian shearer* would have despoiled, and you yourself, Bacchus, would happily let him feast on your vine. A golden Amor straddles the beast; he has a pair of wings, and Pallas' lotus* echoes from his dainty mouth: just so did the dolphin delight in Methymnaean Arion* as he carried his voluble cargo across the languid sea.

sic Methymnaeo gauisus Arione delphin
    languida non tacitum per freta uexit onus.
imbuat egregium digno mihi nectare munus
    non grege de domini, sed tua, Ceste, manus;
Ceste, decus mensae, misce Setina:
    ipse puer nobis, ipse sitire caper.
det numerum cyathis ISTANTI littera RUFI:
    auctor enim tanti muneris ille mihi:
si Telethusa uenit promissaque gaudia portat,
    seruabor dominae, Rufe, triente tuo;
si dubia est, septunce trahar; si fallit amantem,
    ut iugulem curas, nomen utrumque bibam.

53 (55)

Auditur quantum Massyla per auia murmur,
    innumero quotiens silua leone furit,
pallidus attonitos ad Poena mapalia pastor
    cum reuocat tauros et sine mente pecus,
tantus in Ausonia fremuit modo terror harena.
    quis non esse gregem crederet? unus erat,
sed cuius tremerent ipsi quoque iura leones,
    cui diadema daret marmore picta Nomas.
o quantum per colla decus, quem sparsit honorem
    aurea lunatae, cum stetit, umbra iubae!
grandia quam decuit latum uenabula pectus
    quantaque de magna gaudia morte tulit!
unde tuis, Libye, tam felix gloria siluis?
    a Cybeles numquid uenerat ille iugo?
an magis Herculeo, Germanice, misit ab astro
    hanc tibi uel frater uel pater ipse feram?

55 (56)

Temporibus nostris aetas cum cedat auorum
    creuerit et maior cum duce Roma suo,
ingenium sacri miraris desse Maronis
    nec quemquam tanta bella sonare tuba.
sint Maecenates, non derunt, Flacce, Marones

The hand that first fills for me this noble gift with the nectar it deserves—let it not come from your master's rank-and-file, Cestus, but be your own. Cestus, you jewel of the dining-table, mix Setine: the boy and the goat themselves look to us thirsty. Let the letters ISTANTI RUFI lend their number to the refills,* for he is the origin of this great gift. If Telethusa comes and brings her promised delights, Rufus, I shall conserve myself for my mistress by sticking to your four; if she can't make up her mind, I'll pass the time with the seven; if she lets her lover down, I'll murder my cares and drink both your names.

53 (55)

Like the rumbling heard in Africa's trackless wastes, when the forest is seething with innumerable lions, and the herdsman, pale with fright, calls back to his Punic kraal* his frantic cattle and panicked sheep: so loudly did Terror recently roar in the Ausonian arena. Who would not have thought him a pride? He was just one, but one at whose laws the lions themselves would tremble as we did; one whom Numidia, famed for its variegated marble, would crown as king. Oh, what majesty, what glory did the golden shadow of his crescent mane cast across his neck as he made his stand! How nobly his broad chest met the tall hunting-spears! What delight he found in a mighty death! Where, Libya, did your forests find so propitious a glory? Had he come, perhaps, from Cybele's chariot-team? Or, Germanicus, was it rather from Hercules' star* that your brother, or your father even, sent you this beast?

55 (56)

Since our grandparents' generation is giving way to our own times, and Rome has grown in grandeur alongside her Leader, you express surprise that we lack the genius of a holy Maro; that none sounds forth wars from so fine a horn as his. Let there be Maecenases, Flaccus, and you will not want for Maros: your own country estate,

Vergiliumque tibi uel tua rura dabunt.
   iugera perdiderat miserae uicina Cremonae
     flebat et abductas Tityrus aeger oues:
risit Tuscus eques paupertatemque malignam
     reppulit et celeri iussit abire fuga.
'Accipe diuitias et uatum maximus esto;
     tu licet et nostrum' dixit 'Alexin ames.'
adstabat domini mensis pulcherrimus ille
     marmorea fundens nigra Falerna manu,
et libata dabat roseis carchesia labris
     quae poterant ipsum sollicitare Iouem.
excidit attonito pinguis Galatea poetae
     Thestylis et rubras messibus usta genas:
protinus Italiam concepit et 'Arma uirumque',
     qui modo uix Culicem fleuerat ore rudi.
quid Varios Marsosque loquar ditataque uatum
     nomina, magnus erit quos numerare labor?
ergo ero Vergilius, si munera Maecenatis
     des mihi? Vergilius non ero, Marsus ero.

56 (54)

Magna licet totiens tribuas, maiora daturus
     dona, ducum uictor, uictor et ipse tui,
diligeris populo non propter praemia, Caesar,
     te propter populus praemia, Caesar, amat.

61

Liuet Charinus, rumpitur, furit, plorat
et quaerit altos unde pendeat ramos:
non iam quod orbe cantor et legor toto,
nec umbilicis quod decorus et cedro
spargor per omnes Roma quas tenet gentes;
sed quod sub urbe rus habemus aestiuum
uehimurque mulis non ut ante conductis.
quid imprecabor, o Seuere, liuenti?
hoc opto: mulas habeat et suburbanum.

perhaps, will give you a Virgil. His acres lost—too close to poor Cremona—a sorrowful Tityrus* was weeping for his stolen sheep; but his Tuscan knight smiled and thrust back malignant Poverty, ordering her to begone in hurried exile. 'Accept these riches and become the greatest of bards; you may even', he said, 'make love to my Alexis.' That boy, a drop-dead beauty, was standing by his master's table, his marble-white hand pouring the black Falernian; he offered wine-cups touched by rosy lips that could have aroused Jupiter himself.

Sleek Galatea; Thestylis, her cheeks tanned ruddy from harvesting—they vanished from the mind of the smitten poet. There and then he conceived of Italy and 'Arms and the man', though only just before he had sung mournfully and with unpractised tongue of the *Gnat.** Why should I speak of Variuses and Marsuses, all those poets granted wealth? To list their names would be a mighty labour! Will I become a Virgil, then, if you give me presents worthy of a Maecenas? I won't be a Virgil; I'll be a Marsus.*

56 (54)

Though you bestow noble gifts so often, and will give nobler yet—you conqueror of kings, and more, of your own self—you are not the people's favourite because of your bounties, Caesar. The people love your bounties, Caesar, because they're from you.

61

Charinus is jealous. He's gutted, he's incensed, he's actually crying. He's looking for high branches to hang himself from. Not because my poems are sung and read all around the world—not this time; and not because, smartened up with knobs and cedar-oil,* I am broadcast throughout all the nations that Rome rules. No, it's because I have a summer place just outside town, and commute by mule (and they're not rentals like before). What curse, Severus, shall I call down on this jealous man? I wish him this: may he have mules, and a place just outside town.*

63

Thestylon Aulus amat sed nec minus ardet Alexin,
    forsitan et nostrum nunc Hyacinthon amat.
i nunc et dubita uates an diligat ipsos,
    delicias uatum cum meus Aulus amet.

65

Hic ubi Fortunae Reducis fulgentia late
    templa nitent, felix area nuper erat:
hic stetit Arctoi formosus puluere belli
    purpureum fundens Caesar ab ore iubar;
hic lauru redimita comas et candida cultu
    Roma salutauit uoce manuque ducem.
grande loci meritum testantur et altera dona:
    stat sacer et domitis gentibus arcus ouat;
hic gemini currus numerant elephanta frequentem,
    sufficit immensis aureus ipse iugis.
haec est digna tuis, Germanice, porta triumphis;
    hos aditus urbem Martis habere decet.

70

Quanta quies placidi tantast facundia Neruae,
    sed cohibet uires ingeniumque pudor.
cum siccare sacram largo Permessida posset
    ore, uerecundam maluit esse sitim,
Pieriam tenui frontem redimire corona
    contentus, famae nec dare uela suae.
sed tamen hunc nostri scit temporis esse Tibullum
    carmina qui docti nota Neronis habet.

73

Istanti, quo nec sincerior alter habetur
    pectore nec niuea simplicitate prior,
si dare uis nostrae uires animosque Thaliae
    et uictura petis carmina, da quod amem.

63

Aulus loves Thestylus but is every bit as hot for Alexis,* and now I think he's fallen for my own Hyacinthus. Go ahead and doubt that he cares for actual poets, when my Aulus is so keen on the poets' younger boyfriends.

65

Here, where the shining temple of Fortune of Homecomings gleams from afar, was until recently a promising and vacant lot. Here, handsome in the dust of Arctic war, stood Caesar, with brilliant radiance beaming from his face. Here, her hair crowned with laurel and clothed in white, Rome welcomed her Leader with cheering and applause. Other gifts witness the site's noble worth: a sacred Arch* stands in triumph over the conquered tribes. Here, twin chariots muster a host of elephants; he, in gold, handles their massive teams. This, Germanicus, is an entrance worthy of your triumphs: such portals befit the city of Mars.

70

Gentle Nerva* is as eloquent as he is unassuming; but modesty keeps his vigour and talent in check. Though he could have drunk sacred Permessis dry in a single gulp, he has preferred to keep his thirst within modest limits, content to wreath his Pierian brow* with a slender garland and not crowd sail on his reputation. All the same, he who recalls the poems of bookish Nero knows him the Tibullus of our age.

73

Istantius, no one is reckoned purer of heart than you; none outdoes you in snow-white innocence. If you wish to lend vigour and passion to my Muse, and you desire poems that will live on, give my love an object. Cynthia made *you* a bard, saucy Propertius; pretty Lycoris

Cynthia te uatem fecit, lasciue Properti;
  ingenium Galli pulchra Lycoris erat;
fama est arguti Nemesis formosa Tibulli;
  Lesbia dictauit, docte Catulle, tibi:
non me Paeligni nec spernet Mantua uatem,
  si qua Corinna mihi, si quis Alexis erit.

80

Sanctorum nobis miracula reddis auorum
  nec pateris, Caesar, saecula cana mori,
cum ueteres Latiae ritus renouantur harenae
  et pugnat uirtus simpliciore manu.
sic priscis seruatur honos te praeside templis
  et Casa tam culto sub Ioue numen habet;
sic noua dum condis, reuocas, Auguste, priora:
  debentur quae sunt quaeque fuere tibi.

was Gallus' inspiration; fair Nemesis brought fame to clear-voiced
Tibullus; and *you*, bookish Catullus, took dictation from Lesbia.*
Neither Paelignians nor Mantua* will spurn me as a poet, if I can just
get a Corinna or an Alexis.

80

You restore to us the marvels of our pious ancestors, nor, Caesar, do
you permit that hoary antiquity should pass away, when the ancient
rites of the Latin arena are renewed and courage fights bare-handed.
Thus is the charm of olden temples preserved under your steward-
ship, and the Hut retains its sanctity under so revered a Jupiter;* thus
as you build the future do you, Augustus, recall what came before.
Present and past alike are in your debt.

LIBER IX

Haue, mi Torani, frater carissime. epigramma, quod extra ordinem
paginarum est, ad Stertinium clarissimum uirum scripsimus, qui
imaginem meam ponere in bibliotheca sua uoluit. de quo scriben-
dum tibi putaui, ne ignorares Auitus iste quis uocaretur. uale et para
hospitium.

> Note, licet nolis, sublimi pectore uates,
>   cui referet serus praemia digna cinis,
> hoc tibi sub nostra breue carmen imagine uiuat,
>   quam non obscuris iungis, Auite, uiris:
> 'Ille ego sum nulli nugarum laude secundus
>   quem non miraris sed, puto, lector, amas.
> maiores maiora sonent: mihi parua Iocuto
>   sufficit in uestras saepe redire manus.'

I

Dum Ianus hiemes, Domitianus autumnos,
Augustus annis commodabit aestates;
dum grande famuli nomen adseret Rheni
Germanicarum magna lux Kalendarum;
Tarpeia summi saxa dum patris stabunt;
dum uoce supplex dumque ture placabit
matrona diuae dulce Iuliae numen:
manebit altum Flauiae decus gentis
cum sole et astris cumque luce Romana.
inuicta quidquid condidit manus, caeli est.

4

Aureolis futui cum possit Galla duobus
    et plus quam futui, si totidem addideris,
aureolos a te cur accipit, Aeschyle, denos?
    non fellat tanti Galla. quid ergo? tacet.

BOOK 9

[*Preface*] Greetings, my Toranius, dearest brother. The epigram that sits outside the sequence of this book I wrote for Stertinius, a very distinguished fellow who decided to put a portrait of me* in his library. I thought I should write to you about him, so you wouldn't be left wondering who this person I call 'Avitus' is. Farewell, and prepare to welcome a guest!

Famed, though reluctantly so, as a bard of exalted feeling, to whom after long life the grave will grant the distinction you deserve: may this brief poem* dwell under your portrait of me, which you are placing in famous company:
    'It is I, second to none in my reputation for trash; you're not impressed by me but, reader, I think you love me. Let greater poets pour forth greater themes; I speak of small ones, and am content to come back often into your hands.'

1

While Janus bestows winters, Domitian, autumns,* and Augustus, summers to our years; while the glorious light of the Kalends of Germanicus asserts the mighty title of the Rhine enslaved, and the Tarpeian rock of the Father on High still stands; while a beseeching matron still soothes with chant and incense the gentle majesty of Julia deified: so long shall the towering splendour of the Flavian race* endure, while there are sun and stars and Roman daylight. Whatever an invincible hand has built, belongs to heaven.

4

Galla can be fucked for two gold pieces. More than fucked, if you add the same again. So, Aeschylus,* why have you paid her ten? She doesn't charge that much to use her mouth. What's it for, then? To keep her mouth shut.

7 (8)

Tamquam parua foret sexus iniuria nostri
　　foedandos populo prostituisse mares,
iam cunae lenonis erant, ut ab ubere raptus
　　sordida uagitu posceret aera puer:
immatura dabant infandas corpora poenas.
　　non tulit Ausonius talia monstra pater,
idem qui teneris nuper succurrit ephebis,
　　ne faceret steriles saeua libido uiros.
dilexere prius pueri iuuenesque senesque,
　　at nunc infantes te quoque, Caesar, amant.

8 (9)

Nil tibi legauit Fabius, Bithynice, cui tu
　　annua, si memini, milia sena dabas.
plus nulli dedit ille: queri, Bithynice, noli:
　　annua legauit milia sena tibi.

11

Nomen cum uiolis rosisque natum,
quo pars optima nominatur anni,
Hyblam quod sapit Atticosque flores,
quod nidos olet alitis superbae;
nomen nectare dulcius beato,
quo mallet Cybeles puer uocari
et qui pocula temperat Tonanti,
quod si Parrhasia sones in aula,
respondent Veneres Cupidinesque;
nomen nobile, molle, delicatum
uersu dicere non rudi uolebam:
sed tu, syllaba contumax, rebellas.
dicunt Eiarinon tamen poetae,
sed Graeci quibus est nihil negatum
et quos Ἄρες Ἄρες decet sonare:
nobis non licet esse tam disertis
qui Musas colimus seueriores.

7 (8)

As if it were some small infraction against our sex to prostitute males
for customers to defile, the cradle now belonged to the pimp. The
child snatched from the teat begged squalling for his sordid wage.
Unripe bodies payed an unspeakable price. The Ausonian Father
would not tolerate such monstrosities—that same who lately came
to the aid of tender youths, so that brutal lust could not make men
eunuchs. Before, boys and youths and old men favoured you; now,
Caesar, babies love you too.

8 (9)

Fabius has left you nothing in his will, Bithynicus—the man to
whom, if memory serves, you were giving six thousand a year. That's
the most he's left anyone. Bithynicus, stop complaining: he's left you
six thousand a year.*

11

A name that shares birth with violets and roses, for which is named
the best part of the year, that knows Hybla and the flowers of Attica,
that smells of the Phoenix's nest;* a name sweeter than blessed nectar,
by which Cybele's boy would prefer to be called, and he* who mixes
the wine-cup for the Thunderer (if you speak it in the Parrhasian pal-
ace, Venuses and Cupids reply); a name that's noble, gentle, tender
. . . I kept trying to put it into verse that doesn't grate.* But you, you
bastard syllable, keep fighting back. Sure, poets say 'Eiarinos'—but
Greek ones, for whom anything goes; they can declaim 'Āres Ares'
and no one minds. We're not allowed such ways with words, who cul-
tivate more stringent Muses.

15

Inscripsit tumulis septem scelerata uirorum
  SE FECISSE Chloe. quid pote simplicius?

17

Latonae uenerande nepos, qui mitibus herbis
  Parcarum exoras pensa breuesque colos,
hos tibi laudatos domino, rata uota, capillos
  ille tuus Latia misit ab urbe puer;
addidit et nitidum sacratis crinibus orbem,
  quo felix facies iudice tuta fuit.
tu iuuenale decus serua, ne pulchrior ille
  in longa fuerit quam breuiore coma.

18

Est mihi— sitque precor longum te praeside, Caesar—
  rus minimum, parui sunt et in urbe lares.
sed de ualle breui quas det sitientibus hortis
  curua laboratas antlia tollit aquas:
sicca domus queritur nullo se rore foueri,
  cum mihi uicino Marcia fonte sonet.
quam dederis nostris, Auguste, penatibus undam,
  Castalis haec nobis aut Iouis imber erit.

21

Artemidorus habet puerum, sed uendidit agrum;
  agrum pro puero Calliodorus habet.
dic uter ex istis melius rem gesserit, Aucte:
  Artemidorus arat, Calliodorus arat.

31

Cum comes Arctois haereret Caesaris armis
  Velius, hanc Marti pro duce uouit auem;
luna quater binos non tota peregerat orbes,

15

The tombs of seven husbands bear wicked Chloe's byline: HER
COMMISSION.* Could she *be* any more frank?

17

Latona's revered grandson,* you who with soothing herbs prevail
upon the spun wool and short distaffs of the Fates: to you has your
boy sent from the Latin city his long hair, extolled by his Lord. His
vows are now fulfilled.* To these consecrated locks he has added too
a shining disc,* the appraiser and safeguard of his good looks. May
you keep safe the glories of his youth; let him not have been hand-
somer in long hair than in short.

18

I have—and may I long have while you rule, Caesar—a tiny coun-
try seat, and a little place in town. But up from the narrow valley
a stooping foot-pump toils to lift water for my thirsty fields, while my
dry town-house complains that it's not pampered with a single drop,
though I can hear the gush of the Marcia* right next door. The water
you give to my home, Augustus, will be my Castalian spring; it will be
Jupiter's rain.

21

Artemidorus has a boy, but has sold his field; Calliodorus has a field
he's swapped for a boy. Auctus, can you say which got the better deal?
They both have furrows to plough.*

31

Velius was constantly at Caesar's side in the Arctic campaign; he
vowed this bird to Mars for his Leader's safety. The moon had not
yet completed eight cycles, and already the god began to ask for

debita poscebat iam sibi uota deus.
ipse suas anser properauit laetus ad aras
    et cecidit sanctis hostia parua focis.
octo uides patulo pendere nomismata rostro
    alitis? haec extis condita nuper erant:
quae litat argento pro te, non sanguine, Caesar,
    uictima iam ferro non opus esse docet.

32

Hanc uolo quae facilis, quae palliolata uagatur,
    hanc uolo quae puero iam dedit ante meo,
hanc uolo quam redimit totam denarius alter,
    hanc uolo quae pariter sufficit una tribus.
poscentem nummos et grandia uerba sonantem
    possideat crassae mentula Burdigalae.

36

Viderat Ausonium posito modo crine ministrum
    Phryx puer, alterius gaudia nota Iouis:
'Quod tuus ecce suo Caesar permisit ephebo,
    tu permitte tuo, maxime rector' ait;
'iam mihi prima latet longis lanugo capillis,
    iam tua me ridet Iuno uocatque uirum.'
cui pater aetherius 'Puer o dulcissime,' dixit,
    'non ego quod poscis, res negat ipsa tibi:
Caesar habet noster similis tibi mille ministros
    tantaque sidereos uix capit aula mares;
at tibi si dederit uultus coma tonsa uiriles,
    quis mihi qui nectar misceat alter erit?'

37

Cum sis ipsa domi mediaque ornere Subura,
    fiant absentes et tibi, Galla, comae,
nec dentes aliter quam Serica nocte reponas,
    et iaceas centum condita pyxidibus,
nec tecum facies tua dormiat, innuis illo
    quod tibi prolatum est mane supercilio,

a thanksgiving now fallen due: the goose itself bustled cheerfully to its destined altar and fell, a small thank-offering for such hallowed altar-fires. Do you see the eight coins hanging from the bird's gaping beak? Just lately they lay hidden amid its organs. A victim that augurs well for you with silver, not with blood, Caesar, teaches us there is now no need for steel.

32

I want a girl who's easy, who goes around in a coat* and nothing else. I want a girl who's already given it up to my slave. I want a girl where a second denarius buys *everything*. I want a girl who can take on three at a time. But the one who keeps asking for money and talks posh— that prick from dull Bordeaux can have *her*.

36

The Ausonian cupbearer had just lately put aside his long hair. The Phrygian boy, who famously delights the other Jupiter, saw him. 'See what your own Caesar has let his young charge do? Please let yours do the same, almighty ruler! Already the first down hides behind my long locks; already your Juno laughs at me and calls me a man.' The Heavenly Father replied: 'My sweetest boy, it's not me but the facts that turn you down. Our Caesar has a thousand cupbearers who look like you. His whole vast palace teems with gorgeous hunks. But if *your* haircut makes you look grown-up, who else will mix my nectar?'

37

You may be at home, Galla, but your hair is out—out being done in the heart of Subura. You put away your teeth at night, same as you do your imported silks,* and you lie tucked away in a hundred little jars; your face doesn't share your bed. That eyebrow you bat, they delivered this morning; and you feel no reverence* for your grey-haired cunt, which you really could count among your ancestors by now.

et te nulla mouet cani reuerentia cunni,
quem potes inter auos iam numerare tuos.
promittis sescenta tamen; sed mentula surda est,
et sit lusca licet, te tamen illa uidet.

40

Tarpeias Diodorus ad coronas
Romam cum peteret Pharo relicta,
uouit pro reditu uiri Philaenis
illam lingeret ut puella simplex
quam castae quoque diligunt Sabinae.
dispersa rate tristibus procellis
mersus fluctibus obrutusque ponto
ad uotum Diodorus enatauit.
o tardus nimis et piger maritus!
hoc in litore si puella uotum
fecisset mea, protinus redissem.

41

Pontice, quod numquam futuis, sed paelice laeua
uteris et Veneri seruit amica manus,
hoc nihil esse putas? scelus est, mihi crede, sed ingens,
quantum uix animo concipis ipse tuo.
nempe semel futuit, generaret Horatius ut tres;
Mars semel, ut geminos Ilia casta daret.
omnia perdiderat si masturbatus uterque
mandasset manibus gaudia foeda suis.
ipsam crede tibi naturam dicere rerum:
'Istud quod digitis, Pontice, perdis, homo est.'

43

Hic qui dura sedens porrecto saxa leone
mitigat, exiguo magnus in aere deus,
quaeque tulit spectat resupino sidera uultu,
cuius laeua calet robore, dextra mero:
non est fama recens nec nostri gloria caeli;
nobile Lysippi munus opusque uides.

Then again, you're promising me a fortune*. . . But my cock is deaf.
It may be one-eyed, but it can see you.

40

When Diodorus set off from Pharos* to seek Tarpeian wreaths* at
Rome, Philaenis* made a vow for her husband's safe return: that she
would lick—good, wholesome girl!—that thing even chaste Sabine
women enjoy. A violent storm destroyed his ship. Though swamped
by waves and swallowed by the deep, Diodorus swam home to claim
his vow. Such a slow and idle husband—it's uncalled for! If *my* girl
had made such a vow on the shore, I'd have turned round immediately.

41

Ponticus, that you never fuck, but make your left hand your mistress;
that your obliging palm services your lust: do you think this doesn't
matter? Trust me, it's a crime,* and one so grave your mind can scarce
conceive it. Horatius, I am certain, fucked just once to father triplets;
Mars once, that chaste Ilia might give him twins. If either of them had
wanked* and taken his filthy pleasure into his own hands, he would
have thrown it all away. Trust that Nature herself is telling you, 'That
which you squander with your fingers, Ponticus, is a person.'

43

This figure* sitting on a hard rock that he has padded by spreading
a lion-skin, a mighty god in diminutive bronze, gazing with upturned
face on the stars he bore; whose hot left hand grips a club of oak,
his right, strong wine: his is no recent fame, no glory of our sky.* It
is Lysippus' work and craft you see. This deity graced the table of
Pella's tyrant, who lies victorious in the lands he swiftly conquered;

hoc habuit numen Pellaei mensa tyranni,
　　qui cito perdomito uictor in orbe iacet;
hunc puer ad Libycas iurauerat Hannibal aras;
　　iusserat hic Sullam ponere regna trucem.
offensus uariae tumidis terroribus aulae
　　priuatos gaudet nunc habitare lares,
utque fuit quondam placidi conuiua Molorchi,
　　sic uoluit docti Vindicis esse deus.

61

In Tartesiacis domus est notissima terris,
　　qua diues placidum Corduba Baetin amat,
uellera natiuo pallent ubi flaua metallo
　　et linit Hesperium brattea uiua pecus.
aedibus in mediis totos amplexa penates
　　stat platanus densis Caesariana comis,
hospitis inuicti posuit quam dextera felix,
　　coepit et ex illa crescere uirga manu.
auctorem dominumque nemus sentire uidetur:
　　sic uiret et ramis sidera celsa petit.
saepe sub hac madidi luserunt arbore Fauni
　　terruit et tacitam fistula sera domum;
dumque fugit solos nocturnum Pana per agros,
　　saepe sub hac latuit rustica fronde Dryas.
atque oluere lares comissatore Lyaeo
　　creuit et effuso laetior umbra mero;
hesternisque rubens deiecta est herba coronis
　　atque suas potuit dicere nemo rosas.
o dilecta deis, o magni Caesaris arbor,
　　ne metuas ferrum sacrilegosque focos.
perpetuos sperare licet tibi frondis honores:
　　non Pompeianae te posuere manus.

66

Uxor cum tibi sit formosa, pudica, puella,
　　quo tibi natorum iura, Fabulle, trium?
quod petis a nostro supplex dominoque deoque
　　tu dabis ipse tibi, si potes arrigere.

by him the boy Hannibal swore his oath at Libyan altars; he bade
Sulla cease his reign of terror. Displeased with the puffed-up terrors
of diverse courts, he is happy now to dwell in a private home. Once,
the god guested with genial Molorchus; now, he has chosen to stay
with bookish Vindex.

61

In the land of Tartessus is a house of legend, where rich Cordoba
delights in the smooth-flowing Guadalquivir, where fleeces glow pale
gold* with native ore and living gold-leaf covers the Hesperian flock.
At the centre of this mansion, and sheltering the whole dwelling in
its embrace, stands the plane-tree—Caesar's, with thick foliage.*
The right hand of that invincible house-guest planted it, and gave it
luck; from that very hand did the green shoot begin to grow. The tree
seems to follow after its creator and lord, so greenly does it flourish
as its branches reach for the high heavens.* Often under that tree
have drunken Fauns played, and late at night the Pan pipes have ter-
rified the silent household; and as she fled nocturnal Pan through the
deserted fields, often has a rustic Dryad lain hidden beneath these
leafy branches. And the homestead reeked from Bacchus' partying,
and the tree's shade grew, all the merrier for the wine they spilled,
and the grass was red with the trampled garlands of the night before
and no one was able to say which roses were their own. Tree dear to
the gods, tree of great Caesar, you need not fear steel or sacrilegious
hearths. You may justly hope to glory in your leaves forever: it was not
Pompey's hands that planted you.*

66

You have a wife: she's pretty, and modest, and young. So why this
'right of three children'* business, Fabullus? The thing you're going
begging to our Lord and God for, you can award to yourself—if you
can get it up.

67

Lasciuam tota possedi nocte puellam,
    cuius nequitias uincere nulla potest.
fessus mille modis illud puerile poposci:
    ante preces totas primaque uerba dedit.
improbius quiddam ridensque rubensque rogaui:
    pollicita est nulla luxuriosa mora.
sed mihi pura fuit; tibi non erit, Aeschyle, si uis
    accipere hoc munus conditione mala.

68

Quid tibi nobiscum est, ludi scelerate magister,
    inuisum pueris uirginibusque caput?
nondum cristati rupere silentia galli:
    murmure iam saeuo uerberibusque tonas.
tam graue percussis incudibus aera resultant,
    causidicum medio cum faber aptat equo:
mitior in magno clamor furit amphitheatro,
    uincenti parmae cum sua turba fauet.
uicini somnum—non tota nocte—rogamus:
    nam uigilare leue est, peruigilare graue est.
discipulos dimitte tuos. uis, garrule, quantum
    accipis ut clames, accipere ut taceas?

70

Dixerat 'O mores! o tempora!' Tullius olim,
    sacrilegum strueret cum Catilina nefas,
cum gener atque socer diris concurreret armis
    maestaque ciuili caede maderet humus.
cur nunc 'O mores!', cur nunc 'o tempora!' dicis?
    quod tibi non placeat, Caeciliane, quid est?
nulla ducum feritas, nulla est insania ferri;
    pace frui certa laetitiaque licet.
non nostri faciunt tibi quod tua tempora sordent,
    sed faciunt mores, Caeciliane, tui.

67

I had a girl all night long. Horny? She was the filthiest girl who ever
lived. We did it a thousand ways. I was exhausted. Then I asked her
to take it like a boy. I expected to beg, but before I'd got a word in
she gave it *all* up. I smiled, I blushed, and asked for something more
extreme; she didn't even have to think about it, the slut, she just said
yes. But to me, she was pure. She won't be to you, Aeschylus, since
you're willing to get stiffed on the deal.*

68

What have I ever done to *you*, you rotten schoolmaster, figure of hat-
red for boys and girls? The crested cockerels have not yet shattered
the silence, and you're already laying down a backbeat of furious mut-
ters and smacks. Bronze reverberates with just that bass note when
the anvils take a hammering, as the smith rivets *The Lawyer** onto
horseback. The applause that rages in the great Amphitheatre is less
deafening, when a Thracian wins and his fan-club go wild. We, your
neighbours, ask for some sleep—not a full night's worth, lying awake
in the dark is no big deal, but being kept up all night is. Give your
pupils a break, loudmouth. How much do you get paid for yelling,
and can we pay you that much to shut up?

70

O mores! O tempora!, was Cicero's line in days of yore: such morals,
such times, when Catiline* fomented sacrilegious atrocity, when
father- and son-in-law clashed in detestable battle and the sad earth
dripped with civil massacre. So why now do you say *O mores*, why
now *O tempora*? What's got you riled, Caecilianus? What? There are
no brutal generalissimos, no orgies of violence—instead we reap the
benefits of stable peace and prosperity. The morals that make these
times so vile to you aren't ours, Caecilianus: they're your own.

76

Haec sunt illa mei quae cernitis ora Camoni,
    haec pueri facies primaque forma fuit.
creuerat hic uultus bis denis fortior annis
    gaudebatque suas pingere barba genas,
et libata semel summos modo purpura cultros
    sparserat. inuidit de tribus una soror
et festinatis incidit stamina pensis
    absentemque patri rettulit urna rogum.
sed ne sola tamen puerum pictura loquatur,
    haec erit in chartis maior imago meis.

78

Funera post septem nupsit tibi Galla uirorum,
    Picentine: sequi uult, puto, Galla uiros.

79

Oderat ante ducum famulos turbamque priorem
    et Palatinum Roma supercilium:
at nunc tantus amor cunctis, Auguste, tuorum est
    ut sit cuique suae cura secunda domus.
tam placidae mentes, tanta est reverentia nostri,
    tam pacata quies, tantus in ore pudor.
nemo suos—haec est aulae natura potentis—
    sed domini mores Caesarianus habet.

89

Lege nimis dura conuiuam scribere
    cogis, Stella? 'Licet scribere nempe malos.'

95b

Nomen Athenagorae quaeris, Callistrate, uerum:
    si scio, dispeream, qui sit Athenagoras.
sed puta me uerum, Callistrate, dicere nomen:
    non ego sed uester peccat Athenagoras.

76

The face you see is that of my Camonius; this is how he looked at the beginning, as a boy. His features had grown up in twenty years: he looked quite rugged; a beard lent glad colour to his cheeks, and his purple stripe had only once and just now been trimmed of its loose shavings. But one of the Three* cast an evil eye, and as the wool hurried by, she snipped his thread; and the urn brought back to his father the ashes of a pyre far from home. The picture that speaks of his childhood need not stand alone, though; the likeness in my pages will paint him bigger.

78

Galla put seven husbands in the ground, and then she married you, Picentinus; I guess she wants to follow them.

79

Before, Rome hated its emperors' domestic staff. Under that old gang, the Palatine looked down its nose at us. But now, Augustus, we so love all your servants that his own household takes second place in each man's affections. They're so sensible, so concerned to treat us right, so calm and reassuring, so modest in expression. Such is the nature of a mighty court: no man of Caesar's has a style of his own. Each has his master's.

89

You make your guests at dinner write poems, Stella. Is your rule too stringent? 'They can always write bad ones.'

95b

You think I'm using Athenagoras' real name. Callistratus, I'm damned if I know who Athenagoras is. But suppose I *was* using his real name: I'm not the villain here, it's your friend Athenagoras.

LIBER X

I

Si nimius uideor seraque coronide longus
    esse liber, legito pauca: libellus ero.
terque quaterque mihi finitur carmine paruo
    pagina: fac tibi me quam cupis ipse breuem.

2

Festinata prior, decimi mihi cura libelli
    elapsum manibus nunc reuocauit opus.
nota leges quaedam, sed lima rasa recenti;
    pars noua maior erit: lector, utrique faue,
lector, opes nostrae: quem cum mihi Roma dedisset,
    'Nil tibi quod demus maius habemus' ait.
'pigra per hunc fugies ingratae flumina Lethes
    et meliore tui parte superstes eris.
marmora Messallae findit caprificus et audax
    dimidios Crispi mulio ridet equos:
at chartis nec furta nocent et saecula prosunt,
    solaque non norunt haec monumenta mori.'

3

Vernaculorum dicta, sordidum dentem,
et foeda linguae probra circulatricis,
quae sulphurato nolit empta ramento
Vatiniorum proxeneta fractorum,
poeta quidam clancularius spargit
et uult uideri nostra. credis hoc, Prisce?
uoce ut loquatur psittacus coturnicis
et concupiscat esse Canus ascaules?
procul a libellis nigra sit meis fama,
quos rumor alba gemmeus uehit pinna:
cur ego laborem notus esse tam praue,
constare gratis cum silentium possit?

BOOK 10

1

If I seem too much of a book, if I'm too long and 'The End' comes too late, read just a few poems and I'll be a little one. Time and again, one of my little pages ends where a poem does; make me as short as you yourself desire.

2

I was in a hurry, before; I didn't pay attention; and my tenth little book wriggled out of my grasp. It was work in progress, and now it's been recalled. You will read some poems you know, but smoothed by fresh revisions; the majority are new. Reader, look kindly on both—reader, in whom I prosper. When Rome gave me you, she said: 'I have no greater gift for you than this. Through him, you shall escape the sluggish streams of ungrateful Lethe; the better part of you will out-live you. The wild fig-tree splits Messalla's marble, the bold mule-driver laughs at Crispus' halved horses,* but no harm comes to poems from burglaries, and the passing centuries actually make them better. These memorials alone pay death no heed.'

3

The things slaves say; squalid snark;* the filthy slanders of a street-vendor's tongue; stuff that a dealer in broken novelty drinking-cups* wouldn't trade a sulphur match for. Some undercover poet is broadcasting these and making out they're mine. Can you believe it, Priscus? It's like a parrot singing like a quail, or Canus conceiving a passion to become a bagpiper. Grubby Rumour can keep well away from my little books; a jewelled reputation carries them on shining wing. Why would I labour to become a byword for viciousness, when silence costs me nothing?

4

Qui legis Oedipoden caligantemque Thyesten,
  Colchidas et Scyllas, quid nisi monstra legis?
quid tibi raptus Hylas, quid Parthenopaeus et Attis,
  quid tibi dormitor proderit Endymion,
exutusue puer pinnis labentibus? aut qui
  odit amatrices Hermaphroditus aquas?
quid te uana iuuant miserae ludibria chartae?
  hoc lege, quod possit dicere uita 'Meum est.'
non hic Centauros, non Gorgonas Harpyiasque
  inuenies: hominem pagina nostra sapit.
sed non uis, Mamurra, tuos cognoscere mores
  sec te scire: legas Aetia Callimachi.

5

Quisquis stolaeue purpuraeue contemptor
quos colere debet laesit impio uersu,
erret per urbem pontis exul et cliui,
interque raucos ultimus rogatores
oret caninas panis improbi buccas;
illi December longus et madens bruma
clususque fornix triste frigus extendat:
uocet beatos clamitetque felices
Orciniana qui feruntur in sponda.
at cum supremae fila uenerint horae
diesque tardus, sentiat canum litem
abigatque moto noxias aues panno.
nec finiantur morte supplicis poenae,
sed modo seueri sectus Aeaci loris,
nunc inquieti monte Sisyphi pressus,
nunc inter undas garruli senis siccus
delasset omnis fabulas poetarum:
et cum fateri Furia iusserit uerum,
prodente clamet conscientia 'Scripsi.'

4

You read about Oedipus, Thyestes in the dark, Colchises and Scyllas; do you read anything that's not dark fantasy? Snatched Hylas, Parthenopaeus and Attis, Endymion the sleeper: what use to you are *they*,* or the boy who lost his stalling wings, or Hermaphroditus who hates the lusting waters?* Read *this*, of which real life can say, 'It's mine'. You'll find no Centaurs, Gorgons, and Harpies here; my page smells human. But you don't want to be reminded of what you're like, Mamurra, or know yourself—well, you can read Callimachus' *Aetia*.*

5

The individual who holds the matron's gown and senator's purple in contempt, whose sarcastic verses lash out at those he ought to revere: whoever he is, may he wander through the city, barred from bridge and slope;* the lowest among hoarse beggars, may he plead for mouthfuls of poor bread fed to dogs;* may a long December and a wet winter and a walled-up archway* prolong the cold and make him suffer; may he call them blessed and acclaim them fortunate who are carried out to a pauper's grave. But when the threads of his last hour have come, on a day many years from now, may he hear the dogs squabbling over him and wave his rags to keep off carrion birds. And may his sufferings not end with a simple death,* but, now lashed by stern Aeacus' thongs, now struggling under restless Sisyphus' boulder, now parched among the old gabbler's waters, may he wear out all the legends of the poets; and when the Fury commands him to confess the truth, may his conscience give him away and may he cry out, 'I wrote them!'*

6

Felices, quibus urna dedit spectare coruscum
    solibus Arctois sideribusque ducem.
quando erit ille dies, quo campus et arbor et omnis
    lucebit Latia culta fenestra nuru?
quando morae dulces longusque a Caesare puluis
    totaque Flaminia Roma uidenda uia?
quando eques et picti tunica Nilotide Mauri
    ibitis, et populi uox erit una: 'Venit'?

9

Undenis pedibusque syllabisque
et multo sale nec tamen proteruo
notus gentibus ille Martialis
et notus populis—quid invidetis?—
non sum Andraemone notior caballo.

11

Nil aliud loqueris quam Thesea Pirithoumque,
    teque putas Pyladi, Calliodore, parem.
dispeream, si tu Pyladi praestare matellam
    dignus es aut porcos pascere Pirithoi.
'Donaui tamen' inquis 'amico milia quinque
    et lotam, ut multum, terue quaterue togam.'
quid, quod nil unquam Pyladi donauit Orestes?
    qui donat quamuis plurima, plura negat.

13 (20)

Ducit ad auriferas quod me Salo Celtiber oras,
    pendula quod patriae uisere tecta libet,
tu mihi simplicibus, Mani, dilectus ab annis
    et praetextata cultus amicitia,
tu facis; in terris quo non est alter Hiberis
    dulcior et uero dignus amore magis.
tecum ego uel sicci Gaetula mapalia Poeni

6

Fortunate are they to whom the urn has granted to see our Leader glittering in Arctic suns and stars. When will come that day, when field and tree and every window shall light up, decorated by Latium's young wives? When the sweet delays, the long dust-trail that follows Caesar, and all Rome on parade on the Flaminian Way? When, cavalry, will you trot, and the tattooed Moors* in their Egyptian tunics; when will the people shout as one, 'Here he comes'?

9

Known to the nations and their peoples for my eleven feet and eleven syllables and ample wit (that never goes too far), I am that Martial who . . . don't get jealous; I'm no more known than Andraemon the horse.

11

Calliodorus, you talk of nothing but Theseus and Pirithous, and think yourself the equal of a Pylades.* Well, damn me if you're fit to hold a pot for Pylades to piss in, or feed Pirithous' pigs. 'Hang on,' you say, I gave my friend five thousand and a toga that'd only been washed three or four times at most.' What would you say if I told you Pylades never 'gave' Orestes anything? However much a 'giver' gives, there's more he doesn't.

13 (20)

Celtiberian Salo pulls me towards its gold-bearing shores; I have a yen to see the roofs of my mountain town. You, Manius, my dear friend since our years of innocence—*you* make it so; in all Iberia there is none sweeter, none worthier of true love. With you at my side I could guest in the Gaetulian kraal of a parched Carthaginian, or Scythian huts, and love them. If you feel the same, if you return my devotion, then anywhere at all can be our Rome.

et poteram Scythicas hospes amare casas.
si tibi mens eadem, si nostri mutua cura est,
in quocumque loco Roma duobus erit.

20 (19)

Nec doctum satis et parum seuerum,
sed non rusticulum tamen libellum
facundo mea Plinio Thalia
i perfer: breuis est labor peractae
altum uincere tramitem Suburae.
illic Orphea protinus uidebis
udi uertice lubricum theatri
mirantisque feras auemque regis
raptum quae Phryga pertulit Tonanti;
illic parua tui domus Pedonis
caelata est aquilae minore pinna.
sed ne tempore non tuo disertam
pulses ebria ianuam, uideto:
totos dat tetricae dies Mineruae,
dum centum studet auribus uirorum
hoc quod saecula posterique possint
Arpinis quoque comparare chartis.
seras tutior ibis ad lucernas:
haec hora est tua, cum furit Lyaeus,
cum regnat rosa, cum madent capilli:
tunc me uel rigidi legant Catones.

23

Iam numerat placido felix Antonius aeuo
  quindecies actas Primus Olympiadas
praeteritosque dies et tutos respicit annos
  nec metuit Lethes iam propioris aquas.
nulla recordanti lux est ingrata grauisque;
  nulla fuit, cuius non meminisse uelit.
ampliat aetatis spatium sibi uir bonus: hoc est
  uiuere bis, uita posse priore frui.

20 (19)

This little book, less clever and less serious than it should be, but at least not all that oafish—go, my Muse, and deliver it to eloquent Pliny.* It doesn't take long to conquer the steep path at the far side of the Subura. Right there, you'll immediately see Orpheus, slippery at the summit of his watery theatre, and the enraptured animals, and the kingly bird that snatched the Phrygian boy* and carried him off to the Thunderer. Right there's the little house of your friend Pedo,* with its carved relief of a lesser eagle's wing. But take care you don't drunkenly knock on that well-spoken door at a time that's wrong for you: he gives the whole of his days to testy Minerva. He's hard at work for the ears of the Hundred Men* on matter that the centuries and future generations will be able to compare even to Arpine pages.* You'll be safer going in when the late lanterns are lit: this is your hour, when Bacchus rages, when the rose holds sway, when hair is slicked. Then, even stiff Catos may read me.

23

Antonius Primus is happy: he has tallied fifteen completed Olympiads* in a life untroubled. He can look back at the days gone by, at the years he has banked; the waters of Lethe draw closer, but he does not fear them. None of his days fails to please, or is hard to bear, as he reviews it in memory; every last one is a pleasure to recall. The good man broadens for himself the span of his years: to be able to enjoy the life you have spent, is to live it twice.

25

In matutina nuper spectatus harena
    Mucius, imposuit qui sua membra focis,
si patiens durusque tibi fortisque uidetur,
    Abderitanae pectora plebis habes.
nam cum dicatur tunica praesente molesta
    'Ure manum', plus est dicere 'Non facio.'

26

Vare, Paraetonias Latia modo uite per urbes
    nobilis et centum dux memorande uiris,
at nunc Ausonio frustra promisse Quirino,
    hospita Lagei litoris umbra iaces.
spargere non licuit frigentia fletibus ora,
    pinguia nec maestis addere tura rogis.
sed datur aeterno uicturum carmine nomen:
    numquid et hoc, fallax Nile, negare potes?

31

Addixti seruum nummis here mille ducentis,
    ut bene cenares, Calliodore, semel.
nec bene cenasti: mullus tibi quattuor emptus
    librarum cenae pompa caputque fuit.
exclamare libet: 'Non est hic, improbe, non est
    piscis: homo est; hominem, Calliodore, comes.'

33

Simplicior priscis, Munati Galle, Sabinis,
    Cecropium superas qui bonitate senem,
sic tibi consoceri claros retinere penates
    perpetua natae det face casta Venus:
ut tu, si uiridi tinctos aerugine uersus
    forte malus liior dixerit esse meos,
ut facis, a nobis abigas, nec scribere quemquam

25

Recently a sensation in the arena's morning show, that Mucius who put his arm in the fire—if you think he's steadfast and tough and brave, you have the brains of the proles of Abdera.* Because when a man's told 'Burn your hand', and it's that or the Shirt of Woe,* it takes a lot to say 'No'.

26

Varus, you and your Latin vine-staff were lately renowned through the cities of Egypt, a commander worthy of remembrance by your hundred men. But now, promised in vain to Ausonian Quirinus,* you lie in rest, a shade guesting at the Ptolemaic shore. Fate did not allow us to wet your cooling face with tears and add rich incense to your grieving pyre. But it is granted that your name shall live on in eternal verse; treacherous Nile, can you deny us even this?

31

You sold a slave yesterday for two-hundred thousand, Calliodorus, so you could get 'just one good dinner'. And you didn't get one: the high point and *pièce de résistance* of the meal was a three-pound mullet* you'd bought. I feel like shouting, 'This thing isn't a fish, you bastard—it's a man; Calliodorus, you're gobbling up a man.'

33

Munatius Gallus, you are more innocent than the Sabines of old, and you outdo the aged Cecropian in goodness. May chaste Venus keep your daughter's marriage-torch forever burning, and thus grant that you retain the brilliant household of your fellow father-in-law. In return, if wicked Envy should chance to say that verses dipped in green verdigris* are mine, may you herd them away from me, as you are doing, and may you insist that no one who has a readership writes

talia contendas carmina qui legitur.
hunc seruare modum nostri nouere libelli,
parcere personis, dicere de uitiis.

35

Omnes Sulpiciam legant puellae,
uni quae cupiunt uiro placere;
omnes Sulpiciam legant mariti,
uni qui cupiunt placere nuptae.
non haec Colchidos asserit furorem
diri prandia nec refert Thyestae;
Scyllam, Byblida nec fuisse credit:
sed castos docet et pios amores,
lusus, delicias facetiasque.
cuius carmina qui bene aestimarit,
nullam dixerit esse nequiorem,
nullam dixerit esse sanctiorem.
tales Egeriae iocos fuisse
udo crediderim Numae sub antro.
hac condiscipula uel hac magistra
esses doctior et pudica, Sappho:
sed tecum pariter simulque uisam
durus Sulpiciam Phaon amaret.
frustra: namque ea nec Tonantis uxor
nec Bacchi nec Apollinis puella
erepto sibi uiueret Caleno.

38

O molles tibi quindecim, Calene,
quos cum Sulpicia tua iugales
indulsit deus et peregit annos!
o nox omnis et hora, quae notata est
caris litoris Indici lapillis!
o quae proelia, quas utrimque pugnas
felix lectulus et lucerna uidit
nimbis ebria Nicerotianis!
uixisti tribus, o Calene, lustris:

poems of that sort. This rule my little books know to observe: spare persons, skewer vices.

35

All the girls should read Sulpicia* if they want to please their husbands; all the husbands should read Sulpicia if they want to please their brides. Her trademark isn't the Colchian's frenzy, nor does she recount feasts of dire Thyestes; she doesn't think Scylla and Byblis* ever existed. Instead she teaches you how to be faithful lovers—turn-ons and tricks to spice up monogamy. The smart judge of her poetry will say no woman ever had worse morals, or better ones: I could believe Egeria tried such moves in Numa's dripping cave.* If she had been your fellow student or indeed your teacher, Sappho, you would have been more learned—and been modest; but if he had seen her with you, it's Sulpicia that heartless Phaon would have loved. In vain: for even as the wife of Jupiter, Bacchus, or Apollo, that girl would not go on living without her dear Calenus.*

38

How tender have been those fifteen years, Calenus, spent married to your dear Sulpicia! Some god has granted them and seen them to completion! What nights, what hours, and each of them marked by precious pebbles from India's shore! What bouts, what battles your lucky bed has witnessed, and the lamp drenched with Niceros' perfumes!* These three lustra you have *lived*, Calenus: this, you reckon your entire life; your days as a husband are the only ones you count. You would beg long for Atropos to give you back just one of them; and if she did, you would choose that one day over four times Nestor's great old age.

aetas haec tibi tota computatur
et solos numeras dies mariti.
ex illis tibi si diu rogatam
lucem redderet Atropos uel unam,
malles quam Pyliam quater senectam.

43

Septima iam, Phileros, tibi conditur uxor in agro.
  plus nulli, Phileros, quam tibi, reddit ager.

53

Ille ego sum Scorpus, clamosi gloria Circi,
  plausus, Roma, tui deliciaeque breues,
inuida quem Lachesis raptum trieteride nona,
  dum numerat palmas, credidit esse senem.

59

Consumpta est uno si lemmate pagina, transis,
  et breuiora tibi, non meliora placent.
diues et ex omni posita est instructa macello
  cena tibi, sed te mattea sola iuuat.
non opus est nobis nimium lectore guloso;
  hunc uolo, non fiat qui sine pane satur.

61

Hic festinata requiescit Erotion umbra,
  crimine quam fati sexta peremit hiems.
quisquis eris nostri post me regnator agelli,
  manibus exiguis annus iusta dato:
sic lare perpetuo, sic turba sospite solus
  flebilis in terra sit lapis iste tua.

63

Marmora parua quidem, sed non cessura, uiator,
  Mausoli saxis pyramidumque legis.

43

Now a seventh wife lies buried in your field. Phileros,* no man's field
returns a richer harvest than yours.

53

I am the famous Scorpus, idol of the cheering Circus. You applauded
me, Rome, and made me your favourite—for a little while. Jealous
Lachesis* snatched me away when I was not yet thirty. She counted
my trophies and thought I must be old.

59

If a page is expended on a single poem, you skip it; you like the
shorter titles, not the better ones. A rich banquet is laid out for you,
provisioned from every shop in the market, but you limit yourself to
a single antipasto. I have no use for a reader who's such a fussy eater;
I want one who needs to fill up on bread.

61

Here rests Erotion,* too soon a shade, murdered by Fate: her sixth
winter ended her. Whoever you may be, you who are lord and master
of my little farm once I am gone, please make offerings each year to
her tiny ghost; and if you do, may your home endure and your house-
hold be safe. May this stone be the only place on your land where
tears are shed.

63

The marble tomb you are reading may be small, wayfarer, but it will
not yield pride of place to the Mausoleum or the Pyramids. My life

bis mea Romano spectata est uita Tarento,
    et nihil extremos perdidit ante rogos:
quinque dedit pueros, totidem mihi Iuno puellas;
    cluserunt omnes lumina nostra manus.
contigit et thalami mihi gloria rara fuitque
    una pudicitiae mentula nota meae.

68

Cum tibi non Ephesos nec sit Rhodos aut Mitylene,
    sed domus in Uico, Laelia, patricio,
deque coloratis numquam lita mater Etruscis,
    durus Aricina de regione pater;
κύριε μου, μέλι μου, ψυχή μου congeris usque,
    —pro pudor!—Hersiliae ciuis et Egeriae.
lectulus has uoces, nec lectulus audiat omnis,
    sed quem lasciuo strauit amica uiro.
scire cupis quo casta modo matrona loquaris?
    numquid, cum crisas, blandior esse potes?
tu licet ediscas totam referasque Corinthon,
    non tamen omnino, Laelia, Lais eris.

72

Frustra, Blanditiae, uenitis ad me
attritis miserabiles labellis:
dicturus dominum deumque non sum.
iam non est locus hac in urbe uobis;
ad Parthos procul ite pilleatos
et turpes humilesque supplicesque
pictorum sola basiate regum.
non est hic dominus, sed imperator,
sed iustissimus omnium senator,
per quem de Stygia domo reducta est
siccis rustica Veritas capillis.
hoc sub principe, si sapis, caueto
uerbis, Roma, prioribus loquaris.

twice passed scrutiny at Roman Tarentos,* and I took my last rest on
the pyre having wasted none of it: Juno gave me five sons and as many
daughters, and all their hands were there to close my eyes. A rare dis-
tinction of the marriage-bed was granted me: I was so modest, I took
just one cock.

68

You're not from Ephesus. Or Rhodes. Or Mytilene. You live on Senate
Street, Laelia; your mother (who never used make-up) was descended
from the sunburnt Etruscans, your tough old dad's from somewhere
round Aricia. But you're forever stockpiling your Grecisms—*ah
m'sieu! mon amour, mon âme!** Have you no shame? You are a fellow
countrywoman of Hersilia and Egeria. The bed's where such expres-
sions should be heard, and not just any bed, but one spread by a party
girl for her horny boyfriend. You should hear yourself talk—and you
a respectable married lady. Could you be any more of a prick-tease by
twerking?* But even if you get all Corinth by heart and can recite it,
Laelia, you still won't quite be Lais.*

72

In vain, Flatteries, do you come to me, all wretched with your lips
chapped from overuse; for I will not be speaking of a 'Lord and God'.
There is no place for you now, not in this city; take yourselves abroad,
to the Parthians in their fezzes. You're disgusting, servile, wheedling;
go kiss the boot-soles of painted kings. There is no 'Lord' here, only
a Commander in Chief; only the justest senator of them all, by whom
plain-speaking and unadorned Truth has been restored to us from the
house of Styx. A word to the wise, Rome: under this leader, avoid the
verbiage of former times.

76

Hoc, Fortuna, tibi uidetur aequum?
  ciuis non Syriaeue Parthiaeue,
  nec de Cappadocis eques catastis,
  sed de plebe Remi Numaeque uerna,
  iucundus, probus, innocens amicus,
  lingua doctus utraque, cuius unum est,
  sed magnum uitium, quod est poeta,
  pullo Maeuius alget in cucullo,
  cocco mulio fulget Incitatus.

96

Saepe loquar nimium gentes quod, Auite, remotas,
  miraris, Latia factus in urbe senex,
auriferumque Tagum sitiam patriumque Salonem
  et repetam saturae sordida rura casae.
illa placet tellus, in qua res parua beatum
  me facit et tenues luxuriantur opes:
pascitur hic, ibi pascit ager; tepet igne maligno
  hic focus, ingenti lumine lucet ibi;
hic pretiosa fames conturbatorque macellus,
  mensa ibi diuitiis ruris operta sui;
quattuor hic aestate togae pluresue teruntur,
  autumnis ibi me quattuor una tegit.
i, cole nunc reges, quidquid non praestat amicus
  cum praestare tibi possit, Auite, locus.

100

Quid, stulte, nostris uersibus tuos misces?
  cum litigante quid tibi, miser, libro?
  quid congregare cum leonibus uulpes
  aquilisque similes facere noctuas quaeris?
  habeas licebit alterum pedem Ladae,
  inepte, frustra crure ligneo curres.

76

Does this strike you, Fate, as fair? No citizen of Syria or Parthia, no knight off the Cappadocian runways,* but a native son of Remus' and Numa's plebs; a kind and honest man, an upright friend, and whose one crime (a big one) is to be a poet: Mevius shivers in a pauper's shawl, while Incitatus* the mule-driver glistens in scarlet.

96

You are surprised, Avitus, that I often talk of such very far-off peoples, now I've grown old in Latium's city; that I thirst for the gold-bearing Tagus and my native Salo; that my mind turns back to the scruffy fields of a well-provisioned cottage. I love a land where a little money makes me a rich man, where slender means are more than enough. Here, the fields are fed; there, they feed. Here the hearth grudges you a lukewarm fire; there, its blaze lights the room. Here, being hungry costs a fortune, the butcher's bill wipes you out; there, the table can't be seen for the bounty of neighbouring farms. Here, I wear out four togas or more in a summer; there, one does me for four autumns. Go suck up to your lords and masters, Avitus—but there's a place that can give you everything your 'friend' doesn't.

100

Idiot! Why do you mingle your verses with mine? Wretch! What use to you is a book at odds with itself? Why are you trying to slip foxes into a pride of lions, and make little owls resemble eagles? Moron! Even if one of your feet belongs to Ladas, you won't run far with a wooden leg.

104

I nostro comes, i libelle, Flauo
longum per mare, sed fauentis undae,
et cursu facili tuisque uentis
Hispanae pete Tarraconis arces:
illinc te rota tollet et citatus
altam Bilbilin et tuum Salonem
quinto forsitan essedo uidebis.
quid mandem tibi quaeris? ut sodales
paucos, sed ueteres et ante brumas
triginta mihi quattuorque uisos
ipsa protinus a uia salutes,
et nostrum admoneas subinde Flauum
iucundos mihi nec laboriosos
secessus pretio paret salubri,
qui pigrum faciant tuum parentem.
haec sunt. iam tumidus uocat magister
castigatque moras, et aura portum
laxauit melior. uale, libelle:
nauem, scis, puto, non moratur unus.

104

Go, little book; keep Flavus company on his long voyage. With kindly seas, smooth sailing, and the winds in your favour, make for the heights of Spanish Taragona. From there, wheels will carry you; make good speed and perhaps you'll see high Bilbilis and Salo, your home town, with five days' riding. You want to know my orders? Say hello to my friends: not many, but old ones, last seen by my eyes four-and-thirty winters past. Do it at once, as soon as you get in, and right afterwards remind my mate Flavus to sort me out with a nice little hideaway, nothing that needs much work, at a price I'll like: a place that's going to make your Daddy lazy. That's the lot. And now the skipper's getting annoyed: he's yelling and cursing at being held up; the breeze is better, and it's opened the harbour for sailing. Goodbye, little book; I think you know a ship won't wait for one passenger.

LIBER XI

I

Quo tu, quo, liber otiose, tendis
cultus Sidone non cotidiana?
numquid Parthenium uidere? certe:
uadas et redeas ineuolutus.
libros non legit ille, sed libellos;
nec Musis uacat, aut suis uacaret.
ecquid te satis aestimas beatum,
contingunt tibi si manus minores?
uicini pete porticum Quirini:
turbam non habet otiosiorem
Pompeius uel Agenoris puella,
uel primae dominus leuis carinae.
sunt illic duo tresue qui reuoluant
nostrarum tineas ineptiarum,
sed cum sponsio fabulaeque lassae
de Scorpo fuerint et Incitato.

2

Triste supercilium durique seuera Catonis
    frons et aratoris filia Fabricii
et personati fastus et regula morum,
    quidquid et in tenebris non sumus, ite foras.
clamant ecce mei 'Io Saturnalia' uersus:
    et licet et sub te praeside, Nerua, libet.
lectores tetrici salebrosum ediscite Santram:
    nil mihi uobiscum est: iste liber meus est.

3

Non urbana mea tantum Pimpleide gaudent
    otia, nec uacuis auribus ista damus
sed meus in Geticis ad Martia signa pruinis

BOOK 11

1

Where are you headed, you book* with nothing better to do, dressed up in the purple you keep for special occasions? Is it to see Parthenius? Fine; but if you go there, you'll return unopened. He's not reading books, but petitions; and he's not free to spend time with the Muses, else he'd be spending it with his own. Do you reckon yourself lucky enough if lesser hands take you up? Make for the portico of our neighbour Quirinus. Pompey, Agenor's girl, the flighty master of the first ship*—none of them has a crowd with more time on their hands. There are two or three people there who might unroll my bookworm-riddled rubbish, but only when they've run out of bets to place and bullshit to talk about Scorpus and Incitatus.*

2

The stern brow and craggy forehead of Cato, and Fabricia the ploughman's daughter,* and counterfeit disdain, and morals drawn with a ruler—out with whatever we aren't when the lights go down. See, my verses are crying 'io Saturnalia!'; they're allowed and under your rule, Nerva,* they want to. Readers, feel testy? Go learn jolting Santra* till you have him by heart; I have no business with you. This book is *mine*.

3

My recondite Muse* does not beguile just Rome's spare time, nor do these poems reach only the ears of the leisured; no, my book is reread by the tough centurion beside the battle-standard amid Getic frosts.

a rigido teritur centurione liber,
dicitur et nostros cantare Britannia uersus.
quid prodest? nescit sacculus ista meus.
at quam uicturas poteramus pangere chartas
quantaque Pieria proelia flare tuba,
cum pia reddiderint Augustum numina terris,
et Maecenatem si tibi, Roma, darent!

5

Tanta tibi est recti reuerentia, Caesar, at aequi
quanta Numae fuerat: sed Numa pauper erat.
ardua res haec est, opibus non tradere mores
et, cum tot Croesos uiceris, esse Numam.
si redeant ueteres, ingentia nomina, patres,
Elysium liceat si uacuare nemus,
te colet inuictus pro libertate Camillus,
aurum Fabricius te tribuente uolet;
te duce gaudebit Brutus, tibi Sulla cruentus
imperium tradet, cum positurus erit;
et te priuato cum Caesare Magnus amabit,
donabit totas et tibi Crassus opes.
ipse quoque infernis reuocatus Ditis ab umbris
si Cato reddatur, Caesarianus erit.

6

Unctis falciferi senis diebus,
regnator quibus imperat fritillus,
uersu ludere non laborioso
permittis, puto, pilleata Roma.
risisti; licet ergo, non uetamur.
pallentes procul hinc abite curae;
quidquid uenerit obuium loquamur
morosa sine cogitatione.
misce dimidios, puer, trientes,
quales Pythagoras dabat Neroni,
misce, Dindyme, sed frequentiores:
possum nil ego sobrius; bibenti

Even Britain is said to have our poems by heart. And what good does it do? My wallet's never met them. But what immortal pages I could compose, what great battles I could puff on the Pierian war-trumpet, if, when the sacred powers restored Augustus to the earth, they had also given you, Rome, a Maecenas!

5

Your reverence for right and fairness, Caesar, is as great as was Numa's;* but Numa was poor. It is a hard business, not to compromise morals for riches and, when you outdo so many Croesuses, to be a Numa. If the fathers of old, those mighty names, could return, and had permission to vacate the Elysian grove, then Camillus, invincible in liberty's cause, would look up to you. With you as its bestower, Fabricius would wish for gold; with you as his Commander, Brutus would rejoice. Blood-drenched Sulla, on the point of resigning his power, would transfer it to you; Pompey the Great would love you, as would Caesar, now a private citizen; Crassus would give you all his fortune. If Cato himself were returned to us, summoned back from Dis' infernal shades, even he would become a Caesarian.

6

On the feast-days of the sickle-bearing ancient,* days the imperious dice-box rules, then, Rome, clad in your liberty cap, you let me mess around with poems that are work-shy. Or I think you do. You're laughing! It's alright then, I'm not banned. Let pale cares clear right off; I'll speak of whatever crosses my path, without finicky premeditation. Boy, mix my drinks half-and-half, the kind Pythagoras used to fix for Nero—mix them, Dindymus,* and keep them coming. I can't do anything when I'm this sober; when I'm drinking, fifteen poets will come to my aid. Now give me kisses, and make them Catullan ones; and if they're as many as he said, I'll slip you Catullus' *Sparrow.**

succurrent mihi quindecim poetae.
da nunc basia, sed Catulliana:
quae si tot fuerint quot ille dixit,
donabo tibi Passerem Catulli.

13

Quisquis Flaminiam teris, uiator,
noli nobile praeterire marmor.
urbis deliciae salesque Nili,
ars et gratia, lusus et uoluptas,
Romani decus et dolor theatri
atque omnes Veneres Cupidinesque
hoc sunt condita, quo Paris, sepulcro.

16

Qui grauis es nimium, potes hinc iam, lector, abire
    quo libet: urbanae scripsimus ista togae;
iam mea Lampsacio lasciuit pagina uersu
    et Tartesiaca concrepat aera manu.
o quotiens rigida pulsabis pallia uena,
    sis grauior Curio Fabricioque licet!
tu quoque nequitias nostri lususque libelli
    uda, puella, leges, sis Patauina licet.
erubuit posuitque meum Lucretia librum,
    sed coram Bruto; Brute, recede: leget.

18

Donasti, Lupe, rus sub urbe nobis;
sed rus est mihi maius in fenestra.
rus hoc dicere, rus potes uocare?
in quo ruta facit nemus Dianae,
argutae tegit ala quod cicadae,
quod formica die comedit uno,
clusae cui folium rosae corona est;
in quo non magis inuenitur herba
quam Cosmi folium piperue crudum;
in quo nec cucumis iacere rectus

13

Whoever you are, wayfarer, who tread the Flaminian Way, do not pass
by without noting this fine marble tomb. The city's darling, the toast
of the Nile, technique and charm, mischief and delight, the orna-
ment and the sorrow of the Roman stage, and every Venus and every
Cupid,* are buried here, in the grave where Paris lies.

16

If you're one of those terribly serious readers, now is a good time
to leave. Pick somewhere nice. *Those* poems, I wrote for formal oc-
casions; now my page gets saucy with Priapic verse, and clatters its
castanets Cadiz-style. Oh, how often your jutting hard-on will knock
against your philosophic cloak, even if you're a sterner moralist than
Curius and Fabricius!* You too, girl—my little book's so wicked and
mischievous, you'll be wet as you read it, even if you're from Dulls-
ville.* Lucretia blushed and put my book down, but Brutus* was
close by; Brutus, give her space: she'll read it.

18

Lupus, you've given me a country place just outside town; but I have
a bigger 'country place' on my windowsill. A 'country place', you say?
Call this a 'country place'? A rue-plant serves as its grove of Diana;
the wing of a shrill cicada covers it; an ant devours it in a single day;
the petal of a rosebud garlands it. You find no more grass there than
you do Cosmus' leaf* or green pepper; a cucumber can't lie there
straight, nor a snake live there whole. My kitchen-garden struggles
to feed a single caterpillar; my willow-tree can't sustain a gnat; a mole
digs my ditches and ploughs for me. A mushroom can't unfurl, figs
crack a smile, or violets bloom. A mouse ravages my borders—he is

nec serpens habitare tota possit.
urucam male pascit hortus unam,
consumpto moritur culix salicto,
et talpa est mihi fossor atque arator.
non boletus hiare, non mariscae
ridere aut uiolae patere possunt.
finis mus populatur et colono
tamquam sus Calydonius timetur,
et sublata uolantis ungue Procnes
in nido seges est hirundinino;
et cum stet sine falce mentulaque,
non est dimidio locus Priapo.
uix implet cocleam peracta messis,
et mustum nuce condimus picata.
errasti, Lupe, littera sed una:
nam quo tempore praedium dedisti,
mallem tu mihi prandium dedisses.

19

Quaeris cur nolim te ducere, Galla? diserta es:
saepe soloecismum mentula nostra facit.

20

Caesaris Augusti lasciuos, liuide, uersus
sex lege, qui tristis uerba Latina legis:
'Quod futuit Glaphyran Antonius, hanc mihi poenam
Fuluia constituit, se quoque uti futuam.
Fuluiam ego ut futuam? quod si me Manius oret
pedicem? faciam? non puto, si sapiam.
"Aut futue, aut pugnemus" ait. quid quod mihi uita
carior est ipsa mentula? signa canant!'
absoluis lepidos nimirum, Auguste, libellos,
qui scis Romana simplicitate loqui.

23

Nubere Sila mihi nulla non lege parata est;
sed Silam nulla ducere lege uolo.

feared by my tenant as if he were the Calydonian Boar; snatched up
by the claw of winged Procne, our cornfield's crop is in a swallow's
nest; and though he stands without sickle or prick, there isn't half
the space for my Priapus. The harvest we bring in hardly fills a snail-
shell;* we bottle our wine-must in a nutshell we've scaled with pitch.
You've got it wrong, Lupus, but only by one letter: that time you gave
me a ranch, I wish you'd given me a lunch.*

19

You ask why I don't want to marry you, Galla? You're so well spoken;
and my cock so often conjugates improperly.

20

Read six naughty lines by Caesar Augustus, you envious ill-wisher,
who frown when you read plain Latin speech:* 'Because Antony fucks
Glaphyra, Fulvia's passed sentence on me—I have to fuck *her*, too.
Me, fuck Fulvia? What if Manius begged me to bugger *him*? Would I?
I don't think so, not in my right mind. "Fuck me, or it's war between
us," she says. But see, my cock's dearer to me than life itself. Let them
sound the trumpets!' Obviously you absolve my smart little books,
Augustus, since you know how to speak with Roman frankness.

23

Sila isn't prepared to marry me on just *any* conditions; but I *uncon-*
ditionally don't want to marry Sila. When she pressed me regardless,

cum tamen instaret, 'Deciens mihi dotis in auro
    sponsa dabis' dixi. 'quid minus esse potest?
'nec futuam quamuis prima te nocte maritus,
    communis tecum nec mihi lectus erit;
complectarque meam, nec tu prohibebis, amicam,
    ancillam mittes et mihi iussa tuam.
te spectante dabit nobis lasciua minister
    basia, siue meus siue erit ille tuus.
ad cenam uenies, sed sic diuisa recumbes
    ut non tangantur pallia nostra tuis.
oscula rara dabis nobis et non dabis ultro,
    nec quasi nupta dabis sed quasi mater anus.
si potes ista pati, si nil perferre recusas,
    inuenies qui te ducere, Sila, uelit.'

43

Deprensum in puero tetricis me uocibus, uxor,
    corripis et culum te quoque habere refers.
dixit idem quotiens lasciuo Iuno Tonanti:
    ille tamen grandi cum Ganymede iacet.
incuruabat Hylan posito Tirynthius arcu:
    tu Megaran credis non habuisse natis?
torquebat Phoebum Daphne fugitiua: sed illas
    Oebalius flammas iussit abire puer.
Briseis multum quamuis auersa iaceret,
    Aeacidae propior leuis amicus erat.
parce tuis igitur dare mascula nomina rebus
    teque puta cunnos, uxor, habere duos.

45

Intrasti quotiens inscriptae limina cellae,
    seu puer arrisit siue puella tibi,
contentus non es foribus ueloque seraque,
    secretumque iubes grandius esse tibi:
oblinitur minimae si qua est suspicio rimae
    punctaque lasciua quae terebrantur acu.
nemo est tam teneri tam sollicitique pudoris
    qui uel pedicat, Canthare, uel futuit.

I told her: 'As my new fiancée, you'll give me a million in gold as a dowry. Does money even come in smaller denominations? Also, I won't fuck you, even on our wedding-night, nor will we share a bed; I shall carry on sleeping with my girlfriend, and you will not interfere, and you'll send me your maid as well when I tell you to. You'll watch as the boy waiting table gives me hot kisses—whether he's my slave, yours, whatever; you shall come to dinner, but you're to recline far enough away from me that our clothes don't touch. You will kiss me infrequently, and not unless you're told to, and not like a bride does, but like an aged mother. If you can stomach all that, if there's nothing you won't put up with—well, Sila, you'll find *someone* willing to marry you.'

43

Catching me with a boy, you give me a sound scolding and remind me that you have an arse too. Juno used to tell the Thunderer that all the time! But still he lay with full-grown Ganymede. The Hero of Tiryns* would often set his bow aside and give Hylas a good stringing, and do you think Megara had no bum? Phoebus was racked with desire for the fleeing Daphne, but those flames vanished at the Oebalian boy's* command. However much Briseis lay with her back turned to him, Aeacus' son* was more intimate with his beardless friend. So stop giving masculine names to your junk, wife, and reckon yourself the owner of two cunts.

45

When you step across the threshold of a marked-up cubicle, whether your hard-on's for a boy or a girl, you're never happy with doors and a curtain and a bolt; you demand greater secrecy. If there's the smallest crack you don't like the look of, or a tiny hole bored by a voyeur's pin, it's plastered over. No one is so fastidious or so anxious about appearances who just fucks arses or pussies, Cantharus.

48

Silius haec magni celebrat monumenta Maronis,
  iugera facundi qui Ciceronis habet.
heredem dominumque sui tumuliue larisue
  non alium mallet nec Maro nec Cicero.

52

Cenabis belle, Iuli Cerialis, apud me;
  condicio est melior si tibi nulla, ueni.
octauam poteris seruare; lauabimur una:
  scis quam sint Stephani balnea iuncta mihi.
prima tibi dabitur uentri lactuca mouendo
  utilis, et porris fila resecta suis,
mox uetus et tenui maior cordyla lacerto,
  sed quam cum rutae frondibus oua tegant;
altera non deerunt leni uersata fauilla,
  et Velabrensi massa coacta foco,
et quae Picenum senserunt frigus oliuae.
  haec satis in gustu. cetera nosse cupis?
mentiar, ut uenias: pisces, coloephia, sumen,
  et chortis saturas atque paludis aues,
quae nec Stella solet rara nisi ponere cena.
  plus ego polliceor: nil recitabo tibi,
ipse tuos nobis relegas licet usque Gigantas,
  rura uel aeterno proxima Vergilio.

53

Claudia caeruleis cum sit Rufina Britannis
  edita, quam Latiae pectora gentis habet!
quale decus formae! Romanam credere matres
  Italides possunt, Atthides esse suam.
di bene quod sancto peperit fecunda marito,
  quod sperat generos quodque puella nurus.
sic placeat superis, ut coniuge gaudeat uno
  et semper natis gaudeat illa tribus.

48

Silius* assiduously attends this memorial of great Maro, he who holds the acres of eloquent Cicero. No other heir* or keeper of tomb or homestead would either Maro or Cicero choose.

52

You'll dine elegantly at my place, Julius Cerialis; if you have no better offer, do come. You will be able to keep the eighth hour* for yourself; we'll bathe together: you know Stephanus' baths are right next door. First you will be served lettuce, for moving the bowel, and leeks cut into slices, shortly followed by a tunny, larger than a scraggy lizard-fish;* it's getting on a bit, but eggs mixed with rue-leaves will cover it up. Plenty of eggs—we'll have the rest scrambled over warm embers, and a cheese from a Velabran hearth, and olives that have felt Pice-num's frost. That will do for appetizers. You want to know the rest? I'll lie, so that you'll come: fish, rib-eye steaks, sow's udder, fatted birds from kitchen-garden and marsh, things even Stella only serves on special occasions. And I make a further promise: I won't recite anything to you, though you may read me your *Giants* (again, and I won't interrupt), or your pastorals that are so like deathless Virgil.

53

Though Claudia Rufina issues from the woad-painted Britons, how nobly Latin is her heart! How beautiful she is! Italian mothers could think her Roman; Attic ones, their own. The gods have blessed her: she has been a fruitful mother to her lawful husband; though still a girl, she hopes for sons- and daughters-in-law. May it please the powers above that she rejoice in a single husband and rejoice forever in her three children.*

54

Unguenta et casias et olentem funera murram
    turaque de medio semicremata rogo
et quae de Stygio rapuisti cinnama lecto,
    improbe, de turpi, Zoile, redde sinu.
a pedibus didicere manus peccare proteruae.
    non miror furem, qui fugitiuus eras.

63

Spectas nos, Philomuse, cum lauamur,
et quare mihi tam mutuniati
sint leues pueri subinde quaeris.
dicam simpliciter tibi roganti:
pedicant, Philomuse, curiosos.

66

Et delator es et calumniator,
et fraudator es et negotiator,
et fellator es et lanista: miror
quare non habeas, Vacerra, nummos.

69

Amphitheatrales inter nutrita magistros
    uenatrix, siluis aspera, blanda domi,
Lydia dicebar, domino fidissima Dextro,
    qui non Erigones mallet habere canem,
nec qui Dictaea Cephalum de gente secutus
    luciferae pariter uenit ad astra deae.
non me longa dies nec inutilis abstulit aetas,
    qualia Dulichio fata fuere cani:
fulmineo spumantis apri sum dente perempta,
    quantus erat, Calydon, aut, Erymanthe, tuus.
nec queror infernas quamuis cito rapta sub umbras:
    non potui fato nobiliore mori.

54

The ointments and the cassia-bark and the myrrh that whiffs of fu-
nerals and the half-burned frankincense from the middle of the pyre
and the cinnamon you snatched from the Stygian bier—Zoilus, you
scum, take them out of that fold in your toga and put them back. Your
itchy fingers learned from your feet how to be a criminal. I'm not
surprised you're a thief; you used to be a runaway.

63

You watch us, Philomusus, while we're bathing, and you keep asking
me why my beardless boys are so well-hung. Since you want to know,
I'll give you a plain answer: they bugger people who keep asking ques-
tions, Philomusus.

66

You're an informer *and* a lying witness, a defrauder *and* a middle-
man, a cocksucker *and* a provocateur. Vacerra, I can't understand why
you're not rich.

69

A huntress nursed among the trainers of the Amphitheatre, fierce in
the woods but gentle in the home, I was called Lydia—ever faithful
to my master Dexter. He would not have preferred to own Erigone's
hound, or the dog of Dictaean bloodline* that walked at Cephalus'
heel as he voyaged to the stars of the light-bringing goddess. Long
passage of days did not claim me, nor useless old-age, the kind of end
the Dulichian dog met; rather, I fell suddenly to the gleaming tusk of
a frothing boar, one as huge as yours, Calydon, or yours, Erymanthus.
Nor do I complain, though snatched too swiftly to the shades below:
for I could have met no nobler end.

77

In omnibus Vacerra quod conclauibus
consumit horas et die toto sedet,
cenaturit Vacerra, non cacaturit.

78

Utere femineis complexibus, utere, Victor,
 ignotumque sibi mentula discat opus.
flammea texuntur sponsae, iam uirgo paratur,
 tondebit pueros iam noua nupta tuos.
pedicare semel cupido dabit illa marito,
 dum metuit teli uulnera prima noui:
saepius hoc fieri nutrix materque uetabunt
 et dicent: 'Uxor, non puer, ista tibi est.'
heu quantos aestus, quantos patiere labores,
 si fuerit cunnus res peregrina tibi!
ergo Suburanae tironem trade magistrae.
 illa uirum faciet; non bene uirgo docet.

80

Litus beatae Veneris aureum Baias,
Baias superbae blanda dona Naturae,
ut mille laudem, Flacce, uersibus Baias,
laudabo digne non satis tamen Baias.
sed Martialem malo, Flacce, quam Baias.
optare utrumque pariter improbi uotum est.
quod si deorum munere hoc mihi detur,
quid gaudiorum est Martialis et Baiae!

86

Leniat ut fauces medicus, quas aspera uexat
 assidue tussis, Parthenopaee, tibi,
mella dari nucleosque iubet dulcesque placentas
 et quidquid pueros non sinit esse truces:
at tu non cessas totis tussire diebus.
 non est haec tussis, Parthenopaee, gula est.

77

Vacerra's in all the toilets—in there for hours; spends the whole day on his arse. He's not straining to shit; he's straining for a dinner invitation.

78

Have a go at sleeping with a woman, Victor; go on, give it a try. Let your cock learn some new tricks. They're already weaving the bridal veil, and getting the girl ready; soon your new wife will be cropping the hair of those boys of yours. She'll let her eager husband bugger her the once, that time she's afraid of the first stab from his unfamiliar weapon, but her nurse and her mother will ban any repeats: 'She's your wife,' they'll tell you, 'not some *boy*.' Oh, how embarrassed you'll be, what a fuss you'll go through, if cunt is still another country to you! So, hand your little soldier over to a sexpert from the Subura. She'll make a man of you; a virgin is a poor teacher.

80

Baiae—the golden shore of blessed Venus. Baiae—the seductive bounty of prideful Nature. Flaccus, I could write a thousand verses in praise of Baiae and still not praise it enough. But Flaccus, I love Martial even more than Baiae. To ask for both together is the prayer of someone shameless. But if the gods were generous and answered— Martial *and* Baiae! How much fun would *that* be?

86

That nasty cough of yours won't go away, Parthenopaeus, and it's giving you a sore throat. The doctor prescribes honey and pine-kernels and cookies to soothe it, all the things that stop kids being little monsters. But still you cough all day, never a let-up. It's not a cough you've got, Parthenopaeus; it's a throat condition.*

93

Pierios uatis Theodori flamma penates
  abstulit. hoc Musis et tibi, Phoebe, placet?
o scelus, o magnum facinus crimenque deorum,
  non arsit pariter quod domus et dominus!

97

Una nocte quater possum: sed quattuor annis
  si possum, peream, te Telesilla semel.

99

De cathedra quotiens surgis—iam saepe notaui—
  pedicant miserae, Lesbia, te tunicae.
quas cum conata es dextra, conata sinistra
  uellere, cum lacrimis eximis et gemitu:
sic constringuntur gemina Symplegade culi
  et nimias intrant Cyaneasque natis.
emendare cupis uitium deforme? docebo:
  Lesbia, nec surgas censeo nec sedeas.

104

Uxor, uade foras aut moribus utere nostris:
  non sum ego nec Curius nec Numa nec Tatius.
me iucunda iuuant tractae per pocula noctes:
  tu properas pota surgere tristis aqua.
tu tenebris gaudes: me ludere teste lucerna
  et iuuat admissa rumpere luce latus.
fascia te tunicaeque obscuraque pallia celant:
  at mihi nulla satis nuda puella iacet.
basia me capiunt blandas imitata columbas:
  tu mihi das auiae qualia mane soles.
nec motu dignaris opus nec uoce iuuare
  nec digitis, tamquam tura merumque pares:
masturbabantur Phrygii post ostia serui,
  Hectoreo quotiens sederat uxor equo,

93

The Pierian halls of the bard Theodorus—fire has snatched them
away. Does this please you, Muses? You, Apollo? What wickedness,
what atrocity, what guilt we may charge against the gods, that the fire
didn't take house and master both!

97

I can do it four times in a night; but I'm damned if I can do *you*,
Telesilla,* once in four years.

99

Every time you get up from your chair—and I've noticed it a lot,
Lesbia—your wretched dresses take you up the arse. You try with
your left hand, you try with your right; you quarry them out, weep-
ing and moaning. That's how tightly they get wedged in the Symple-
gades* of your bum, when they sail between the Clashing Rocks that
you call buttocks. Keen to mend your ugly fault? I'll tell you how:
Lesbia, my advice is don't get up or sit down.

104

Wife, either clear out or live my way. I'm not a Curius, a Numa,
or a Tatius.* My pleasure is in nights drawn out by wine-cups that
cheer; all you drink is water, and then you grimace and can't wait to
leave the table. You like it dark; what pleases me is to frolic with the
lantern as our witness, and shoot my load with the sun coming in.
Your bra and tunics hide you away, a cloak covers you over; but no girl
lies down naked enough for my liking. The kisses that addict me are
like cooing doves; but you kiss me the way you'd kiss your grandma
in the morning. You don't encourage my hard-on by wiggling, or by
talk—or with your fingers; it's as if you're preparing incense and wine
for a sacrifice. The slaves of Phrygia would wank behind the door
every time Hector's wife saddled up her steed, and even when the
Ithacan* was snoring, chaste Penelope always used to keep her hand
there. You deny me buggery: Cornelia granted this to Gracchus, Julia

et quamuis Ithaco stertente pudica solebat
   illic Penelope semper habere manum.
pedicare negas: dabat hoc Cornelia Graccho,
   Iulia Pompeio, Porcia, Brute, tibi;
dulcia Dardanio nondum miscente ministro
   pocula Iuno fuit pro Ganymede Ioui.
si te delectat grauitas, Lucretia toto
   sis licet usque die: Laida nocte uolo.

108

Quamuis tam longo possis satur esse libello,
   lector, adhuc a me disticha pauca petis.
sed Lupus usuram puerique diaria poscunt.
   lector, solue. taces dissimulasque? uale.

to Pompey, and Porcia, Brutus, to you; when the Trojan page-boy was
not yet mixing their soothing wine-cups, Juno played Ganymede to
Jupiter. If you're so fond of your dignity, you can be a Lucretia all day
long; at night, I want a Lais.*

108

A little book this long *could* satisfy your appetite, reader, but still you
ask me for a few couplets more; but Lupus wants his interest, and my
boys, their rations. Reader, clear my slate.* Nothing to say? Pretend-
ing you're deaf? Get lost.

LIBER XII

VALERIUS MARTIALIS PRISCO SUO SALUTEM

Scio me patrocinium debere contumacissimae trienni desidiae; quo absoluenda non esset inter illas quoque urbicas occupationes, quibus facilius consequimur ut molesti potius quam ut officiosi esse uideamur; nedum in hac prouinciali solitudine, ubi nisi etiam intemperanter studemus, et sine solacio et sine excusatione secessimus. accipe ergo rationem: in qua hoc maximum et primum est, quod ciuitatis aures, quibus adsueueram, quaero et uideor mihi in alieno foro litigare; si quid est enim, quod in libellis meis placeat, dictauit auditor: illam iudiciorum subtilitatem, illud materiarum ingenium, bibliothecas, theatra, conuictus, in quibus studere se uoluptates non sentiunt, ad summam omnium illa, quae delicati reliquimus, desideramus quasi destituti. accedit his municipalium robigo dentium et iudici loco liuor, et unus aut alter mali, in pusillo loco multi; aduersus quod difficile est habere cotidie bonum stomachum: ne mireris igitur abiecta ab indignante quae a gestiente fieri solebant. ne quid tamen et aduenienti tibi ab urbe et exigenti negarem—cui non refero gratiam, si tantum ea praesto quae possum—imperaui mihi, quod indulgere consueram, et studui paucissimis diebus, ut familiarissimas mihi aures tuas exciperem aduentoria sua. tu uelim ista, quae tantum apud te non periclitantur, diligenter aestimare et excutere non graueris; et, quod tibi difficillimum est, de nugis nostris iudices nitore seposito, ne Romam, si ita decreueris, non Hispaniensem librum mittamus, sed Hispanum:

BOOK 12

VALERIUS MARTIAL TO HIS FRIEND PRISCUS: GREETINGS

[*Preface*] I've been stubbornly sitting on my arse* for three years, and I know it's high time I presented the case for my defence; but it wouldn't get me off the hook if I were additionally distracted by those city affairs, by pursuing which we more easily appear bothersome than obliging—and still less in this provincial solitude, where, unless I keep myself unreasonably busy with writing, my time as a hermit will have lacked both consolation and pretext. Well, see how I account for myself.

The first and most important thing is that I'm missing the city audience I'd grown accustomed to. I feel like I'm pleading a case in a forum full of strangers; because anything people enjoy in my little books, I learned from my audience. Those penetrating judgements, that brilliant material; the libraries, the theatres; and those parties, at which the pleasures didn't realize the education they were getting: in sum, all those things I'd 'moved on from' and was 'so over', I now miss as if *they'd* dumped *me*. And then there's small-town life: the teeth (all that plaque); small-mindedness in place of judgement; and one or two bad sorts, which in a poxy little place is a lot. When you live with that lot in your face every day it's hard not to get an ulcer— so don't be surprised if Grumpy Martial has tossed aside the stuff Perky Martial was always into.

But rather than disappoint you when you arrive from Rome and demand what's owed—because I'm not repaying you for your friendship if I only deliver what I'm capable of—I've put myself under strict orders to do what I used to do for kicks. I've been hard at work writing these last few days, so that I may captivate your ears (ones I know so well) with the welcome feast they deserve. Yours is the only company in which these poems are in no danger, and I hope you won't find it an imposition to weigh them carefully—give them a good pat-down. It's the most difficult thing for you, but please set aside your kindness when you form a judgement of my trashy efforts, so that (if you find in its favour) I don't end up sending Rome a book that's not so much made in Spain as Spanish through and through:*

I

Retia dum cessant latratoresque Molossi
　et non inuento silua quiescit apro,
otia, Prisce, breui poteris donare libello.
　hora nec aestiua est nec tibi tota perit.

4 (5)

Longior undecimi nobis decimique libelli
　artatus labor est et breue rasit opus.
plura legant uacui, quibus otia tuta dedisti:
　haec lege tu, Caesar; forsan et illa leges.

10

Habet Africanus miliens, tamen captat.
Fortuna multis dat nimis, satis nulli.

12

Omnia promittis, cum tota nocte bibisti;
　mane nihil praestas: Pollio, mane bibe.

16

Addixti, Labiene, tres agellos;
emisti, Labiene, tres cinaedos:
pedicas, Labiene, tres agellos.

17

Quare tam multis a te, Laetine, diebus
　non abeat febris, quaeris et usque gemis.
gestatur tecum pariter pariterque lauatur;
　cenat boletos, ostrea, sumen, aprum;
ebria Setino fit saepe et saepe Falerno,
　nec nisi per niueam Caecuba potat aquam;

I

While the nets are idle, and the barking Molossians,* and the wood is quiet (no sign of the boar), you can give over your break to this very short book, Priscus. It's not summer, but you won't lose a whole hour* to it.

4 (5)

The longer labour of my eleventh and tenth books has been condensed; a shave has made it concise. Let the unoccupied read more, to whom *you* have given leisure free from danger. You, Caesar, read *these* poems;* then maybe you will read the others, too.

10

Africanus has a hundred million, and still he's hunting legacies. Fortune gives too much to many, but 'enough' to none.

12

You promise it all when you've been drinking all night; in the morning, you come through on none of it. Pollio, start drinking in the mornings.

16

Sold, by Labienus: three small fields.
Purchased, by Labienus: three bum-boys.
Buggered, by Labienus: three small fields.*

17

Why hasn't your fever gone away after all these days, you ask; moan, moan, moan. Laetinus, it likes the lifestyle! It takes a drive with you, goes to the baths with you; dines on mushrooms, oysters, sow's udder, boar; gets tipsy on Setine and Falernian whenever it fancies, and *only* drinks Caecuban when it's cooled with snow; reclines for dinner garlanded in roses, and black with expensive balsam;* sleeps

circumfusa rosis et nigra recumbit amomo,
    dormit et in pluma purpureoque toro.
cum sit tam pulchre, cum tam bene uiuat apud te,
    ad Damam potius uis tua febris eat?

18

Dum tu forsitan inquietus erras
clamosa, Iuuenalis, in Subura,
aut collem dominae teris Dianae;
dum per limina te potentiorum
sudatrix toga uentilat uagumque
maior Caelius et minor fatigant:
me multos repetita post Decembres
accepit mea rusticumque fecit
auro Bilbilis et superba ferro.
hic pigri colimus labore dulci
Boterdum Plateamque—Celtiberis
haec sunt nomina crassiora terris—
ingenti fruor improboque somno
quem nec tertia saepe rumpit hora,
et totum mihi nunc repono, quidquid
ter denos uigilaueram per annos.
ignota est toga, sed datur petenti
rupta proxima uestis a cathedra.
surgentem focus excipit superba
uicini strue cultus iliceti,
multa uilica quem coronat olla.
uenator sequitur, sed ille quem tu
secreta cupias habere silua;
dispensat pueris rogatque longos
leuis ponere uilicus capillos.
sic me uiuere, sic iuuat perire.

20

Quare non habeat, Fabulle, quaeris
uxorem Themison? habet sororem.

on a down mattress in a purple bed. Since it's enjoying the high
life so much as your guest, do you expect your fever to go stay with
Dama* instead?

18

I guess right now, Juvenal, you're wandering restless through the yell-
ing Subura, or trudging up the hill of our lady Diana;* your sweaty
toga flaps as you haunt the thresholds of the mighty, and the Greater
and Lesser Caelian wear you out. Me? The place I've come back to
after many Decembers has taken me in and turned me into a yokel:
Bilbilis, that glories in its gold and iron. Here at ease I potter round
Boterdus and Platea—Celtiberian places have these lumpen names;
it's nice to get the exercise. I get a huge, an obscene amount of sleep,
often right through the third hour of the day; I'm paying myself back
now for all those all-nighters I pulled over thirty years. No one here
knows what a toga is; when I ask, they give me whatever clothing's to
hand from a broken chair. When I get up, a hearth welcomes me; some
thoughtful soul has left a splendid stack of logs from my neighbour's
grove of holm-oaks; the steward's wife has crowned it with a bunch
of pots. Afterwards there's the huntsman, but one you'd fancy having
with you in the depths of the forest. My smooth-cheeked steward
weighs out the boys' rations, and asks to put aside his long hair. This
is how I want to spend my life and end my days.

20

Fabullus, you wonder why Themison has no wife? He has a sister.

31

Hoc nemus, hi fontes, haec textilis umbra supini
   palmitis, hoc riguae ductile flumen aquae,
prataque nec bifero cessura rosaria Paesto,
   quodque uiret Iani mense nec alget holus,
quaeque natat clusis anguilla domestica lymphis,
   quaeque gerit similes candida turris aues,
munera sunt dominae: post septima lustra reuerso
   has Marcella domos paruaque regna dedit.
si mihi Nausicaa patrios concederet hortos,
   Alcinoo possem dicere 'Malo meos.'

33

Ut pueros emeret Labienus uendidit hortos:
   nil nisi ficetum nunc Labienus habet.

35

Tamquam simpliciter mecum, Callistrate, uiuas,
   dicere percisum te mihi saepe soles.
non es tam simplex, quam uis, Callistrate, credi.
   nam quisquis narrat talia, plura tacet.

42

Barbatus rigido nupsit Callistratus Afro,
   hac qua lege uiro nubere uirgo solet.
praeluxere faces, uelarunt flammea uultus,
   nec tua defuerunt uerba, Talasse, tibi.
dos etiam dicta est. nondum tibi, Roma, uidetur
   hoc satis? expectas numquid ut et pariat?

43

Facundos mihi de libidinosis
legisti nimium, Sabelle, uersus,
quales nec Didymi sciunt puellae

31

This wood, these springs, this woven shade of trellised vines, this channelled stream of water for the fields, and these meadows, and the rose-beds that concede nothing to Paestum's twice-yearly flowering, and the cabbages that bloom in January and don't feel the cold, and the tame eel that swims in its tank, and the white dovecot that bears white birds: these are the gifts of my mistress. When I came back after seven lustra,* Marcella gave me this home, this little kingdom. If Nausicaa* offered me her father's gardens, I could tell Alcinous, 'I like mine better.'

33

Labienus sold his estate so he could buy some boys. Now all Labienus has is a fig-orchard.*

35

As though we were an item, Callistratus, you can't stop telling me how you've taken it up the arse. You're not as candid as you want me to think, Callistratus. Anyone who shares stories like that has more they're not telling.

42

Bearded Callistratus has got married to rugged Afer. The deal was the same as when girls get married to men: the torches lit the way, the flame-red veil hid his face; and you delivered your lines just fine, Talassus. There was even a dowry contract. Is that still not enough for you, Rome? Are you waiting for him to have babies?

43

You read me some poetry you've written. *Prisoners of Lust* is good, Sabellus; maybe too good: stuff Didyma's girls* don't know, or the sex-manuals of Elephantis. It describes positions so outlandish that

nec molles Elephantidos libelli.
sunt illic Veneris nouae figurae,
quales perditus audeat fututor,
praestent et taceant quid exoleti,
quo symplegmate quinque copulentur,
qua plures teneantur a catena,
extinctam liceat quid ad lucernam.
tanti non erat esse te disertum.

52

Tempora Pieria solitus redimire corona,
    nec minus attonitis uox celebrata reis,
hic situs est, hic ille tuus, Sempronia, Rufus,
    cuius et ipse tui flagrat amore cinis.
dulcis in Elysio narraris fabula campo,
    et stupet ad raptus Tyndaris ipsa tuos:
[tu melior, quae deserto raptore redisti;
    illa uirum uoluit nec repetita sequi.]
ridet et Iliacos audit Menelaus amores:
    absoluit Phrygium uestra rapina Parim.
accipient olim cum te loca laeta piorum,
    non erit in Stygia notior umbra domo:
non aliena uidet, sed amat Proserpina raptas:
    iste tibi dominam conciliabit amor.

56

Aegrotas uno decies aut saepius anno,
    nec tibi, sed nobis hoc, Polycharme, nocet:
nam quotiens surgis, soteria poscis amicos.
    sit pudor: aegrota iam, Polycharme, semel.

57

Cur saepe sicci parua rura Nomenti
laremque uillae sordidum petam, quaeris?
nec cogitandi, Sparse, nec quiescendi
in urbe locus est pauperi. negant uitam

only a hopeless sex addict would dare try them, things male prosti-
tutes don't admit they offer: how to choreograph a five-way, how to
daisy-chain even more, what you can get away with when the light
goes out. Becoming a good poet wasn't worth all that.

52

He often wreathed his brow in the Muses' garland, and his voice was
no less well known to terrified defendants. Here he lies, Sempronia;
here lies your Rufus, whose very ash glows with love for you. He tells
the sweet story of you in the Elysian Fields, and Helen herself is
open-mouthed at your elopement. [But you are better than she: you
left your abductor and returned; she did not wish to accompany her
husband even when he reclaimed her.]* Menelaus grins as he hears
a love-story worthy of Troy; the stealing of you acquits Phrygian
Paris. When one day the happy regions of the virtuous shall receive
you, there shall be no more famous shade in the hall of Styx. Proser-
pina takes your side; she loves snatched women: this love of yours will
make the Queen your friend.

56

You fall ill ten or more times in any one year, but it's not you who
suffers, Polycharmus; it's us, because every time you rise from
your sickbed, you demand your friends throw a shower.* Enough is
enough: fall ill, Polycharmus, and stay ill.

57

You wonder why I often escape to my little estate at dry Nomentum,
to the scruffy hearth of my place in the country? Sparsus, there's no
space at Rome for a poor man to think in peace and quiet. In the
morning the schoolmasters make life impossible; at night, it's the

ludi magistri mane, nocte pistores,
aerariorum marculi die toto;
hinc otiosus sordidam quatit mensam
Neroniana nummularius massa,
illinc balucis malleator Hispanae
tritum nitenti fuste uerberat saxum;
nec turba cessat entheata Bellonae,
nec fasciato naufragus loquax trunco,
a matre doctus nec rogare Iudaeus,
nec sulphuratae lippus institor mercis.
numerare pigri damna quis potest somni?
dicet quot aera uerberent manus urbis,
cum secta Colcho Luna uapulat rhombo.
tu, Sparse, nescis ista, nec potes scire,
Petilianis delicatus in regnis,
cui plana summos despicit domus montis,
et rus in urbe est uinitorque Romanus
nec in Falerno colle maior autumnus,
intraque limen latus essedo cursus,
et in profundo somnus, et quies nullis
offensa linguis, nec dies nisi admissus.
nos transeuntis risus excitat turbae,
et ad cubile est Roma. taedio fessis
dormire quotiens libuit, imus ad uillam.

61

Versus et breue uiuidumque carmen
in te ne faciam, times, Ligurra,
et dignus cupis hoc metu uideri.
sed frustra metuis cupisque frustra.
in tauros Libyci fremunt leones,
non sunt papilionibus molesti.
quaeras censeo, si legi laboras,
nigri fornicis ebrium poetam,
qui carbone rudi putrique creta
scribit carmina quae legunt cacantes.
frons haec stigmate non meo notanda est.

bakers; and all day long, the hammers of the coppersmiths. Over here the bored moneychanger is making his grubby table rattle with Neronian bullion; over there someone's hammering Spanish gold-dust,* thrashing the worn-down stone with a glistening maul; and those fired-up disciples of Bellona* aren't letting up, nor is the shipwreck victim with his bandaged torso and his sob-story, nor the Jew who learned to beg from his mother, nor the sore-eyed vendor flogging sulphured firewood. What man can count all the things that stop us sleeping in? *He* will tell us how many pots and pans the hands of the city bash about, when the bisected moon is assaulted by the magic rhombus* of Colchis.

Sparsus, you don't know these things; you can't know, tucked up as you are in the spread you got off Petilius. Its ground floor looks down on the heights of the hills; it's a country estate, but in town—your vineyard's worked by a Roman, and yet Falernian slopes don't yield a bigger vintage; a broad driveway for your runabout* loops through your front porch; and at the heart of the place, you sleep in peace and quiet. No intruding conversations; daylight only by invitation. Me? The jostle of the passing crowd jolts me awake; all Rome is at my bedside. When I'm exhausted, when I can't stand it, whenever I feel like some sleep—I go to my place in the country.

61

You're afraid I'll write lines with you as their target, Ligurra—some poem as vigorous as it's short. *And* you're keen for people to think you're right to be afraid. But your fear is pointless, and so's your desire. Lions of Libya aim their roars at bulls; they don't maul butterflies. My advice to you is, if you're so desperate to be read about, find some drunken poet in a soot-darkened archway, one who writes his poems with a lump of charcoal and crumbling chalk—the kind of poem people read while they're shitting. This brow hasn't earned a branding from *my* iron.

62

Antiqui rex magne poli mundique prioris,
    sub quo pigra quies nec labor ullus erat,
nec regale nimis fulmen nec fulmine digni,
    scissa nec ad Manes, sed sibi diues humus:
laetus ad haec facilisque ueni sollemnia Prisci
    gaudia: cum sacris te decet esse tuis.
tu reducem patriae sexta, pater optime, bruma
    pacifici Latia reddis ab urbe Numae.
cernis ut Ausonio similis tibi pompa macello
    pendeat et quantus luxurietur honos?
quam non parca manus largaeque nomismata mensae,
    quae, Saturne, tibi pernumerentur opes?
utque sit his pretium meritis et gratia maior,
    et pater et frugi sic tua sacra colit.
at tu sancte—tuo sic semper amere Decembri—
    hos illi iubeas saepe redire dies.

68

Matutine cliens, urbis mihi causa relictae,
    atria, si sapias, ambitiosa colas.
non sum ego causidicus nec amaris litibus aptus,
    sed piger et senior Pieridumque comes;
otia me somnusque iuuant, quae magna negauit
    Roma mihi: redeo, si uigilatur et hic.

69

Sic tamquam tabulas scyphosque, Paule,
omnes archetypos habes amicos.

73

Heredem tibi me, Catulle, dicis.
non credam nisi legero, Catulle.

62

Great King of the heavens of old,* of the world that went before, whose
rule saw sleepy repose and knew no toil; no thunderbolt of overweening
kingship, nor any deserving it; nor earth split down to the Underworld,
but guarding its wealth for itself: be propitious, show favour, and at-
tend the traditional festivities that Priscus is hosting. You deserve to be
present at rites dedicated to you. Best of fathers, you restore him to his
fatherland in the sixth winter of his sojourn in the Latin city of peace-
loving Numa. Do you see how the piñata* is swinging, as well stocked
as an Ausonian market, and how they've made the place special with all
those treats? See how unstinting his hand has been, and the tickets for
that lavish spread? Do you see, Saturn, what wealth is being counted
out in your name? And to make these good deeds more precious, more
pleasing, it's a father (and a frugal one) who's showing such devotion
to your rites. But you, holy one—and may you always be loved for it in
your own month of December—please command these days to come
around again for him many times over.

68

You early-morning client—you're the reason I left Rome. If you had
sense, you'd hang around the lobbies of people who care about ap-
pearances. I'm no barrister, I've no head for bitter litigation: I'm
sleepy, I'm getting old, I hang out with the Muses; what I like is free
time and sleep, the very things that mighty Rome wouldn't let me
have. If there are early mornings even *here*, I'm going back.

69

You're convinced your paintings and plate are the real deal, Paulus.
You're convinced your friends are, too.

73

You say I'm your heir, Catullus.* Catullus, I'll believe it when I see it
in writing.

92

Saepe rogare soles, qualis sim, Prisce, futurus,
  si fiam locuples simque repente potens.
quemquam posse putas mores narrare futuros?
  dic mihi, si fias tu leo, qualis eris?

94

Scribebamus epos; coepisti scribere: cessi,
  aemula ne starent carmina nostra tuis.
transtulit ad tragicos se nostra Thalia cothurnos:
  aptasti longum tu quoque syrma tibi.
fila lyrae moui Calabris exculta Camenis:
  plectra rapis nobis, ambitiose, noua.
audemus saturas: Lucilius esse laboras.
  ludo leuis elegos: tu quoque ludis idem.
quid minus esse potest? epigrammata fingere coepi:
  hinc etiam petitur iam mea palma tibi.
elige quid nolis—quis enim pudor, omnia uelle?—
  et si quid non uis, Tucca, relinque mihi.

95

Musseti pathicissimos libellos,
qui certant Sybariticis libellis,
et tinctas sale pruriente chartas
istanti lege Rufe; sed puella
sit tecum tua, ne thalassionem
indicas manibus libidinosis
et fias sine femina maritus.

96

Cum tibi nota tui sit uita fidesque mariti,
  nec premat ulla tuos sollicitetue toros,
quid quasi paelicibus torqueris inepta ministris,
  in quibus et breuis est et fugitiua Venus?
plus tibi quam domino pueros praestare probabo:

92

You keep asking me, Priscus, what sort of person I'd turn into if I suddenly got rich and powerful. Do you really think anyone can tell you how they'd behave then? Tell me, Priscus, if you turned into a lion, what sort of lion would you be?

94

I tried to write an epic once. You started writing one; so I stopped, so my poetry wouldn't compete with yours. Then my Muse redirected herself to the thigh-boots of Tragedy. You tried on the trailing robe yourself. I plucked lyre-strings brought to a pitch of art by Calabrian Muses;* fired with ambition, you grab my plectrum before I even get going. I dare Satire; you throw yourself into becoming Lucilius. I unwind with some light elegies; you copy me and unwind just the same. How low *won't* you go?* Now I've started composing epigrams, but even my success with these is in your sights. Decide what you *don't* want—because wanting it all would just be embarrassing—and if there *is* anything you don't want for yourself, Tucca, leave it for me.

95

Mussetius' little books are queer as fuck. Serious rivals to the ones from Sybaris. Their pages *drip* with pornographic genius. Istantius Rufus, you should read them; but make sure your girlfriend's around, so your horny hands don't strike up 'Here comes the bride' and make a husband of you without a wife.

96

You know how your husband lives. You know he's faithful. No other woman's putting a dent in your bed and threatening your marriage. So why torment yourself over his page-boys, as if they were mistresses making their move? Silly woman: our passion for boys is brief and fleeting. I will prove to you that you get more out of these boys than

hi faciunt, ut sis femina sola uiro;
hi dant, quod non uis uxor dare. 'Do tamen,' inquis,
    'ne uagus a thalamis coniugis erret amor.'
non eadem res est: Chiam uolo, nolo mariscam:
    ne dubites quae sit Chia, marisca tua est.
scire suos fines matrona et femina debet:
    cede sua pueris, utere parte tua.

97

Uxor cum tibi sit puella, qualem
uotis uix petat improbis maritus,
diues, nobilis, erudita, casta,
rumpis, Basse, latus, sed in comatis,
uxoris tibi dote quos parasti.
et sic ad dominam reuersa languet
multis mentula milibus redempta;
sed nec uocibus excitata blandis,
molli pollice nec rogata surgit.
sit tandem pudor, aut eamus in ius.
non est haec tua, Basse: uendidisti.

98

Baetis oliuifera crinem redimite corona,
    aurea qui nitidis uellera tinguis aquis;
quem Bromius, quem Pallas amat; cui rector aquarum
    Albula nauigerum per freta pandit iter:
ominibus laetis uestras Istantius oras
    intret, et hic populis ut prior annus eat.
non ignorat, onus quod sit succedere Macro:
    qui sua metitur pondera, ferre potest.

he does. They're the ones who ensure you're the only woman for him; they're the ones who give him what, as his wife, you won't. 'But I *do* give it up to him,' you say, 'so my husband's love won't stray footloose from our bedroom.' It's not the same thing. I want a Chian fig,* not a big cheap one; and just so you're clear which one is the Chian, yours is the big cheap one. A housewife and lady ought to know her limits: leave the boys *their* part* and make the most of your own.

97

Your wife's the kind of girl a husband would hardly dare ask for in his most shameless prayers.* She's rich, well-born, educated, faithful. And you shoot your load, Bassus—into long-haired boys instead. You bought them with her dowry! And now when your cock comes back to the mistress who laid out so many thousands for it, it's limp. It doesn't twitch at dirty talk or rise at the prompting of a gentle thumb. Enough is enough: behave, or I'm taking you to court. It's not *yours*, Bassus: you sold it.

98

Guadalquivir, with your hair crowned in a garland of olive, you who dye fleeces golden in your gleaming waters; beloved of Bacchus, beloved of Minerva; for whom Tiber, ruler of waters, opens a shipping lane across the deep: may Istantius sail your banks amid prosperous omens, and may this year go for your peoples just as the last one did. He is well aware what a weighty task it is to succeed Macer; but the man who can gauge his own burden, is capable of carrying it.

XENIA

I

Ne toga cordylis et paenula desit oliui
  aut inopem metuat sordida blatta famem,
perdite Niliacas, Musae, mea damna, papyros:
  postulat ecce nouos ebria bruma sales.
non mea magnanimo depugnat tessera telo
  senio nec nostrum cum cane quassat ebur:
haec mihi charta nuces, haec est mihi charta fritillus:
  alea nec damnum nec facit ista lucrum.

3

Omnis in hoc gracili XENIORVM turba libello
  constabit nummis quattuor empta tibi.
quattuor est nimium? poterit constare duobus,
  et faciat lucrum bybliopola Tryphon.
haec licet hospitibus pro munere disticha mittas,
  si tibi tam rarus quam mihi nummus erit.
addita per titulos sua nomina rebus habebis:
  praetereas, si quid non facit ad stomachum.

4. Tus

Serus ut aetheriae Germanicus imperet aulae
  utque diu terris, da pia tura Ioui.

5. Piper

Cerea quae patulo lucet ficedula lumbo
  cum tibi sorte datur, si sapis, adde piper.

7. Faba

Si spumet rubra conchis tibi pallida testa,
  lautorum cenis saepe negare potes.

PARTY FAVOURS

Whitebait need their jackets,* and olives their oilskins—and we
don't want the undiscriminating bookworm worrying he'll starve.
So, Muses, write off these Nile papyri: count them among my losses.
Look, boozy midwinter is calling for new jokes. *My* die isn't battling
it out with the high-spirited knucklebone, a six and a one aren't rat-
tling *my* ivory; this page is my nuts, this page, my dice-box. *This* kind
of game brings neither loss nor winnings.

3

The job-lot of *Doggy-bags* assembled in this slender little book will
cost you four sesterces to buy. Is four too much? It could cost two, and
Tryphon the bookseller would still make a profit. You can send these
two-liners to your guests in place of a gift, if you don't see a sesterce
any more often than I do. You'll find each gift is labelled—there are
headings;* so if one isn't to your taste, you can skip to the next.

4. Incense

Want Germanicus to rule the palace of heaven, but not for a good
while yet? Want him long on earth? Offer ritual incense to Jupiter.

5. Pepper*

When the lottery gives you a glossy, fat-loined figpecker, if you're
smart, add pepper.

7. Bean

If you have a pale bean simmering in an earthenware pot, you can
keep turning down the dinners of the smart set.

9. Lens

Accipe Niliacam, Pelusia munera, lentem:
uilior est alica, carior illa faba.

13. Betae

Vt sapiant fatuae, fabrorum prandia, betae,
o quam saepe petet uina piperque cocus!

14. Lactucae

Cludere quae cenas lactuca solebat auorum,
dic mihi, cur nostras inchoat illa dapes?

16. Rapa

Haec tibi brumali gaudentia frigore rapa
quae damus, in caelo Romulus esse solet.

29. Vas Damascenorum

Pruna peregrinae carie rugosa senectae
sume: solent duri soluere uentris onus.

32. Caseus Fumosus

Non quemcumque focum nec fumum caseus omnem,
sed Velabrensem qui bibit, ille sapit.

35. Lucanicae

Filia Picenae uenio Lucanica porcae:
pultibus hinc niueis grata corona datur.

36. Cistella Olivarum

Haec quae Picenis uenit subducta trapetis
inchoat atque eadem finit oliua dapes.

9. Lentil

Accept the Nile lentil, a gift from Pelusium;* cheaper than emmer groats, but dearer than beans.

13. Beets

To give bland beets, the workmen's lunch, some kick, oh, how often will the cook ask for wine and pepper!

14. Lettuces*

Lettuce always concluded our ancestors' feasts. So tell me, why does it introduce ours?

16. Turnip

This turnip I'm giving you, that loves the winter frost: it's what Romulus has for tea in heaven.

29. Jar of Prunes

Take plums, wrinkled by drying in old age overseas: they're just the thing for constipation.

32. Smoked Cheese

The cheese that has drunk up not just any hearth and not your everyday smoke, but the smoke of the Velabrum*—*that* cheese has a kick to it.

35. Lucanian Sausages

I'm a Lucanian sausage, daughter of a sow from Picenum. Slices of me make a lovely topping for white porridge.

36. Punnet of Olives

This one kind of olive, filched from the presses of Picenum, both introduces a feast and marks its end.

41. Porcellus Lactans

Lacte mero pastum pigrae mihi matris alumnum
ponat, et Aetolo de sue diues edat.

50. Terrae Tubera

Rumpimus altricem tenero quae uertice terram
tubera, boletis poma secunda sumus.

59. Glires

Tota mihi dormitur hiems et pinguior illo
tempore sum quo me nil nisi somnus alit.

72. Phasinae

Argoa primum sum transportata carina.
ante mihi notum nil nisi Phasis erat.

77. Cycni

Dulcia defecta modulatur carmina lingua
cantator cycnus funeris ipse sui.

82. Ostrea

Ebria Baiano ueni modo concha Lucrino:
nobile nunc sitio luxuriosa garum.

92. Lepores

Inter aues turdus, si quid me iudice certum est;
inter quadripedes mattea prima lepus.

93. Aper

Qui Diomedeis metuendus saetiger agris
Aetola cecidit cuspide, talis erat.

41. Suckling Pig

If a rich man serves me the milk-fed offspring of a sluggish mother, he can gorge on Aetolian boar* for all I care.

50. Truffles*

We truffles that poke a delicate head through the earth that nurses us are a crop second only to mushrooms.

59. Dormice

I hibernate all winter. I'm fattest then, when nothing feeds me but sleep.

72. Pheasants

I was first shipped abroad in the *Argo*'s hold.* Before, all I knew was Phasis.

77. Swans

Sweet melodies it sings, with fading voice—the swan, dirge-singer at its own funeral.

82. Oysters

I am a fresh delivery of shellfish, sozzled in Baiae's Lucrinus.* Self-indulgent, I thirst for the very best garum.*

92. Hares*

Among birds it's the thrush, if I'm a sure judge of anything; but among four-footed beasts, the number-one delicacy is hare.

93. Boar

The bristly beast that terrorized Diomedes' fields, and fell to an Aetolian spear, was such a boar as this.

99 (98). Dorcas

Delicium paruo donabis dorcada nato:
iactatis solet hanc mittere turba togis.

102. Garum Sociorum

Exspirantis adhuc scombri de sanguine primo
accipe fastosum, munera cara, garum.

103. Amphorae Muriae

Antipolitani, fateor, sum filia thynni:
essem si scombri, non tibi missa forem.

107. Picatum

Haec de uitifera uenisse picata Vienna
ne dubites, misit Romulus ipse mihi.

108. Mulsum

Attica nectareum turbatis mella Falernum;
misceri decet hoc a Ganymede merum.

111. Falernum

De Sinuessanis uenerunt Massica prelis.
condita quo quaeris consule? nullus erat.

122. Acetum

Amphora Niliaci non sit tibi uilis aceti:
esset cum uinum, uilior illa fuit.

126. Vnguentum

Vnguentum heredi numquam nec uina relinquas:
ille habeat nummos, haec tibi tota dato.

99 (98). Gazelle

You will give this gazelle to your little boy as a pet; the crowd likes to let her go free, waving their togas.*

102. Garum of the Associates*

Made from the fresh blood of a still-gasping mackerel: accept this haughty garum, a pricy gift.

103. Jar of Muria*

I am the daughter of a tunny from Antipolis and I don't deny it. If my mother had been a mackerel, I wouldn't have been sent to *you*.

107. Pitch-Flavoured Wine

You needn't doubt that this pitch-flavoured wine came from the vineyards of Vienne; Romulus himself* sent it to me.

108. Honeyed Wine

You honeys of Attica, you muddy the nectar-like Falernian. This heady brew is fit to be mixed by Ganymede.

111. Falernian Wine

This Massic has come from the presses of Sinuessa. Laid down under which consul, you ask? Back then, there weren't any.*

122. Vinegar

Don't think this jar of Nile vinegar is cheap: when it was wine, it was cheaper still.

126. Ointment

Never leave ointment or wine to your heir. He can have the money, but will all that stuff to yourself.*

127. Coronae Roseae

Dat festinatas, Caesar, tibi bruma coronas:
quondam ueris erat, nunc tua facta rosa est.

127. Garlands of Roses

Winter gives you forced garlands, Caesar.* Once a sign of spring, the
rose now shows your power.

APOPHORETA

1

Synthesibus dum gaudet eques dominusque senator
   dumque decent nostrum pillea sumpta Iouem;
nec timet aedilem moto spectare fritillo,
   cum uideat gelidos tam prope uerna lacus:
diuitis alternas et pauperis accipe sortes:
   praemia conuiuae dent sua quisque suo.
'Sunt apinae tricaeque et si quid uilius istis.'
   quis nescit? uel quis tam manifesta negat?
sed quid agam potius madidis, Saturne, diebus,
   quos tibi pro caelo filius ipse dedit?
uis scribam Thebas Troiamue malasue Mycenas?
   'Lude' inquis 'nucibus'. perdere nolo nuces.

2

Quo uis cumque loco potes hunc finire libellum:
   uersibus explicitum est omne duobus opus.
lemmata si quaeris cur sint adscripta, docebo:
   ut, si malueris, lemmata sola legas.

12. Loculi Eborei

Hos nisi de flaua loculos implere moneta
   non decet: argentum uilia ligna ferant.

13. Loculi Lignei

Si quid adhuc superest in nostri faece locelli,
   munus erit. nihil est; ipse locellus erit.

28. Vmbrella

Accipe quae nimios uincant umbracula soles:
   sit licet et uentus, te tua uela tegent.

DOGGY-BAGS

I

So long as the knight and our important friend the senator are having
fun in their party clothes; so long as liberty caps get our Jupiter's seal
of approval, and while the born slave isn't afraid to look the aedile* in
the eye as he shakes his dice-box, though he sees the icy pools so close
by: accept these presents, meant for rich man and poor man by turns.
May each reader give the right one to the right guest. 'They're junk!
Rubbish! Worse, if that's possible!' We all know *that*; no one would
deny it; it's obvious. But what else should I be doing, Saturn, in these
boozy days that your own son gave you as a trade for the heavens? You
want me to write about Thebes, or Troy, or wicked Mycenae? 'Go
play with your nuts,' you say: well, I don't want to lose my nuts.

2

You can make this little book end whenever you like: each of my pro-
ductions is over and done with in two lines.* If you're wondering why
the poems have titles, I'll tell you: if you prefer, you can just read the
titles.*

12. Ivory Cash-boxes

You've no business filling these cash-boxes with anything less than
yellow coinage: cheap wood can carry silver.

13. Wooden Cash-boxes

If there's anything left in the fluff at the bottom of my cash-box, it can
be the present. No, nothing there. The box can be the present.

28. A Parasol

Accept this parasol that can keep off the sun when it's too strong; and
if it's windy,* too, you'll have your own awning to shade you.

29. Causea

In Pompeiano tecum spectabo theatro:
nam flatus populo uela negare solet.

30. Venabula

Excipient apros expectabuntque leones,
intrabunt ursos, sit modo firma manus.

31. Culter Venatorius

Si deiecta gemas longo uenabula rostro,
hic breuis ingentem comminus ibit aprum.

51. Strigiles

Pergamon has misit. curuo destringere ferro:
non tam saepe teret lintea fullo tibi.

52. Gutus Corneus

Gestauit modo fronte me iuuencus:
uerum rhinocerota me putabas.

53. Rhinoceros

Nuper in Ausonia domini spectatus harena,
hic erit ille tibi, cui pila taurus erat.

54. Crepitaculum

Si quis plorator collo tibi uernula pendet,
haec quatiat tenera garrula sistra manu.

97. Lances Chrysendetae

Grandia ne uiola paruo chrysendeta mullo:
ut minimum, libras debet habere duas.

29. A Macedonian Hat

I will watch the plays with you in the Theatre of Pompey, because the breeze often denies the people their awning.

30. Hunting-Spears

They will meet boar head-on, they will ambush lions, they will skewer bears—just let the grip be firm.

31. Hunting-Knife

If you're sorry you've dropped your long-bladed hunting-spears, this short blade will go toe-to-toe with a massive boar.

51. Strigils

Pergamum has sent these. Use their curved steel to exfoliate, and the laundry won't have to scrub your towel so often.

52. A Flask Made of Horn*

A bullock carried me about on his forehead not long ago. You will think I am genuine rhinoceros.

53. Rhinoceros*

Lately the star attraction in our Lord's Ausonian arena—to you this will be he, to whom a bull was but a ball.

54. A Little Rattle

If a little home-grown slave hangs bawling round your neck, let him shake this chatty rattle in his infant hand.

97. Gold-Inlaid Platters

Don't insult grand gold-inlaid dishes with a paltry mullet. He ought to weigh two pounds, minimum.

98. Vasa Arretina

Arretina nimis ne spernas uasa monemus:
lautus erat Tuscis Porsena fictilibus.

124. Toga

Romanos rerum dominos gentemque togatam
ille facit, magno qui dedit astra patri.

125. Idem

Si matutinos facile est tibi perdere somnos,
attrita ueniet sportula saepe toga.

161. Pluma

Lassus Amyclaea poteris requiescere pluma,
interior cycni quam tibi lana dedit.

162. Faenum

Fraudata tumeat fragilis tibi culcita mula:
non uenit ad duros pallida cura toros.

172. Sauroctonos Corinthius

Ad te reptanti, puer insidiose, lacertae
parce: cupit digitis illa perire tuis.

174. Hermaphroditus Marmoreus

Masculus intrauit fontis, emersit utrumque:
pars est una patris, cetera matris habet.

185. Vergili Culex

Accipe facundi Culicem, studiose, Maronis,
ne nucibus positis ARMA VIRVMQVE legas.

98. Arretine Ware

Don't turn your nose up at Arretine ware. I'm serious: Porsena* dined in style off Tuscan crocks.

124. A Toga

'Lords of Nature, the toga-wearing race':* he makes Romans so, who gave his great father the stars.*

125. Ditto

If losing your morning sleep is no big deal, wearing out your toga gets you regular handouts.

161. Feathers

Tired? Now you can lie at ease on feathers from Amyclae, that the swan's inner down has given you.

162. Hay

May your crackling mattress bulge with what you robbed from the mule. Pallid care steers clear of hard bunks.*

172. *Lizard-Slayer** in Corinthian Bronze

Spare the lizard, treacherous boy, as it crawls towards you; it craves death at your fingers.

174. Hermaphrodite in Marble

He entered the fountain a male; he emerged double-sexed. One part is his father's, the rest, his mother's.

185. Virgil's *Gnat*

Accept, avid reader, the *Gnat* of eloquent Maro, so you needn't read 'Arms and the Man' when you've put away your nuts.*

186. Vergilius in Membranis

Quam breuis immensum cepit membrana Maronem!
ipsius uultus prima tabella gerit.

188. Cicero in Membranis

Si comes ista tibi fuerit membrana, putato
carpere te longas cum Cicerone uias.

194. Lucanus

Sunt quidam, qui me dicant non esse poetam:
sed qui me uendit bybliopola putat.

203. Puella Gaditana

Tam tremulum crisat, tam blandum prurit, ut ipsum
masturbatorem fecerit Hippolytum.

205. Puer

Sit nobis aetate puer, non pumice leuis,
propter quem placeat nulla puella mihi.

217 (216). Accipiter

Praedo fuit uolucrum: famulus nunc aucupis idem
decipit et captas non sibi maeret aues.

222. Pistor Dulcarius

Mille tibi dulces operum manus ista figuras
extruet: huic uni parca laborat apis.

223. Adipata

Surgite: iam uendit pueris ientacula pistor
cristataeque sonant undique lucis aues.

186. Virgil on Parchment*

What a compact parchment has fitted in vast Maro! The front page bears his portrait.

188. Cicero on Parchment

If this parchment will be your travelling-companion, tell yourself you are taking a long trip with Cicero.

194. Lucan*

There are some who say I am no poet—but the bookseller who stocks me counts me as one.

203. A Girl from Cadiz

She twerks so twitchily, she's such a prick-tease, she'd have made a wanker of Hippolytus* himself.

205. A Boy

Give me a boy who's smooth because he's young, not from pumice:* one who'll ruin me for girls.

217 (216). Hawk

He was a pirate among birds; now he's the bird-catcher's slave.* As he snatches the birds, he grieves they're not caught for himself.

222. Confectioner

This hand will craft for you a thousand kinds of sweets. For him alone does the thrifty bee labour.

223. Lardy-Cake

Get up! Already the baker is selling the boys their breakfast, and from all sides the crested fowl cry daybreak.

EXPLANATORY NOTES

ABBREVIATIONS

The following abbreviations are used:

AP   *Anthologia Palatina*, the 'Greek Anthology' (see Introduction, pp. ix and xiii)

SB   Shackleton Bailey's Loeb edition of Martial (see Note on the Text, p. xxix)

Often a note will direct the interested reader to further scholarship, most frequently the English-language commentaries on individual books of Martial. These references take the form 'Name (date: page(s))' and refer to items listed in the Select Bibliography. The numbers in the left-hand column are the book and epigram number, or the epigram number only in the case of the three unnumbered books.

LIBER SPECTACULORUM/BOOK OF SHOWS

1   *the Wonders*: as noted by Coleman (2006: 3), this poem responds to a Greek model by Antipater (*AP* 9.58) that praised the Seven Wonders of the Ancient World. Martial is not the first Roman poet to slight the Pyramids; cf. the famous opening to Horace, *Odes* 3.30, 'I have erected a monument more enduring than bronze, and loftier than the Pyramids' royal tomb'. Martial again flatteringly contrasts the Pyramids to Roman engineering achievements at 8.36.

the Crossroads Goddess: Artemis, worshipped at her world-famous temple at Ephesus. She was goddess of the hunt, but also had a connection to the underworld; crossroads were associated with witchcraft and the supernatural.

to Delos: the island of Delos was the great cult centre of Apollo; in his sanctuary was a famous altar made of animal horns. Legend said the god himself had built it from the horns of animals hunted by his sister, Artemis. It is only sometimes included in lists of the Seven Wonders.

2   *Colossus of the Sun*: erected by Nero, this giant statue originally stood beside the lake in his Golden House complex. After his fall the Flavians built an amphitheatre on the lake's site; the amphitheatre subsequently became known as the Colosseum because the statue was still an identifying landmark. In this poem it is 'close' to the stars both physically (like the Mausoleum in poem 1, it is very tall) and by virtue of family relationship (sun and stars).

gifts to the people: the Latin is *munera*, which means both public benefactions and shows (including arena entertainments)—the baths are spectacular as well as useful.

3   *Orpheus' Haemus*: a mountain range in Thrace, where the legendary
    musician mourned his lost wife Eurydice; cf. *Book of Shows* 24.

    a Sarmatian: these Scythian nomads were increasingly seen as a military
    threat (Coleman 2006: 44), and later books celebrate Domitian's victory
    over them.

    farthest Tethys: Tethys is partnered with Oceanus in myth, and Coleman
    (2006: 46) points to Martial's use of her name to signal the seas off Scot-
    land at 10.44.1–2.

    the Sabaeans too . . . drenched in their native mists: the Sabaeans are the
    inhabitants of Arabia Felix; Cilicia is where Rome got its saffron, prized
    for its scent as much as its flavour (3.65). A saffron-perfumed mist of
    water droplets could be used to cool the crowd at public events.

6 (5)   *the ancient tale*: Roman arena entertainments sometimes reproduced
    scenes from myth and ancient history (see Coleman 1990), and a re-
    enactment of the myth of Pasiphae is attested under Nero (Suetonius,
    Nero 12.2). The offspring of her mythical coupling with the bull was the
    Minotaur; cf. *Book of Shows* 32. Coleman's own commentary on this
    poem (2006: 64–5) speculates that one of the Flavian emperors restaged
    the myth in an attempt to outdo Nero's version, and supplies gruesome
    physiological detail.

8   *a woman's hand*: the Latin, *manus*, evokes personal courage in close com-
    bat. The word used for shows, *munera*, recalls the public baths given as
    an amenity in poem 2.

9 (7)   *a Caledonian bear*: this is another fatal charade, as in poem 6; the Scot-
    tish bear is another visitor from the far North (cf. poem 3). Latin authors
    were showing increasing interest in Scotland in the later first century
    AD; see Coleman (2006: 90).

12 (10)   *under such a leader*: the Latin word is *princeps*, 'first citizen', a title of
    the emperors since Augustus.

20   *the pious elephant*: Imperial authors were fascinated by elephants: see
    Coleman (2006: 156–7), citing Plutarch and Pliny the Elder.

24 (21)   *Rhodope . . . in Orpheus' theatre*: Latin poets habitually associated
    the legendary musician with this Thracian (now Bulgarian) mountain
    region, e.g. Virgil, *Georgics* 4.461, *flerunt Rhodopeiae arces*, 'the heights
    of Rhodope wept'.

    against the script: Martial goes into Greek here, παρ' ἱστορίαν, echoing
    Lucillius, *AP* 11.254, which ends with the same words in the same position.

30 (26)   *trident*: the trident's usual role in the arena is as the weapon of the net-
    man, the *retiarius*; here it is the customary attribute of Neptune.

    the Spartan boys: Castor and Pollux, the Dioscuri, demigod brothers
    of Helen and traditional protectors of sailors. Coleman (2006: 212–14)
    is fascinatingly informative on ancient aquatic displays, a type of show
    that drove the moralists of the early Church to paroxysms of outrage.

4

30 (26) *Thetis*: a Nereid (sea-nymph) and the mother of Achilles. Catullus 64 takes her marriage to the human Peleus as its theme.

32 (28; 27) *Porthaon's beast*: Porthaon was a legendary king of Calydon, where roamed the Calydonian Boar, slain by Meleager.

> *He could yoke . . . Pasiphae's beasts*: Carpophorus the *bestiarius* (a professional fighter of wild animals in the arena) outdoes all the heroes of myth, including Hercules and Jason (the 'Colchian woman' is Medea, cf. e.g. 10.35). 'Pasiphae's beasts' are the bull that mounted her and the Minotaur to which she subsequently gave birth; cf. poem 6.

> *Hesione and Andromeda*: mythical princesses rescued from sea-monsters by Hercules and Perseus respectively.

34 (30; 28) *the trumpet of sea-battle*: Augustus did lay on mock sea-battles in Rome in a specially built pool (the *Stagnum*), which Titus reused (Suetonius, *Titus* 7.3); but these opening lines might also make readers think of Actium, the real sea-battle that secured his rule.

BOOK 1

PREFACE

and doesn't assign headings: surviving copies of ancient epigram-books sometimes preface each poem with a descriptive title (called a *lemma* or *titulus*); whether such headings formed part of the author's original design is usually a matter of guesswork. Many modern translators insert suppositious titles when working with ancient collections of short poems, and one may note that Martial's term for 'critic', *interpres*, can also mean 'translator'.

spectators at Flora's Games. Cato can stay out: this immediately ties Book 1 to Martial's earlier *Book of Shows*. Flora's Games, the *Floralia*, were an ancient Roman tradition and offered spectacular and naughty entertainment. The name 'Cato' is shorthand for stern patrician conservatism, conjuring up not one but two famous holders: 'the Elder' (234–149 BC, opponent of Hellenization) and his great-grandson 'the Younger' (95–46 BC, renowned Stoic and opponent of Caesarianism).

1.2 *parchment binds them between narrow boards*: the special travel-sized copies described in the poem are parchment codices: they have spines, covers, and pages, like the books of today. Codices did not catch on as a mainstream way of publishing literature for centuries after Martial's time, so his typical ancient reader will have read this poem in a book-roll—a scroll made of papyrus.

the threshold of Peace and the Forum of Pallas: Vespasian's temple of AD 75 celebrated the end of the Jewish revolt and looked out over a colonnaded garden. The relatively narrow urban corridor between the Temple of Peace complex (sometimes called the 'Forum of Peace') and the Forum of Augustus was subsequently turned into the Forum of Nerva, which takes its name from Domitian's short-lived successor. However, the project was begun under Domitian and included a temple of his favourite goddess, Minerva.

1.4 *Thymele and Latinus*: this knockabout double-act reappears at Juvenal 1.36.

As Censor: one of Domitian's offices, making him guardian of public morals.

but my life is clean: a Catullan pose, cf. *Carmen* 16.5–6, *Nam castum esse decet pium poetam | ipsum, uersiculos nihil necesse est*, 'You see, a reverend bard ought to be chaste, but that's just him—his ditties needn't be.'

1.6 *Though the eagle . . . the heavens*: the boy is Ganymede, Zeus' favourite; Martial often alludes to his myth. Martial's description of the eagle carrying him off through the 'airy vault of the heavens' (*aetherias . . . auras*) adds pseudo-epic grandeur by echoing Virgil, *Aeneid* 1.545-6, *aurā | aetheriā*.

1.7 *if Verona hears it . . . Catullus' Sparrow*: Verona was Catullus' birthplace, cf. 1.61, where again Stella's poem is preferred to Martial's allegedly revered poetic predecessor. Two poems by Catullus (*Carmina* 2 and 3 in the transmitted text) take as their topic the death of Lesbia's pet sparrow; here Martial appears to take *Sparrow* to be the title of a Catullan book.

1.22 *a Dacian boy would not fear Caesar's arms*: Rome went to war with Dacia in AD 85, and Books 1 and 2 are traditionally dated to the following year. 'Arms' is the first word of the *Aeneid* (*arma uirumque cano*), so is appropriately applied to Domitian as a late heir to Aeneas' mission. It is no coincidence that this poem invokes the *Aeneid* while praising Domitian's mercy to non-combatants: Virgil's epic famously assigns Rome a divine mandate 'to be merciful to the surrendered and crush the proud in war', *parcere subiectis et debellare superbos* (6.853).

1.25 *Pandion's Cecropian citadel*: 'Cecropian' as a synonym for 'Athenian' recurs several times in Martial. Cecrops is the mythical king under whose rule Athens *became* Athens, by securing Athena's patronage. Pandion was another of the city's legendary kings, and father of Procne and Philomela (1.53).

The glory . . . comes too late: the contrast between living and posthumous fame is picked up from 1.1, with similar wording.

1.27 *I loathe . . . a recollective guest*: the sententious final line is an old saying, presented by Martial in its original Greek.

1.30 *Diaulus used to be a surgeon . . . undertaker*: a *uispillo* is an undertaker who buries paupers; a *clinicus* is a doctor who visits patients in bed. This is one of many poems in which Martial borrows from skoptic epigram, where comically bad doctors are a favourite topic (*AP* 11.112–26). Martial draws attention to his appropriation of the Greek motif by returning to it not long after, at 1.47, and again at 6.53. Doctoring was a Greek trade in antiquity, and much of its technical vocabulary is still Greek-derived.

1.34   *Lesbia*: a name-*cum*-characterization appropriated from Catullus and made even more publicly promiscuous than in his *Carmen* 58.

Chione: another recurring figure whose poems (e.g. 3.82) can be called a 'cycle'. Her name is humorously inappropriate: 'Snow White'.

professional cock-sucking bitches: Adams (1982: 199) finds that in Martial, *purus* implies avoidance of oral sex; its opposite, *spurcus*, would thus imply habitual and frequent oral sex. *Lupa*, 'she-wolf', is specifically used of low-end prostitution.

1.44   *both large and small*: when *libellus*-theory reigned (Introduction, pp. xxiii–xxvi), this was read as a reference to the distinction between Martial's supposed pamphlets for patrons (the *libelli*) and his larger and more miscellaneous *libri*, but already at 1.2 Martial's reader has been encouraged to purchase extra copies of his books in travel-sized codex editions.

frolicking hares and playful lions: this recalls 1.22 but also the *Book of Shows*. Hare was a particular delicacy (cf. 5.29, *Xenia* 92).

1.52   *I entrust my little books to your care*: a close echo of Catullus, *Carmen* 1.1–3; see p. xxiv.

the plagiarist: Martial plays on a word's historic meaning here. *Plagiarius* carried the literal meaning of 'kidnapper' before it came to mean 'plagiarist' by metaphorical extension. The relationship between a text and its putative author is again mapped on to that between slave and master in the immediately following poem, 1.53; this is an Ovidian gesture, cf. *Tristia* 1.1.2, 3.7.2.

1.53   *a Lingonian kaftan*: the Lingones were a Celtic people; effectively Martial just means 'Gaulish'. The *bardocucullus* (a rare word in Latin and an obvious barbarism) was a long, hooded cloak in coarse wool that muffled its wearer against the foul northern weather; Martial speaks slightingly of it again at *Apophoreta* 128.

if a black raven . . . Philomela's birds: the river Cayster in Lydia (modern Turkey) was renowned for its swans; cf. Philostratus, *Imagines* 1.11. Philomela is here identified by allusion as 'the Attic woman' (*Atthis*), but at 5.67 the exact same paraphrase identifies her sister Procne, who turns not into a nightingale but a swallow.

1.61   *Verona . . . blessed with Maro*: Verona was Catullus' home town; Mantua, Virgil's. As very often in Martial, Virgil is identified by his short and metrically easy third name or *cognomen*; cf. 'Naso' for Ovid.

Aponus' land . . . and no less for Stella: Aponus, a god of health-giving springs, had his main sanctuary near Livy's home town of Patavium (modern Padua). Stella's *Dove* has already been singled out for praise at 1.7.

the Paelignians: the Paeligni were a people of Abruzzo; Ovid was from their capital, Sulmo.

gay Cadiz: famous for its sexy dancing girls; see note on 6.71. At 11.6, introducing a book we are told will be saucy, Martial warns the prudish reader that it will shake its castanets 'Cadiz-style'.

1.70 *its painted Corybant*: a Corybant was a dancing priest of Cybele. The reference is generally understood as meaning that this round temple (*tholos*) was painted with frescos depicting worship, although it could instead mean that the priest himself was 'painted', e.g. tattooed; cf. the Moorish cavalry of 10.6, where again some guesswork is required. See the Introduction, p. xxi.

Phoebus and the learned sisters: Apollo, god of poetry, and the Muses.

1.72 *a windfall mulberry*: the mulberry is proverbial for blackness at e.g. Horace, *Satires* 2.4.22.

1.77 *Charinus licks cunt—and still he's pale*: the Latin word (*cunnus*) is meant to be shocking; outside Martial, it appears mostly in graffiti. Adams (1983: 80–1) has a useful note. The joke of the poem hinges on two different senses of the Latin verb *palleo*: to grow pale, because one is sick or is doing something that makes one feel sick; and to be pale, despite doing something that ought to make anyone blush with shame.

1.104 *big as Calydon's in legend*: the legendary Calydonian boar was slain by Meleager; the hunt makes a well-known episode in the eighth book of Ovid's *Metamorphoses*.

1.107 *his Flaccus and his Virgil*: Maecenas was patron to a circle of on-message poets in the early years of the Augustan regime. 'Flaccus' is Quintus Horatius Flaccus, the poet known to modern readers as Horace, and Martial's conditional offer of undying verse looks back to his *Epistles* 2.1 and *Odes* 3.30.

1.109 *her portrait in miniature*: as at 7.84, the small-scale portrait is painted on a piece of board (*tabella*). Numerous examples of such portraits survive from the Fayum in Egypt, where Graeco-Roman portraiture was combined with Egyptian mummification.

1.110 *Swifty*: this is an example of Martial's use of so-called 'speaking names': comically appropriate or inappropriate names that deliver a quick laugh and some instant characterization. His source for the technique is Lucillius.

1.113 *the hick stuff*: the Latin has *apinas*. Apina was a small town in Apulia, proverbial for pointlessness and triviality.

1.114 *the name you read*: the implied context is a roadside tomb, but 'you read' also recalls the reception Martial anticipates from the Avid Fan reading his little books in 1.1.

1.117 *if he's wanting the Pear Tree*: a spot on the Quirinal.

popping down to the Argiletum: an area known for its shopping.

If you ask for Atrectus: the transmitted text begins *Nec*, 'And don't ask . . .'. This seems to make no sense, and I follow SB in marking the Latin as probably corrupt.

1.117 *smoothed down with pumice*: at the end of the book, as at its start, Martial pays literary homage to Catullus, *Carmen* 1; like Catullus' *libellus*, his little book has been buffed with pumice. Cf. the specified absence of pumice at Ovid, *Tristia* 1.1.11, a book sent (putatively) to Rome from barbarous Tomis with neither literal nor metaphorical polish.

BOOK 2

2.1 *book-roll*: Martial addresses the papyrus scroll (a *liber*) onto which book 2 (a *libellus* of epigrams) is copied; cf. the similarly introductory 11.1.

going lukewarm: wine could be served hot in winter, and this is the likely context here. In summer, the wealthy might enjoy it chilled with snow.

2.12 *Postumus*: this name-*cum*-characterization appears frequently in Martial (e.g. 6.19), leading critics to identify his poems as a 'cycle', particularly here in Book 2. As well as 2.12 and 2.23, he is encountered at 2.10 and 2.21 (not in this selection). Postumus' typical motif is *os impurum*, the 'impure mouth' dirtied by oral sex, which Romans viewed as demeaning to the person giving pleasure.

2.23 *kisses*: Postumus' kisses are *basationes*, a mock-grandiose term that evokes Catullus, *Carmen* 7.

2.29 *See his cloaks*: cloaks (*lacernae*) were worn in the theatre when the weather was bad; cf. 6.82.

Peel off . . . the answer: this senatorially dressed theatregoer (the purple-striped toga, the badged shoe—cf. Juvenal 7.191, Statius, *Silvae* 5.2.27–8) has a past: he was once a slave, recaptured after running away and branded on the forehead. Martial repeatedly revisits the theme of the social-climbing freedman: compare e.g. 2.29 (now he wears the iron ring of the *eques*; formerly he wore iron shackles), and 11.54 (a former runaway slave who is still a compulsive petty thief). Martial comes back to the allocation of seating in the Theatre of Marcellus in Book 5, where he praises Domitian for introducing strict segregation between social classes and rooting out fraudulent claimants of equestrian status (5.8, 5.35).

2.32 *she's a widow*: Ponticus keeps refusing to speak on Martial's behalf in lawsuits because he hopes for favours from the parties Martial is suing. The theme of the legacy-hunter, currying favour with wealthy old men and women in the hope of being remembered in their wills, is a favourite of Roman satirical authors: cf. e.g. Juvenal 12.93–130 and the Croton episode in Petronius' *Satyrica*, fr. 116. Martial returns to it often, as e.g. at 4.56 and 9.8 (9). As a widow, Laronia is legally entitled to manage her own finances.

2.37 *you pass them . . . to take home*: i.e. to the slave who has accompanied him from home as his attendant and now stands behind him as he reclines to dine. Martial gets the idea for this poem from Lucillius, but his version is more elaborate: cf. *AP* 11.205 and 207. He comes back to the same topic at 3.23.

2.48   *even in Butuntum*: an insignificant inland city of Apulia, in the far south of Italy; Martial uses it again as an exemplar of provincial dullness at 4.55 (not in this selection).

2.53   *gold-inlaid dinner service*: *chrysēndeta*, a quite rare and technical term taken from the Greek, as was so much of the terminology of the good life in Rome; Martial uses it twice in quick succession, at 2.43 (not in this selection) and here, and it recurs as an expensive gift at *Apophoreta* 97.

   the Lower Pleasures: technically, a cultic distinction: Venus Plebeia as opposed to Venus Pronuba.

   freer than the king of Parthia: this could be an otherwise lost saying, but Williams (2004: 186) notes that Parthian and Persian kings referred to themselves by the title 'King of Kings'; such a title assigns total freedom to its holder (and none to anyone else).

2.57   *the Saepta*: the Saepta Julia in the Campus Martius had begun a century earlier as a voting enclosure but was now an upmarket shopping-centre.

   his hand studded with amethysts: as in 2.53, Martial uses a rarefied term with a Greek root (*amethystinatus*); his attentive reader will spot a connection back to 2.29, where the social climber's hand is described with an identically formed adjective, *sardonychata*.

   long hair: likely to indicate youthful male attendants, like the 'gorgeous hunks' who swarm in Domitian's palace at 9.36; cf. 4.7.

2.65   *came with a million in dowry*: the theme of the widower who has inherited a fortune from his wealthy wife, and whose grief fails to convince, is revisited at 5.37.

2.71   *work you'd written*: the apparent compliment at the end is nicely double-edged: is Martial encouraging Caecilianus to display his own talent, or insinuating that his own poetry would look even better when placed against Caecilianus' rubbish?

2.75   *a hand to be put in his mouth*: this poem subverts the reader's memory of tame and gentle lions in Book 1 (1.22, 44, 104).

   The martial sand: the sandy floor of the Colosseum. The Latin for 'sand' (*harena*) is synonymous with the arena, and persists (minus its 'h') into modern English.

   our she-wolf: a she-wolf (*lupa*) legendarily nursed Romulus and Remus, but note that the term has already been used in Book 1, where its meaning is much seedier (1.34).

2.77   *Brutus' Boy*: a statuette owned by Brutus and taking its name from him (Pliny, *Natural History* 34.82).

2.89   *this vice was Cicero's*: the Late Republican orator wrote a famously bad epic about his own consulship (Quintilian 11.1.24).

2.89   *That you throw up, Antony's*: Cicero, in his second *Philippic* (2.63), excoriated Antony for being so hung over he vomited while presiding over an official meeting; 'Martial's brief allusion suggests that the incident became famous' (Williams 2004: 268–9).

2.90   *Quintilian, unequalled teacher*: this is the famous author of the *Institutio oratoria*, a manual of Roman rhetoric; his students included the younger Pliny.

2.92   *At my request*: this and the preceding poem are clearly meant to be enjoyed as a pair, and the juxtaposition flatters Domitian as an ideally or even impossibly attentive patron, with no passage of time (marked by intervening poems) between request and gift.

       My master's: Martial must mean Domitian. Fathering three children earned legal perks (cf. 4.27). On hearing he has been granted them for 'fathering' little books instead (2.91), Martial immediately divorces his wife on the comic pretext that it would be a snub to Domitian if he then went and had three children anyway. Since Domitian is Censor (1.4) in charge of public morals, this is clearly not a poem intended to be taken seriously as a statement about Martial's domestic arrangements.

2.93   *you can always take one 'i' off the title*: this turns the Roman numeral for 2 (II) into the numeral for 1 (I).

BOOK 3

3.1   *named for the Roman toga*: Martial sends his book to Rome from 'Togaed Gaul' (*Gallia Togata*), another name for Cisalpine Gaul in northern Italy; the toga is the emblem of Roman citizenship.

3.2   *some soot-blackened kitchen*: the culinary uses of papyrus are real, but also a literary echo of Catullus, *Carmen* 95, where the poet anticipates that Volusius' *Annals* are destined to 'often provide loose jackets for mackerel'. Martial closely echoes this line of Catullus later in the book, at 3.50; and cf. *Xenia* 1, where some of Martial's own books are used to cover whitebait. The poem again echoes *Carmen* 1 (see p. x).

3.5   *little book*: the word (*paruus*) is used not just of physical size but of maturity (the book is childish), and of value and importance (the book is inconsequential).

       Julius: this poem is part of the Julius Martial cycle (Introduction, pp. xiii and xv).

3.9   *Cinna*: Martial's epigrammatic rival shares a name with (although obviously cannot be) the Late Republican 'Cinna the poet' of Shakespeare's *Julius Caesar*, author of the epyllion *Zmyrna* (Catullus, *Carmen* 95); much later (6.17), he will turn out to have been a lower-class rogue.

3.10   *left you penniless*: because he will quickly squander it and there will be no more handouts; cf., with a piquantly different scenario, 4.66.

3.11 *Sextus*: Quintus and Sextus are both common Roman forenames; the joke is that Quintus means 'fifth' and Sextus means 'sixth'.

3.12 *Fabullus . . . he's really stiffed*: Fabullus appears often enough (e.g. 4.87, 5.35, 9.66) that his appearances can be called a 'cycle'. Sweet-smelling ointment made dinner parties more pleasant, but was also used to anoint the dead.

3.19 *pretty Hylas*: Hercules' young boyfriend in myth (Martial alludes to him often), making 'Hylas' an obvious name to give a pretty slave-boy.

     not true: in two senses: it is not a real bear (just a statue), and it is deceptive (a nasty surprise lurks inside).

3.20 *Canius Rufus*: like Postumus and Fabullus, Rufus appears often in the dodecalogy.

     that reprobate Phaedrus: a Greek freedman of the first century BC who introduced Aesop's fables to Roman readers by composing versions in Latin verse. These got him into trouble with the emperor Tiberius because of supposed political allusions.

     delightful Europa: the Porticus of Europa (cf. 11.1) is mentioned only in Martial, a slender basis indeed for attempts at reconstruction.

     shameless Tigellinus: the Praetorian prefect who famously abetted Nero's worst crimes.

     rowing his little boat on Lake Lucrinus: this saltwater lagoon, famous for its farmed shellfish—Martial often praises its oysters (e.g. 6.11)—was an easy outing from the upscale coastal resort of nearby Baiae (1.62, 6.68). When Rufus 'rows his little boat' there, he does so in a Latin verb, *nauculor*, that is only attested in this poem.

3.22 *Apicius*: this legendary gourmet first appeared at 2.89. This and the immediately following poem, 3.23, are thematically paired.

3.23 *next to your feet*: because Romans reclined on couches to dine, facing inwards around the dining-room, and their attending slaves stood behind them by the walls. See note on 2.37. Lucillius, *AP* 11.207, complains of a greedy diner who passes 'everything' he cannot eat to a slave standing 'behind him', 'at his feet' (πάντα δίδως ὀπίσω . . . πρὸς πόδας), and this is surely Martial's immediate source.

3.26 *Candidus*: this speaking name, 'Shiny', recurs at 3.46.

     murrine-ware: very expensive tableware, imported from Parthia; Dalby (2000: 188–9) identifies it as fluorspar. Martial's reader encounters it again at 3.82, again as a sign of flashy wealth.

     Opimius' Caecuban: the year of Lucius Opimius' consulship (121 BC), a proverbially excellent vintage for any and all wines, takes us back to the Republic (Gaius Gracchus was killed that same year); see Pliny the Elder, *Natural History* 14.55. Massic was a full-bodied Campanian wine that improved with ageing (Dalby 2000: 47, 141).

3.28   *Nestor*: a comically inappropriate name, since the Homeric Nestor is famous for sage advice.

3.29   *his old set of rings*: Zoilus passes himself off as an equestrian, a status marked by an iron ring, but he used to wear iron rings of a very different kind—the shackles of a slave.

3.32   *I can do Hecuba, I can do Niobe*: Hecuba (Greek Hecabe) was a standard exemplar of extreme old age, as e.g. at Lucian, *AP* 11.408. She illustrates the same theme later in the book (3.76). Invective against and mockery of old women (especially if they are sexually active) is frequent in skoptic epigram, as e.g. at *AP* 11.71–4, 256, 417. Niobe, daughter of Tantalus, doubted the gods and was turned to stone after they killed her children in punishment; Martial may have got her myth from Lucillius, *AP* 11.253–5.

3.36   *my wooden sword*: the symbol of a gladiator's manumission and retirement from the ring. Gladiators were typically slaves, and Martial may be hinting that the 'toga-work' of clientage (3.46) is degrading for a free citizen.

3.38   *a Naso*: on 'Maro' and 'Naso' for Virgil and Ovid, see note on 1.61.

3.39   *half-blind Lycoris*: the second one-eyed girlfriend in this book—the first is Thais (3.8 and 3.11).

       the Trojan cup-bearer: Ganymede.

3.43   *Proserpina*: queen of the Underworld; no matter who else he fools, Laetinus cannot fool nature and fate.

3.46   *toga-work*: a client attending on his patron had to put on formal wear and be clean and presentable. Martial revisits this detail frequently (e.g. 4.26), often putting the toga into a diminutive form (*togula*— 'stupid toga', 'wretched toga') to indicate his distaste for the whole social ritual.

3.47   *the Small Hercules*: a Roman cult of this name is attested in a couple of inscriptions.

       he was carrying eggs: on foot, because otherwise they would arrive broken. Roman carts had no suspension.

       Quite the opposite: Roman satire conventionally contrasts the vice-ridden metropolis with the virtuous self-sufficiency of country life; here though, as repeatedly in Martial, the productive countryside is over-written by the consumer lifestyles of wealthy commuters.

3.50   *we're served lettuce*: as an appetizer, lettuce was thought to help the digestion; cf. 5.78, 11.52, *Xenia* 14. It could be served as a salad or a purée (Apicius 3.15.3, 4.2.3).

       donate . . . to the mackerel: on the culinary uses of papyrus, see note on 3.2.

3.57   *he served it neat*: the wine is unbelievably bad; cf. e.g. Lucillius, *AP* 11.396, where the wine is so acidic it would be best used to make a vinaigrette for lettuce, just as in Martial 3.50.

3.58 *a proper, scruffy farm*: Faustinus' villa is at Baiae, where one might expect an estate given over to leisure and ostentatious display of wealth; instead Martial presents a vivid picture of a working farm. On the scenography and ethical meanings of the elite villa garden, see usefully Spencer (2010).

the pheasant of the depraved Colchians: the pheasant is so named after its place of origin in Roman eyes, Phasis in Colchis—Medea country (cf. 10.35 and *Xenia* 32).

your Priapus: the rustic god whose images, like scarecrows, guarded Italian orchards, warning off thieves with his sickle and erect phallus.

3.59 *The cobbler Cerdo*: probably a speaking name, but in any case passable as a working name: it is a Greek loan-word meaning 'artisan'.

3.65 *Corycian saffron*: reckoned the best.

an Arabian reaper: Arabia was called *Arabia Felix*, Happy or Fortunate Arabia, because it was the source or intermediary for so many precious spices and perfumes (4.13, and see Dalby 2000: 167, 182–4).

slick with spikenard: this crushed root of a plant of the Valerian family was an expensive aromatic, used to make nard oil (cf. 4.13). It also had culinary uses: Apicius includes a delicious recipe for an 'extraordinary' spiced wine (1.1) made with spikenard, pepper, and saffron.

Diadumenus: this beautiful young slave, named after a famous Greek statue by Polyclitus, reappears at 5.46 and 6.34.

3.68 *Up to this point, Madam*: Martial addresses the respectable female reader of Book 3 again at poem 86: 'I warned you in advance, bashful lady. I told you . . .'. These ironic disclaimers count on the book-roll format: a codex might fall open at any page, but a papyrus scroll can only be read sequentially, and its reader has only him- or herself to blame if s/he ignores the author's warnings and goes 'further in'.

that thing: no one seems to know what the custom or ritual is whereby Venus gets given a phallus; cf. 4.64.

avidly: Martial's wording (*studiosa*) evokes the *lector studiosus* ('Avid Fan') of 1.1.

3.80 *Apicius*: met as a speaking name at 3.22, and here given a different spin: the addressee is a glutton, like his famous namesake, but not for food. The *os impurum* motif is implied here (see note on 2.12).

3.82 *in his green suit*: the colour green (cf. the 'leek-green fan') was thought to connote effeminacy, in much the same way that yellow (as, for instance, in the title of the self-consciously avant-garde periodical, the *Yellow Book*) suggested Decadence in the Victorian *fin de siècle*.

the smoke-rooms of Marseilles: the city's stinky smokeries also feature at 10.36 and *Apophoreta* 14.118 (neither poem included in this selection).

Cosmus' little bottles: Cosmus is *the* maker of unguents in Roman satire: cf. Juvenal 8.86. Martial (cf. 12.55, 11.15) typically alludes to his products using adjectival forms that turn his name into a designer brand.

3.83   *'Do me like Chione does'*: the ultra-concise (half-line) epigram with which Martial imagines putting Cordus in his place, i.e. 'suck my cock'.

3.86   *the mimes*: Roman mime (*mimus*) was popular entertainment, less scripted and more physical than comedy. Men and women performed in it, without masks, and the content was often sexually explicit.

3.99   *Cerdo . . . you got away with murder*: Book 3's reader will immediately think of Cerdo, the cobbler of 3.59 who sponsored gladiatorial games in an attempt to improve his social standing.

3.100   *the sky was falling*: quite a downpour. 'The sky is falling' was used proverbially of anything very improbable.

BOOK 4

4.1   *Life-giving day of Caesar*: the book opens with praise of Domitian under the pretext of his approaching birthday, 24 October.

  honour Minerva . . . countless oak-wreaths: wreaths of oak-leaves were the prizes awarded at the Capitoline Games, refounded by Domitian; the stadium built for the athletic contests is now the Piazza Navona, and there was an *odeum* (conservatory) next door for musical events. Domitian also founded a poetry contest in honour of Minerva.

  Romulus' own Tarentos: cf. 10.63, 'Roman Tarentos', part of the Campus Martius. The Secular Games were held here, once every *saeculum* (110 years). It was called 'Roman Tarentos' to distinguish it from the Calabrian town of the same name.

4.4   *Tiber*: Albula was the ancient name for the Tiber.

  than what you smell of: the poem is another variation on a theme by Lucillius, *AP* 11.239.

4.5   *tout vapourware*: in Latin, to 'sell smoke' (*fumum uendere*) is idiomatic for taking money for something that's never delivered.

  Philomelus: a Greek name that Martial's readers will recognize from 3.31 as a *nouveau-riche*.

4.7   *Hyllus, my boy*: like that of Hylas, Hyllus' name is taken from the myth of Hercules, suggesting he is a slave; cf. 2.51. The characters have different roles in Hercules' story but the close similarity of the names is suggestive.

  your hair: previously the long hair of adolescence, now cut short as a sign of entry into manhood; cf. 12.18 and Persius 4.5.

  it has turned me into an old man: the Latin is ambiguous: does Hyllus become the 'old man', or is it Martial? Probably the latter: in ancient poetry one of the very worst things about becoming old is that young people will find you sexually repulsive and spurn your advances, as Hyllus is spurning Martial's here (cf. e.g. Mimnermus, fragment 1).

4.8   *The first hour and the second*: on the hours of the Roman day, see note on 11.52.

Euphemus: a Greek name, placing the addressee as one of the Imperial freedman who ran things for Domitian.

4.9   *Dr Saver*: the doctor's name, Sōtas, relates to the Greek for saving lives; on medicine as a Greek trade, see note on 1.9. His daughter has a Latin name but dissolutely (ἀσώτως) chases a Greek lover.

4.10   *my little book is . . . not yet trimmed*: Martial again echoes the famous opening of Catullus, *Carmen* 1, *Cui dono lepidum nouum libellum . . .?* The word for 'trim' also means 'shave', so there may be a play on the idea of the book's immaturity; either way, it is not yet ready for circulation.

a Punic sponge: a sponge could work as an eraser while the ink was still wet (Martial is sending Faustinus his work the instant he's finished writing it), but Romans also used sponges on sticks to wipe after going to the toilet. Martial self-deprecatingly suggests that it will be easier to wipe the book-roll clean and start again than try and fix what's there.

fix my jokes: Martial's terminology of correction (*emendare*) consciously nods to Ovid's (Galán Vioque 2002: 103 on 7.11.2).

4.13   *Pudens*: the name means 'modest' or 'bashful'.

Massic wines with Theseus' honeycombs: the honey of Attica (Theseus was a legendary king of Athens) was acknowledged to be the best (6.34); on Massic wine, see note on 3.26. Moreno Soldevila (2006: 171) points out that honeyed wine, *mulsum*, had a reputation as an aphrodisiac; and that nard was a fragrance for men (with sympotic associations), cinnamon for women. *Mulsum* is a choice Saturnalia gift at *Xenia* 108.

4.14   *the Castalian sisterhood*: Apollo turned the nymph Castalia into a spring and dedicated it to the Muses; it was a literal fount of inspiration for poets.

the mighty Scipios: Silius Italicus' *Punica*, an epic on the wars against Carthage, does not in fact include both the Scipiones Africani, just the elder. Perhaps the plan of his work was not yet clear, or Martial's vagueness is deliberate exaggeration to make the in-progress poem sound grander. Martial praises the *Punica* again at 7.63 (not in this selection).

a loaded knucklebone: Martial's word, *tropa*, transliterates a Greek term for a game played with knucklebones. The word is vanishingly rare in either language, and dictionary-makers on both sides are in the dark as to how the game was played. The *Sparrow* as a presumptive title for the (or a) book of Catullus first appeared at 1.7, and again at 1.109; it recurs at 11.6, in a dirty *double entendre*.

Just so, perhaps . . . to great Maro: SB points out that Virgil was a child when Catullus was writing; Martial must know this, and that his readers (presumably including the real Silius) will know it too.

4.17   *Lycisca*: a Greek name—'Little Wolf'—that stereotypes her as a prostitute; see note on 1.34.

4.18   *Where the gate drips with rain . . . and the stone is slippery-wet*: the scenario envisaged by SB is that the icicle formed under a leaky aqueduct, 'perhaps the Aqua Virgo'. Moreno Soldevila (2006: 201) notes the mourning associations of the opening lines: the 'stone' (*lapis*) could as well be a tombstone, and is 'wet' (*madet*) as though soaked with tears.

4.22   *her husband . . . in the glittering waters*: is the husband Martial, or is Martial in this poem an opportunistic interloper? Is the encounter in a bath-house, or in some secluded lake? These deliberate ambiguities help create an atmosphere of fantasy, and the waters are muddied further when the 'real' Cleopatra shows up at 4.59 (not in this selection). One could even read this poem as an add-on to the Julius Martial cycle: Martial awards himself a Cleopatra to go with his Caesarian pretensions.

4.23   *Callimachus*: the most famous of the Hellenistic poets, Callimachus wrote in the early third century BC. He was an influential literary propagandist for concise, bookish poetry and was among the pioneers of epigram as a poetic genre. He was also the inventor of library cataloguing. He is thus ideally qualified to rank epigrammatists. Martial invokes him again as the *ne plus ultra* of ivory-tower poets at 10.4 (see note).

        Bruttianus: not otherwise attested, and perhaps invented for this poem; since his name is not Greek, presumably Martial's reader is meant to think of him as a Roman writing epigrams in Greek after the manner of Gaetulicus. The theme of contest under Minerva's patronage may make readers think of 4.1 (see note), and Domitian's literary festival in the goddess's honour.

4.25   *Altinum*: an ancient coastal town in the north-east of Italy; its remains now lie a little inland. After its sack by Attila the Hun in 452, its inhabitants, the Veneti, relocated to islands in the lagoon where their descendants would one day build Venice.

4.26   *all year, Postumus*: the addressee has stopped rewarding Martial's service as a client with the expected gifts and invitations, but he was so mean to begin with that the loss is not great—Martial was already running at a deficit, merely by incurring the expense of having his toga cleaned so he could visit and pay his respects. Martial returns to Postumus' failure as a patron in 4.40.

4.27   *the presents you gave me*: these must be the *ius trium liberorum*, the legally privileged status that came with having fathered three children; see 2.91–2. At 8.31 Martial, having secured it for himself, mocks another petitioner who keeps trying to do the same.

4.29 *silly Marsus*: Domitius Marsus is an unlikely epic poet here; see note on 8.55 (56). Roses in winter: cf. *Xenia* 127.

4.32 *Phaethon's drop*: in myth, Phaethon's sisters were turned into trees and their tears at his death became nuggets of amber. Martial and his readers know the story best from Ovid, *Metamorphoses* 2.340–66.

She lies unseen . . . casked in her own nectar: the bee is encased in a lump of amber. There are close verbal echoes here of the reluctant Cleopatra whom Martial ambushes while bathing at 4.22: *latere, lucere, conditus*.

4.40 *When the mansion of the Pisos still stood . . . a house thrice noteworthy*: the opening lines backdate Postumus' patronage of Martial to the reign of Nero, when the failure of a conspiracy by Gaius Calpurnius Piso (AD 65) brought down many famous names. The house of Seneca is 'thrice noteworthy' for the two Senecas, Elder and Younger, and for Lucan (see note on 7.23), all famous authors; the latter two were implicated in Piso's plot and were left with no choice but suicide.

4.42 *when I'm saying 'No'*: cf. 4.38 (Galla), 71, and 81 (Galla again). Martial returns to the theme of stealing kisses from a pretty boy at 5.46.

Let him beware of the boys: as up-and-coming rivals for his master's affection, since an adolescent male's period of peak attractiveness was held to be so short.

4.44 *Here was Venus' seat . . . famous for its Herculean name*: Venus was the divine patron of Pompeii, Hercules of Herculaneum, which was named after him.

4.46 *a Faliscan haggis*: made with a pig's stomach and not necessarily from Faleria, any more than every 'Lucanian sausage' came from Lucania (Varro, *On the Latin Language* 5.111). Lucanian sausages are a Saturnalia gift at *Xenia* 35.

and a napkin titivated with a broad stripe: a comic *reductio ad absurdum* of the senatorial toga, likewise distinguished by a broad stripe (*latus clauus*). This list shares many items with the list of Saturnalia gifts passed on to Martial by Umber at 7.53.

4.49 *'ditties' and 'jokes'*: Martial here disallows a characterization of epigrams that elsewhere he happily endorses.

the trailing robe of Tragedy: the *syrma* (the letter *y* flags up the word's Greek origin), a long robe with a train, worn especially by tragic actors. Martial recycles it at 12.94, and Juvenal too uses it as a shorthand for the pretensions of tragedy at 15.30.

4.62 *Lycoris*: Martial introduced a one-eyed Lycoris at 3.39 (cf. Thais at 3.8), but this dark-skinned Lycoris recurs at 7.13, a variant on 4.62. Her famous namesake, the 'pretty Lycoris' who inspired the elegies of Cornelius Gallus, is introduced as part of a catalogue of examples justifying Martial's argument (the scholarly term for such a catalogue is 'priamel') at 8.73. The equation of pale skin with feminine beauty was standard in antiquity; and cf. 4.42, where Martial's ideal toy-boy is also pale-skinned.

4.62   *everything turns white there*: Tivoli itself (Latin Tibur), where Hercules Victor had a major cult centre, is a hill-town; but the sulphur springs on the plain below can still be smelled from the train that takes you there from Roma Tiburtina station, stopping at Tivoli Bagni (spa) on the way.

4.64   *every cool spot*: cooled by water or shade and thus pleasant in the heat of summer.

that delights in virgin's blood: the reference is obscure. There have been various attempts to emend the text or to explain it as it stands (an atavistic and otherwise unattested outdoor-sex custom? Something to do with pomegranates?); none of them are wholly persuasive.

Alcinous' godfearing home, or Molorchus': two examples of legendarily considerate hosts. Alcinous was king of the Phaeacians in Homer's *Odyssey*; Molorchus, the peasant with whom Hercules stayed the night (cf. 9.43) before his first labour, the slaying of the Nemean Lion.

lofty Setia: an ancient town of old Latium (the Latium of the Latin League, back in the day before Rome took over). It was an out-of-the-way place: at one point Rome stashed Carthaginian hostages there for that reason.

4.66   *Linus . . . you pulled it off*: Linus has gone on a spree and spent the lot, because his simple country upbringing has left him with no idea how to manage money; this poem makes an ironic pair with 3.10, where a dissolute city upbringing has the exact same effect. Linus' name is comically inappropriate for his bumpkin persona; the Linus of myth, son of Apollo and one of the Muses, was the inventor of music and teacher of Orpheus.

BOOK 5

5.2   *Germanicus . . . in company with his girl*: the reference is to Domitian's special relationship with the virgin goddess Minerva; cf. 6.10, 8.1. Domitian adopted the title 'Germanicus' in 84: Galán Vioque (2002: 356) on 7.61.3 summarizes the sources and bibliography.

5.3   *Degis, dweller on a riverbank*: the river is the Danube; Degis was the brother of Decebalus, king of the Dacians, with whom Domitian made a deal that was then glossed as conquest.

5.5   *the heavenly poem of the Capitoline War*: flattery of Domitian as a poet. Martial stands to Catullus as Virgil ('Maro') stands to the emperor's juvenilia (a detail extorted by SB from Suetonius, *Domitian* 2.2).

5.7   *sloughed her former skin*: for the idiom, compare Pliny the Elder, *Natural History* 8.111. The presumptive context is recent fire-damage to Rome, followed by rebuilding; Howell makes this the fire of AD 80, described by

Cassius Dio 66.24, which caused widespread destruction in the Campus Martius.

your well-known grudge: Vulcan was, of course, the god of fire; the mythological reference is to his chaining of his wife Venus and Mars when he caught them in adultery, a punishment that famously backfired. Lemnos was the centre of his cult. Martial anticipates further fires at 5.42.

5.8   *Phasis*: the name suggests a servile origin in the semi-Hellenized East, at the far end of the Black Sea (where the pheasants come from, 3.58).

    Leitus: this theatre usher reappears at 5.35. The poem is all one sentence in the Latin.

5.10   *Pompey's ancient portico . . . Catulus' excuse for a temple*: dating from 55 BC and 69 BC respectively. Howell 1995: 86–7 gives useful background on both. It is worth noting that the approximate date for Book 5 is AD 89–90, and that Domitian had rebuilt Catulus' temple of Capitoline Jupiter, sparing no expense, in the early 80s. The old men (*senes*) are thus praising the temple as they remember it from younger days.

    none but Corinna: the beloved of Ovid's *Amores*.

    I'm in no rush: this poem contradicts Martial's assertions (e.g. in 1.1) that his *libelli* have already made him a legend in his own lifetime. Three poems later (5.13) the contradiction is contradicted.

5.11   *Sardonyxes . . . jaspers*: see note on 4.32 (poetic gems). The poem makes an obvious pair with 5.12.

5.12   *hard to pull off*: identical phrasing to 4.66, where Linus got through his mother's million.

    Stella can carry ten girls: the intended meaning is obscure; one explanation is the nine Muses plus Minerva. Stella appears often in Martial; see note on 1.61.

5.13   *Callistratus*: his Greek name immediately stereotypes him as a freedman made good.

    all round the world: Martial's self-description here directly and obviously samples his self-introduction back in 1.1.

    Gaulish Parma: so called because it lies in Cisalpine Gaul (see note on 3.1).

5.18   *damsons*: Latin *Damascenos*. They came from, and were named after, Damascus; cf. *Xenia* 29.

    the greedy parrot-wrasse: on the *scarus* (parrot-wrasse), a delicacy of a fish, see SB's note on 13.84.

5.20   *dear Martial*: this poem is part of the Julius Martial cycle (Introduction, pp. xiii and xv).

    haughty ancestor-masks: displayed in the atrium of a patrician townhouse (*domus*) to illustrate the family tree (*stemma*).

5.20   *They're gone, they've been debited from our account*: Howell (1995: 101) adds the fascinating aside that this Latin tag (*pereunt et imputantur*) has since been adopted as a motto for inscription on sundials.

5.22   *where rustic Flora looks on ancient Jupiter*: the temple of Flora and the Capitolium Vetus both stood on the Quirinal. On the Subura, see note on 7.31.

no human feeling: at 5.18, a few poems previously this was the charge against Martial himself for being a Scrooge at Saturnalia.

5.29   *you've never eaten hare*: on the superstition that eating hare made one pretty, see Pliny the Elder, *Natural History* 28.260; the belief is likely to have arisen because 'hare' and 'charm' are the same word in Latin, *lepos*, *leporis*, and 'decline identically, apart from the scansion' (Howell 1995: 113).

5.34   *father Fronto and mother Flaccilla*: although the Latin is not explicit, it makes more sense to take Fronto and Flaccilla as Martial's parents (at least for the purposes of this poem) than Erotion's—they have respectable Roman names and she is a slave-girl. Alternatively, Fronto and Flaccilla could be the deceased former *paterfamilias* and *materfamilias* of the household (*familia*) to which Erotion belonged.

she plays and skips now: the translation follows SB in preferring *iam*, 'now [she plays]', to the not very satisfactory *tam* 'so very [old]' of the manuscript tradition. Martial returns to Erotion's death a few poems later (5.37) and again at 10.61.

5.35   *a naughtier key*: if Euclides really had the status he pretends to, he would not need to carry possessions around (he would have staff for that), and certainly not his front-door key (he would have a doorman at home). Ancient keys were large, and dropping one would be very noticeable. As so often in Martial, the ambitious and pretentious social climber wears a Greek name.

5.36   *turning a deaf ear . . . he's a fraud*: this poem closes identically to 4.40 (the last word is *imposuit*; cf. *Postumus imposuit*, 'Postumus is an imposter'), but looks forward as well as back: 'turning a deaf ear' (*dissimulat*) will be echoed at 11.108, 'pretending you're deaf'.

5.37   *ageing swans*: swans legendarily sang just before they died, hence 'swan-song'; cf. *Xenia* 77.

Phalantine Galaesus: 'Phalantine' is a poetic equivalent for Tarentine, referring to Tarentos in Calabria (4.1). The little river Galaesus flowed into the gulf of Tarentum. Virgil mentions it in *Georgics* 4 and subsequently has 'Galaesus' as one of the first casualties of the Italian war in the *Aeneid* (7.535): see Putnam (1998: 111–12).

fleeces of Baetica, and braids of the Rhine: Baetica's sheep were proverbially golden-fleeced: cf. 9.61. The Suebi and Sygambri (*Liber Spectaculorum* 3.9) wore their hair up in a knot: cf. Juvenal 13.164, Tacitus, *Germania* 38.

And Paetus tells me: the name is chosen because it is aristocratic, with distinct Stoic overtones. Two of its famous first-century bearers set noble examples of principled resistance to the tyranny of 'bad' emperors: A. Caecina Paetus committed suicide in AD 42 after falling under suspicion of conspiracy against Claudius, and his son-in-law P. Clodius Thrasea Paetus in AD 66 under Nero (Tacitus' incomplete *Annals* end with the latter's showily philosophical suicide). Martial's Paetus thus has a lot to live up to, and is instead revealed as a self-justifying hypocrite.

5.43 *Laecania bought hers; Thais' are her own*: the basic joke is out of Lucillius, probably *AP* 11.68, a poem that Martial imitates more closely at 6.12. Thais' name immediately stereotypes the women as prostitutes.

5.46 *struggling kisses*: a close allusion to Ovid, *Metamorphoses* 4.358; Martial's scenario looks back to Catullus, *Carmen* 99 (kisses stolen from Juventius).

5.56 *Tutilius*: a teacher of rhetoric; Quintilian, the addressee of 2.90, married his daughter (Pliny, *Letters* 6.32).

a guitarist: a *citharoedus* sang while playing the *cithara*, a multi-stringed variant on the lyre, played with a plectrum; the instrument's name lives on in our 'guitar'.

5.58 *you're running out of time*: it is ironic that Martial preaches to Postumus about the importance of living for today, when at 5.20 he has admitted that he and Julius Martial never get around to it themselves.

5.65 *the Libyan wrestling-ring*: Libya was where Hercules defeated the giant Antaeus. 'His stepmother' is Juno; the 'Terror of Nemea' is the Nemean Lion, his first labour.

Maenalian swine: the mention of Mt Maenalus in Arcadia aligns Domitian's beast-hunts with Hercules' labour of the slaying of the Erymanthean Boar.

a man who could defeat Geryon: usually read as meaning Carpophorus, the phenomenal beast-fighter from *Liber Spectaculorum* 32. The 'herdsman' is Geryon, who owned magnificent cattle; Hercules' tenth labour was to defeat him and capture them. The duel is 'threefold' because Geryon had, depending on the tradition one followed, either three heads or three bodies.

5.69 *Pothinus; your list*: Pothinus was the politically influential eunuch who in 48 BC arranged for Pompey to be murdered on his arrival in Egypt, and presented his head to Julius Caesar; the scene is an important moment in the civil-war epic of Martial's fellow Spaniard, Lucan. Five years later Marc Antony had Cicero proscribed as an enemy of the state ('your list') and murdered. Cicero had become Antony's bitter political enemy in the aftermath of Caesar's assassination, and denounced him in the speeches he called the *Philippics*. Martial comes back to Pompey in 5.74.

5.69   *even Catiline*: the great villain of Late Republican history, against whom Cicero had fearlessly spoken out and prevailed, only to be semi-judicially murdered when he tried the same trick on Antony: see note on 10.70.

5.74   *around the world*: Pompey's presumptively scattered remains replicate the readership distribution of Martial's *libelli*, as reported in 1.1.

5.78   *single-serving meals at home*: the Latin word, *domicenium*, seems to be Martial's own coinage. He only uses it twice.

       potted tunny will lurk in halved eggs: *cybium*, chopped and salted pieces of young tunny-fish. Tunny is again combined with eggs at 11.52, where the eggs disguise a fish that is past its best.

       branches at Picenum: the olives of Picenum, first encountered in the list of Saturnalia presents at 4.46 and recurring in the overlapping list at 7.53, are praised at *Xenia* 36; cf. 11.52.

       You'll go . . . next to me?: the closing lines propose a seating (or rather reclining) plan for the couches at dinner, with two diners on each couch.

5.84   *pleading with the aedile*: the aedile enforces the law that forbids gambling except at Saturnalia: cf. *Apophoreta* 1.3.

       the first of March: the Matronalia, when women expect to receive gifts, but also Martial's own birthday.

BOOK 6

6.2   *even eunuchs committed adultery*: the theme is picked up again at 6.67.

6.3   *Come to birth, you earnest pledged to Dardan Iulus*: the tone and content of this poem echo Virgil, *Eclogue* 4, the famous 'Messianic Eclogue'. Iulus, son of Aeneas of Troy ('Dardan') and mythic progenitor of the Julian *gens*, is familiar from Virgil's epic of Roman origins, the *Aeneid*. 'Earnest': the Latin *nomen*, 'name', sometimes has the figurative sense of a debt, a sum offered as guarantee, or an entry in a ledger; the anticipated child is owed to the Imperial line by Fate.

      Julia herself will draw out golden threads for you: the deified niece of Domitian, but her name also reminds readers of the Julian Law against adultery, established by Augustus in 17 BC and revived by Domitian, and to which the surrounding poems (6.2, 6.4, and cf. 6.7 and 6.22) allude. Mentioning her also helps prop up the 'Julian' pedigree optimistically trailed in line 1 (the Flavians were of modest country stock, with no blood connection to the great patrician families). The three Fates or Parcae legendarily spun threads that measured out the lifespan of each mortal; here the dead Julia assumes their role, spinning a special thread for the expected Imperial heir from the Golden Fleece of legend.

6.5   *a really expensive one*: Martial's cash-flow crisis continues at 6.10 and 6.20.

6.7   *Telesilla*: the name derives from a famous female poet of Argos, but Martial's immediate source is probably Lucillius, *AP* 11.239; see note on 11.97.

6.10   *those submissive Dacians*: the Domitianic phase of the Dacian conflict concluded in a truce following Roman victory in the Battle of Tapae, AD 88.

      to the Capitol and back: Domitian is ascending the Capitoline on the Via Triumphalis as a *triumphator*, but of course the road also takes him to the temple of the Capitoline Triad, home of his particular confidante, Minerva (5.2, 8.1).

      when he says "No": Martial's phrasing makes Domitian echo the girls who ought to say 'No'—but not *keep* saying 'No'—to sex at 4.71 and 81.

6.11   *no Pylades, no Orestes*: Martial again presents the mythic Greek comrades as an ideal of mutuality in friendship at 7.24 and 10.11. Pylades was the childhood friend who, when Orestes returned from exile to avenge the murder of his father Agamemnon, shared in the deed and in his subsequent wanderings.

6.12   *is she lying?*: this epigram is closely modelled on Lucillius, *AP* 11.68. Several epigrams in this book (e.g. 6.19) denounce theft or disguise, but turn out on closer inspection to be the product of literary theft or disguise on Martial's part; his attentive reader must be meant to find deliberate irony in this. The name Martial has chosen for his target here, Fabulla, is very close to the Latin *fabula*, 'tale'.

6.16   *little patch*: a few *iugera*, says Martial. A *iuger* is a little over half an acre. The addressee is of course Priapus, the rustic god who guards orchards from thieves; Book 6 comes back to him several times.

6.17   *You tell us to call you 'Cinna', Cinnamus*: Cinnamus (the name is Greek and immediately suggests servile origin) is told off for shortening his name in an attempt to pass himself off as old money. 'Cinna' is a fine Roman name with a proud history. Cinnamus reappears at 6.64 (not in this selection) as a make-up artist, at 7.64 as a barber, and at 9.92 (not in this selection) as a loan-shark. A 'Cinna' featured as a would-be rival poet at 3.9, as a slave to his expensive possessions at 2.53, and as a haughty patron and miserly diner at 5.57 and 76 respectively.

      a barbarous way with words: Martial's 'barbarism', *barbarismus*, is a word imported (like Cinnamus himself) from the Greek world.

      you'd now be 'Fur': *fur* is Latin for 'thief'.

6.19   *my three little goats*: the direct model for this poem in the Postumus cycle is Lucillius, *AP* 11.141.

6.20   *a loan of a hundred thousand*: Martial is still after the money he wanted in 6.5.

6.32   *Otho*: briefly ruled during the 'year of the four emperors' following

Nero's downfall. The year ended with Vespasian as Rome's ruler and founder of a new dynasty, the Flavians (see Chronology).

6.32   *Cato*: his Stoic indifference to defeat, and heroic suicide, were major themes of Lucan's epic on the civil war; cf. 5.74 and see note on 7.23.

6.34   *Give me kisses, Diadumenus*: the Diadumenus cycle continues, this time riffing obviously on Catullus, *Carmen* 7.

the Cecropian mountain: Hymettus in Attica, famed for its honey (cf. 4.13).

6.53   *Dr Hermocrates*: as always in Martial, the doctor's name is Greek, and there may be a bit of a joke in it—'Power of Hermes', when one of Hermes' main roles is to convey the souls of the dead to the Underworld. Terrible doctors are a staple of Greek skoptic epigram; see note on 1.30. The most immediate model here is Lucillius, *AP* 11.257.

6.65   *an epigram out of hexameters*: this immediately follows 6.64, a long poem (thirty-two lines) uncharacteristically written in hexameters as a literary experiment; sequencing is important.

6.67   *eunuchs, Pannychis*: this poem picks up on the adultery/fertility theme in the book's opening sequence. Pannychis means 'All-nighter', and is clearly a working name. It is Greek, as naughty things so often were; Lucian's *Dialogues of Courtesans* (second century AD) has a hetaira called Pannychis.

6.68   *Eutychos . . . Castricus . . . inseparable friend*: the poet is otherwise unattested and perhaps only ever existed in this poem. The Greek name of his beloved marked the boy as a slave, and now carries bitter irony—it means 'Lucky'.

the Alexis of our bard: a name out of Virgil's *Eclogues*, which respond closely to Theocritean pastoral. Elsewhere (8.55 (56)), Martial affects to read the 'Corydon' of *Eclogue* 2 as Virgil himself in poetic disguise, and 'Alexis' as a pretty male slave of Maecenas with whom Virgil was infatuated.

send Hercules back his Hylas: Hercules' love for Hylas is a Hellenistic poetic theme; it features in Apollonius' *Argonautica* and is the subject of Theocritus' thirteenth *Idyll*, and Martial comes back to it at e.g. 7.50 and 11.43.

6.71   *Cadiz*: Gades, 'gay Cadiz' (1.61, and cf. 11.6), was a famous exporter of female slaves trained to dance provocatively to the accompaniment of seductive music. Compare Statius, *Silvae* 1.6.67–9 and especially Juvenal 11.162-4, skewering the prurience of a stereotypical Roman dinner-guest who expects to see such girls 'shaking their booty down to the floor' (*ad terram tremulo descendant clunae puellae*, 164); Martial too (5.78) suggests they were something of a cliché. Martial proposes such a girl as an extravagant Saturnalia gift at *Apophoreta* 203.

Hecuba's husband: Priam; imitating Lucillius, Martial repeatedly uses Hecuba as a byword for extreme old age (see note on 3.32).

his mistress: a *domina* is, in the word's most technical sense, the mistress of a household; but she is also the harsh 'mistress' who turns Roman erotic elegists (especially Tibullus) into slaves for love. Martial's word choices have already highlighted this connection for his attentive reader: the 'adept' girl (*docta puella*) is an elegiac staple, and 'tortures' (*excruciat*) recalls Catullus' famous *Carmen* 85, 'I love and I hate, and I am in torment' (*Odi et amo . . . et excrucior*).

6.72 *Cilix*: 'the Cilician', a likely slave-name that points to an origin in what is now southern Turkey, an area formerly notorious for piracy (put down by Pompey in 67 BC).

a marble Priapus: the scenario of this epigram is straight out of Lucilius (*AP* 11.174–9, cf. 11.184) but with a Roman twist in the identity of the god whose statue is being stolen, delivering bathetic closure on the book's Priapus/orchards cycle that began at 6.16. At 8.40 Martial will threaten to burn his Priapus for failing in its duties.

6.76 *the barracks*: the *Castra* were the barracks of the Praetorian Guard and a significant landmark; modern Rome still calls a metro station after them.

The Dacian is tamed: Commodus' Dacian wars were a running theme in Book 5; this poem, an imaginary epitaph on a far-away grave, supplies a quiet coda.

6.82 *such rotten coats*: the *lacerna* was a military-style cloak worn over the toga in foul weather; to wear one at all was a bit of an embarrassment. Cf. 6.11, 'in an itchy blanket' (Latin *sagatus*), where likewise Martial complains of having to wear a type of rough wool cloak (the *sagum*) typical of soldiers and barbarians.

6.85 *but you are not here to see it*: Rufus is dead—or *a* Rufus is, since it's business as usual with Martial's 'Rufus' (cf. 6.82) four poems later at 6.89. The tone of the poem recalls Catullus, *Carmen* 101.

Alpheus' prizes: he had seen out five Olympiads; SB notes that in Martial these typically indicate a five-year span rather than four.

BOOK 7

7.5 *citizens of Rome*: literally 'the Latin toga'. The *toga* is the emblem of and a synonym for civilian life, as at 6.76.

7.6 *Ausonian*: a poetic equivalent for 'Italian', familiar from Virgil's *Aeneid*; cf. e.g. *Apophoreta* 53. A Virgilian mood is also evoked by summoning Rumour, *Fama* (cf. *Aeneid* 4.173–97).

7.8 *Janus*: patron god of the month of January.

laurel-decked cavalry: Martial's language in this poem, and in the opening sequence of which it is a part, is celebratory (an emphasis on play: *ludo*, *lusus*) but also solemnizes Domitian's Sarmatian victories with a gloss of religiosity. The 'laurel-decked' cavalry recall the spears 'twined with laurel' of 7.6—the Latin word, *laurigerus*, is the same.

7.13   *the air of high Tivoli*: this poem is a variant on 4.62.

7.17   *all round the world*: as at 5.74, this samples Martial 1.1; now his name-sake's library will share his fame, by virtue of Martial's dedicatory poem.

7.23   *the second plectrum . . . who thundered forth Wars*: this poem ends a three-poem sequence (7.21–3) that, like Statius, *Silvae* 2.7, posthumously celebrates the birthday of the poet Lucan, a fellow countryman of Martial (cf. 5.74). Galán Vioque (2002: 168) suggests they were written at the request of his widow, Argentaria Polla. Lucan was 'second' to Virgil in date and importance, and 'Wars' is the first word of his epic, *Pharsalia* or *Bellum Civile*. Identifying a poem by its first few words (its *incipit*) was commonplace, and Martial boils the practice down further. Compare 1.22, where Virgil's *Aeneid* is identified by its very first word 'Arms', *arma*, instead of the usual *arma uirumque cano*.

    so great a light: Martial's phrasing supports more than one reading at once. Phoebus Apollo is the god of the sun whose rise inaugurates Lucan's birthday, but a brilliant person can be a 'light' too, and Lucan was brilliant.

7.24   *my dear Juvenal*: one of several poems addressing in friendly terms the younger contemporary who was later to become Rome's most famous satirist; another comes shortly afterward, at 7.31, and cf. 7.91.

    the Sicilian brothers . . . and Leda's brood: Amphinomus and Anapius were 'models of fraternal love and filial piety' (SB); the Atreides (ordinarily not names to conjure with) are Agamemnon and Menelaus; Leda's sons are the Dioscuri, Castor and Pollux.

    may you do that thing: the final line hints accusingly at *os impurum* (see note on 2.12).

7.27   *many holm-oaks . . . the Beast of Aetolia*: compare *Apophoreta* 70 (not in this selection), a pig fat on holm-oak acorns. Acorns were a foraged food of the rural poor. The 'Beast of Aetolia' is the Calydonian boar (cf. e.g. 1.104); this is its second appearance in book 7 (7.2, not in this selection).

    Pepper . . . Falernian . . . fish sauce: pepper came all the way from India; it was a bankable commodity (Dalby 2000: 195), is ubiquitous in the recipes of Apicius, and reappears as a regrettably expensive cooking-spice at *Apophoreta* 13. Falernian was a strong Campanian wine, highly rated by connoisseurs and 'ubiquitous in Roman poetry . . . the single word that proves it was a good wine and a good party' (Dalby 2000: 49); Galán Vioque (2002: 200–1) has a thorough note, and compare 12.57 and *Xenia* 108 and 111. At 8.55 (56) Martial imagines Maecenas impressing Virgil by serving Falernian. *Garum* is the fish sauce without which no Roman kitchen could operate, like *nam pla* in Thai cooking (and this Thai fish sauce is reckoned a fair substitute for garum by re-creators of Roman recipes). It came in several different grades: see notes on *Xenia* 102–3.

7.31 *Chian figs . . . blanched by icy frosts*: small, tender Chian figs were prized ('Chian' identifies the variety rather than where a particular fig happened to be grown; Chians recur in a sexual *double entendre* at 12.96). But these ones are not properly ripened, the olives should have been harvested earlier in the autumn to be at their best, and greens (*holus*) in satire are proverbially cheap fodder, even when they are not late-season: Martial cannot afford to eat well (Galán Vioque 2002: 221).

My little patch: presumably Martial's reader is meant to read this pitiful estate as the one the poet overextended himself to purchase in 6.5.

the broad Subura: Martial 'harvests' his 'crops' in the busy commercial and residential district next to the Fora. It had good shopping and other services, including a lot of prostitution. Martial's route to visit a patron at 5.22 takes it in; cf. 9.37 (on which Henriksén 2012: 164–5 has a useful note), 10.20 (19), and 11.78. At 12.18 Martial, from his quiet retirement in Spain, imagines Juvenal (who was perhaps just then beginning his famous *Satires*, see Chronology) still slogging through 'the yelling Subura' on his way to pay his respects to a patron.

7.36 *rainy Jupiter*: in his aspect of rain-god, Pluvius, as for instance at Tibullus 1.7.26.

clothe . . . its farmer: to dress a person or to cover an object is the same word in Latin, *tego* (and roof-tiles are 'little covers', *tegula*).

7.50 *Ianthis*: a Greek name. Ianthis is a minor recurring character (6.21), married to Stella the poet.

so many Hylases: Hercules and Hylas recur from 6.68.

7.53 *all the presents*: this list of cheap presents closely echoes the list at 4.46 (see note).

Picene olives . . . Laletanian grape syrup: Picenum, now Ancona, was known for its fruit and olive oil; see note on 5.78, and cf. 11.52, *Xenia* 36. Laletania in Hispania Tarraconensis (also found as e.g. *Laiet-*) was known for cheap wine in bulk: Martial at 1.26 (not in this selection) refers contemptuously to *faex Laletana*, 'Latetanian dregs'.

7.61 *Flagons . . . razor . . . smoke-blackened cantina*: verbal echoes tie this poem to 7.53: the flagon (*lago*), and the black colour (*niger*) of the smoky cantina. (A *popina* was an inexpensive neighbourhood bar or trattoria: on *popinae, cauponae,* and the like see Grant 1999: 84–92.) There are connections forward as well as back: the dangerous barber anticipates Cinnamus/Cinna in 7.64 (cf. the barkeeps that make a pair of 3.58 and 59).

7.64 *the Forum's stern laws*: Martial leaves the details vague, but Cinnamus is by now a familiar figure and readers will be unsurprised that he has got into trouble.

in Sicilian theatres: this implies that one *can* make money by hiring out as a flatterer in *Roman* theatres, as at 4.5.

7.67   *Butch Philaenis*: this sexually dominant lesbian (*tribas*) is revisited at 7.70. Her name speaks volumes: Philaenis of Samos was the supposed female author of an ancient sex manual of which, alas, only a small and uninformative fragment survives. It can be no coincidence that one of Martial's very few mentions of the famous Lesbian poet Sappho, notionally respectful enough (7.69), is sandwiched between Book 7's two Philaenis poems. The name is re-purposed for a loving and sexually obliging wife at 9.40.

   a good six pints: as often, Martial's sums take some puzzling out. Philaenis drinks seven *deunces*. A *deunx* is eleven *cyathi*; a *cyathus* is one-twelfth of a *sextarius*; a *sextarius* is 546 ml. By Martial's reckoning, Philaenis therefore drinks and sicks up 3.5035 litres of unmixed wine; just over six pints, or three-quarters of a gallon. Taking wine neat was the sign of a problem drinker (cf. 6.89, not in this selection), and cheap wine was nasty that way (3.57).

   sixteen rib-eyes: the exact cut is guesswork; the Latin is *coloephium*, a Greek-derived term (κωλύφιον). It was especially associated with the red-meat diet of athletes in training, so is likely to have been a cut of beef. At 11.52 Martial ironically promises a friend *coloephia* if he comes to dinner, while making it clear he cannot actually afford to buy them in. Juvenal's use of the term at 2.53 may well come out of Martial.

7.68   *Curius and Fabricius*: Manius Curius Dentatus, tribune of the plebs some time in the 290s BC and consul in 290, was a frugal and incorruptible hero of wars against Pyrrhus of Epirus and various Italian tribes; when the Samnites sent envoys with lavish gifts they famously found him roasting turnips. Gaius Fabricius Luscinus was similarly legendary for his austerity and integrity. Cicero often name-checks them as paired *exempla* of old-fashioned virtues. Martial revisits the cliché at 11.16.

7.69   *Cecropian*: a synonym for 'Attic' or 'Athenian' much favoured by Martial; see note on 1.25.

   Your own Pantaenis: a Greek-flavoured female name, otherwise unattested.

   woman-lover: Latin *amatrix*, a strikingly rare word.

7.84   *Getic Peucē*: 'Getic' is used poetically as a synonym for Thracian; it properly refers to an area on the Danube, bordering on Dacia. Domitian campaigned there as well as in Sarmatia; see e.g. 7.2. Peucē is an island in the delta of the Danube; the river's Latin name is *Hister*.

   a more faithful likeness will be found in my verse: the conceit is Ovidian; cf. *Tristia* 1.7.11–14.

   the work of Apelles: this Greek painter was a byword for great art in Roman connoisseurship.

7.90   *Creticus*: perhaps a speaking name, cueing up the epigram's reflection on poetics: cretics were a category of metre.

BOOK 8

PREFACE

GERMANICUS: Domitian had awarded himself this title in AD 83, when Martial was just starting out as an author, after victories against the Chatti, a Germanic tribe described by Tacitus (*Germania* 30). Martial's frequent use of this title in Book 8 (8.4, 26, 39, 53 (55), 65, and cf. 9.1) emphasizes his emperor's record of success as a military leader (Latin *dux*—8.4.2, 56 (54).2) as he celebrates his new triumph over the Dacians.

8.1   *Caesarian Pallas*: Pallas Minerva, Domitian's favourite deity (5.2, 6.10); the cult name is reused later in the book, at 8.50 (51). The adjective 'Caesarian' is surprisingly rare in Latin authors.

8.4   *in its Leader's name*: SB dates the occasion to 3 January, when vows for the emperor were taken and discharged (Suetonius, *Nero* 46.2).

8.29   *when they're a book*: the physical form of the papyrus roll meant that ancient books tended to be pretty uniform in length. Martial's term here, *liber*, tends to apply either to other authors' works or to his own when viewed as material objects.

8.30   *utmost glory*: Gaius Mucius (early sixth century BC) is one of the historical *exempla*, of no clear relevance to his legal case, about which Martial complains at 6.19. Apprehended while trying to assassinate Lars Porsena, king of Clusium, Mucius thrust his hand into a sacrificial fire to prove the indifference of Romans to pain; Porsena sued for peace. Mucius gained the *cognomen* 'Scaevola' (Southpaw) for his deed. The re-enactment of the Mucius story as a not-quite-fatal charade in the arena (see note on *Liber Spectaculorum* 6) is ironically revisited at 10.25.

8.31   *the perks of fatherhood*: Martial gloated at having secured the *ius trium liberorum* for himself at 4.27.

     wheedling petitions: the Latin for petition (cf. 11.1) is *libellus*, which is of course also Martial's own word for his own books of epigrams, when considered as texts rather than material objects. Martial's *libelli* won Domitian's favour; Dento's have not. Dento's name may be intended to shade his characterization: *dens* ('tooth') was used figuratively of jealous resentment (see note on 10.3).

8.36   *the Pyramids*: see note on *Liber Spectaculorum* 1.

     the works of Dawn: Memphis had many temples and statues, well known to Greek and Roman authors, but this vague reference also suggests the singing Colossus of Memnon, son of the Dawn, at Egyptian Thebes.

     the Parrhasian palace . . . the labour of Mareotis: 'Parrhasian' is a poetic equivalent for Arcadian; the Palatine is Arcadian because Evander came from Arcadia to settle there (Virgil, *Aeneid* 8.51–5). The recondite synonym emphasizes the hill's very ancient mythic associations. The brackish

Lake Mareotis abuts Alexandria, the site of another ancient wonder, the Pharos.

8.36   *Ossa bore Thessalian Pelion*: two mountains in Thessaly; in myth, the giants piled Pelion on Ossa in an attempt to storm Olympus.

8.50 (51)   *or yours, Polyclitus?*: the epigram begins with a display of connoisseurship, name-checking famous Greek artists.

stippled silver: very pure silverware was called 'stippled' (*pustulatus*), 'because of the ridges which appear on the surface during the process of purification' (Galán Vioque 2002: 462 on 7.86.7, citing Suetonius, *Nero* 44.2).

Theban Phrixus: Phrixus and Helle escaped their stepmother Ino on a golden-fleeced ram that took them across the Dardanelles (Aeolia is roughly speaking north-western Asia Minor); Helle fell off and drowned (hence Hellespont), but Phrixus was taken in by Aietes of Colchis. The ram's Golden Fleece was the object of Jason's quest. The conceit or paradox here is that the cup is pseudo-electrum, so *any* goat it shows is going to have a 'golden fleece' and can thus be subsumed into, or serve as a pretext for, mythic footling.

Cinyphian shearer: Cinyphus was a vaguely defined African location known for its long-haired goats; cf. Virgil, *Georgics* 3.311. Dalby (2000: 110) has a note on the uses to which their harvested hair was put.

Pallas' lotus: a flute, because lotus-wood was used to make flutes; cf. Ovid, *Fasti* 4.190.

Methymnaean Arion: the legendary musician Arion was from Methymna, a prosperous city of Lesbos.

lend their number to the refills: the name of the giver, Istantius Rufus, is inscribed on the cup in the genitive case to indicate his ownership: *ISTANTI RUFI*—seven letters and four letters respectively.

8.53 (55)   *Punic kraal*: Martial's term is *mapalia*, a Punic loan-word used to refer to African huts or temporary, portable dwellings; he reuses it at 10.13 (20).

from Hercules' star: the Nemean Lion, slain as Hercules' first labour, became the constellation Leo. Hercules is presented as Domitian's brother because they share a father, Jupiter. Domitian is again 'Germanicus' the conquering hero, as at 5.2.

8.55 (56)   *a sorrowful Tityrus*: Tityrus' expulsion from his smallholding, 'too close to poor Cremona', is straight out of Virgil, *Eclogue* 1; Maecenas here assumes the role of that poem's unnamed 'god', who is usually interpreted as the young Octavian. On Tityrus-as-Virgil, see note on 6.68.

'Arms and the man' . . . the Gnat: referring to a poem by quoting its opening or 'incipit' (here, the first three words of Virgil's instantly recognizable *Aeneid*) was common practice in epigram: see note on 7.23.

The *Gnat* is a parodic mini-epic of unknown authorship, proposed as light reading at *Apophoreta* 185; ancient readers reckoned it among Virgil's juvenilia.

I'll be a Marsus: Domitius Marsus, a friend of Virgil and Tibullus, wrote a book of epigrams, the *Cicuta* ('Hemlock'), elegies, and other works; from the prose preface to Book 1 onwards, Martial cites him from time to time as an important predecessor. A handful of fragments survive, all in elegiac couplets.

8.61   *knobs and cedar-oil*: Martial identifies himself with the physical form of his books, in luxury copies.

may he have . . . a place just outside town: 'with all their worries' (SB) and associated expenditure, or just because Martial's mules and suburban villa are really bad ones?

8.63   *Aulus . . . hot for Alexis*: Thestylus is the toy-boy of the poet Voconius Victor at 7.29 (not in this selection); 'Alexis too must be (or at least be thought of as) a living boy, not Virgil's favourite' (SB), but Virgil's Alexis is fresh in the reader's mind from 8.55 (56). In that poem, too, Alexis' female rival for Virgil's attention wore the feminine form of Thestylus' name—*Thestylis*. Their identities blur intriguingly.

8.65   *a sacred Arch*: sacred because it is dedicated to a divinity, viz, Domitian himself.

8.70   *Gentle Nerva*: the future emperor, although of course Martial has no way of knowing that.

Permessis . . . Pierian brow: the Permessis was a river sacred to Apollo and the Muses; like the Pierian Spring near Mt Olympus, and the Castalian Spring (4.14), its waters inspired poets. The Muses are sometimes called *Pierides*, daughter of Pieria.

8.73   *Cynthia . . . from Lesbia*: this poem name-checks the immortalized beloveds of Rome's greatest love-poets as justification for why Martial should be given one too; see note on 4.62. Catullus is 'bookish' or learned (*doctus*), but so three poems earlier (8.70) was Nero.

Neither Paelignians nor Mantua: see note on 1.61.

8.80   *the Hut . . . so revered a Jupiter*: Domitian is a god on earth; cf. for instance 9.18. The 'Hut' is the Hut of Romulus, a frequently restored ancient monument on the Palatine.

BOOK 9

PREFACE

a portrait of me: like the library-bound portrait of 7.84, painted on board for Caecilius Secundus.

this brief poem: the preface takes the form of a poem, within a poem, within a letter, and proposed as a caption (*titulus*) to be inscribed below a painting.

9.1   *Domitian, autumns*: under Domitian, September and October became 'Germanicus' and 'Domitianus', after the pattern of 'July' (Julius Caesar) and 'August' (Augustus). They reverted to their traditional names (which we still use) after his assassination.

the towering splendour of the Flavian race: Domitian erected a temple to the cult of the dynasty that ended with him.

9.4   *Aeschylus*: the name is comically inappropriate—Aeschylus the father of tragedy was near-proverbial for his moral impeccability. Like Galla, Martial in 9.4 keeps his mouth shut about the exact nature of Aeschylus' sexual transgression, but 9.67 will make everything clear.

9.8 (9)   *Bithynicus . . . he's left you six thousand a year*: Fabius (a noble name) has maintained a high-spending lifestyle all this time by acting as though he is rich; greedy legacy-hunters have unknowingly been bankrolling the whole charade. Bithynicus is implied to be another of Martial's ambitious social climbers; as so often, his name ('the Bithynian') sketches in a servile origin in the Greek East.

9.11   *the Phoenix's nest*: actually not nearly so plainly spelled out. Martial's actual words ('the proud bird', *alitis superbae*) pick up an identical wording placed at the same line-position in 6.55 (not in this selection). In that poem the astute reader knows the bird is the phoenix only because of the first line's 'cassia and cinnamon', which Pliny (*Natural History* 12.85) tells us are found in the nest of the phoenix. This is, then, an extremely recondite reference, firstly intratextual (to 6.55) and then to the Avid Fan's extensive further reading.

Cybele's boy . . . and he: the two jealous boys upstaged by Earinus are Attis and Ganymede.

verse that doesn't grate: Martial is unable to fit the name of Domitian's favourite into the metres of Latin poetry, though Greeks (who allow themselves greater liberties in scansion) have no trouble. Henriksén (2012: 53–6) discusses Book 9's Earinus 'cycle'.

9.15   HER COMMISSION: this poem turns on a word-play on the standard inscriptional formula that records who erected a tomb: [name] *FECIT*. The Latin verb, *facio*, means 'make'—but also 'do', including 'commit a crime'.

9.17   *Latona's revered grandson*: this poem opens like a hymn; Henriksén (2012: 78–9) identifies useful parallels in Horace. The addressee is Aesculapius, invoked (as so often hymns do invoke their deities) by ancestry, powers, and deeds rather than name.

His vows are now fulfilled: Earinus has entered manhood. The entirety of Statius, *Silvae* 3.4 is dedicated to the occasion of the consecration of Earinus' boyish long hair to Aesculapius.

a shining disc: a mirror, made of polished metal.

9.18   *the gush of the Marcia*: the Aqua Marcia came into Rome along the Via Tiburtina; as the Acqua Felice, much of it is still in use today.

9.21 *They both have furrows to plough*: the transmitted text begins *Artemidorus amat* ('Artemidorus loves'). At some point in the history of transmission, a copyist failed to get the joke and erroneously emended it. See Adams (1982: 154). Much the same agricultural euphemism recurs at 12.16.

9.32 *a coat*: the Greek *pallium*, the cloak that characterized philosophers (as at 11.16), was also the conventional dress of courtesans, a custom that carried over into Roman culture.

9.37 *your imported silks*: *Serica*, notes Henriksén (2012: 165–6), is real silk, imported from China—extremely expensive.

no reverence: the implicit judgement is that old women should not depilate their genitalia, because a sexualized identity is not age-appropriate (see note on 3.32).

a fortune: literally 600,000, but Henriksén (2012: 167) points to parallels where Martial is clearly using the same number more or less figuratively. The implied scenario is that Galla is hinting she will make Martial her heir if he sleeps with her.

9.40 *from Pharos*: the famous lighthouse immediately sets the scene as Alexandria, a great seaport and also famous for sexual opportunities (Dalby 2000: 125–6).

Tarpeian wreaths: prizes in Domitian's Capitoline Games, also called Tarpeian Games; the Tarpeian Rock is on the Capitoline.

Philaenis: a name that promises satisfaction: see note on 7.67. Her vow for the safe return home of a loved one smuttily undermines the patriotic topos of 9.31.

9.41 *it's a crime*: Henriksén (2012: 176–7) comments thoughtfully on how this epigram fails to square with what Martial says elsewhere about masturbation, and draws out the comic incongruity in its *faux*-philosophical features—the mini-priamel, the quasi-Stoic appeal to Nature.

If either of them had wanked: again, Henriksén (2012: 180) usefully notes that *masturbor* is a peculiarly Martialic verb, perhaps a choice by him to resurrect an obsolescent term; Adams's discussion (1982: 209–10) rests on examples from Martial.

9.43 *This figure*: Statius 4.6 expands on this same little statue; Newlands (2010: 73–87) has an excellent discussion.

His is no recent fame, no glory of our sky: a line lifted almost verbatim from *Apophoreta* 93 (not in this selection).

9.61 *where fleeces glow pale gold*: on the golden fleeces of Baetica in Spain, see also 5.37.

Caesar's, with thick foliage: the word for foliage is the same as that for hair, so there may be a tiny joke here on the male-pattern baldness that Caesar did his best to disguise with a comb-over.

reach for the high heavens: because Caesar is up there, a god.

9.61   *not Pompey's hands that planted you*: Lucan in Book 1 of his epic on the
        civil war describes Pompey using the elaborate simile of an old oak that
        has no strength left in its roots and must soon fall.

9.66   '*right of three children*': the *ius trium liberorum* for which Martial had him-
        self successfully petitioned; cf. 2.91–2, 4.27.

9.67   *But to me . . . stiffed on the deal*: the closing couplet was first explained
        (albeit in the decent obscurity of Latin) in an article of 1907 by the
        scholar and poet A. E. Housman, reprinted at Diggle and Goodyear
        (eds.) 1972: 711–39. 'Purity' in Martial often implicitly hinges on avoid-
        ing *os impurum*—see note on 1.34. Martial has asked the girl to perform
        oral sex on him; she has said she will, if he returns the favour; he balks at
        this, and the exchange does not go ahead. Aeschylus, on the other hand,
        is welcome to go ahead and make the trade: he is morally so far gone that
        not only does he not mind going down on a woman, he likes it (at 9.4, so
        much that he'll pay extra).

9.68   *The Lawyer*: cf. Juvenal 7.125, on a lawyer who celebrates his successes
        by putting up a bronze equestrian statue of himself in the atrium of his
        house.

9.70   *Catiline*: the reference is to the famous Catilinarian conspiracy, put
        down by Cicero in 63 BC. The famous phrase *o tempora! o mores!* is from
        Cicero's second speech to the Senate denouncing Catiline and calling
        for his execution.

9.76   *the Three*: the three Fates, as at 6.3 and 10.53 (see note).

BOOK 10

10.2   *Crispus' halved horses*: presumably carved in high relief on a monument.

10.3   *snark*: literally 'tooth' (*dens*), used figuratively of the gnawing of envy or
        resentment. Compare the jealous detractor of Martial biting his nails
        at 4.27.

        a dealer in broken novelty drinking-cups: Vatinius the shoemaker appears
        as a maker of four-nozzled drinking-cups at *Apophoreta* 96.

10.4   *Snatched Hylas . . . what use to you are they?*: the aridity of myth as liter-
        ary inspiration is a commonplace of Roman satire. There is some irony
        in Martial disdaining poetry about Hylas when he himself uses the story
        frequently; see note on 6.68.

        the lusting waters: the nymph Salmacis turned the handsome boy
        Hermaphroditus into the original hermaphrodite, a myth alluded to
        again at *Apophoreta* 174.

        Callimachus' Aetia: Callimachus (third century BC) was head librarian
        of the Library of Alexandria, and the *Aetia* epitomizes the self-con-
        sciously 'academic' nature of his poetry. This miniature epic was packed
        with recondite retellings of local myths associated with the foundation

of Greek cities and cults. Martial invokes it as a byword for poetry that has nothing to do with real life.

10.5   *bridge and slope*: SB notes that steep streets are where homeless beggars hang out in Martial; even today, Rome's homeless camp under Tiber bridges to get out of the weather.

poor bread fed to dogs: dogs were fed on a bread made from spelt (Juvenal 5.11).

a walled-up archway: the arches of Rome's ancient aqueducts were notorious for squalid transactions (their Latin name, *fornix*, gives us 'fornication') and have served as shanty housing in modern times as well.

a simple death: far preferable to one drawn out by torture (Livy 40.24.8). SB identifies the 'old gabbler' as Tantalus. Martial is wishing on his target all the legendary torments of the Underworld's worst sinners.

'I wrote them!': at issue are the pseudo-Martial epigrams of 10.3, and returned to at 10.33.

10.6   *the tattooed Moors*: most of Rome's cavalry after the Punic Wars until the third century AD at least were Moors (*Mauri*) from the provinces of Mauretania and Africa Proconsularis; they were unarmoured missile troops equipped with javelins and small leather shields. The cavalry shown on Trajan's Column are Moors.

10.11   *Theseus and Pirithous . . . Pylades*: Martial repeatedly invokes Orestes and Pylades as exemplars of heroic comrades who share everything, in good times and bad; see note on 6.11. Here they are joined by a second legendary pairing. Theseus and Pirithous swore undying friendship and undertook many adventures together, including participating in the hunt for the Calydonian boar, an Ovidian episode to which Martial frequently alludes (e.g. 1.104).

10.20 (19) *eloquent Pliny*: this is Pliny the Younger, who quotes the poem in a letter to his friend Cornelius Priscus after Martial's death (Introduction, p. vii).

the Phrygian boy: Ganymede, snatched up by an eagle and carried off to serve Jupiter's pleasures. Here he is part of the sculptural scheme of an elaborate, stepped water-feature to which Martial's poem is the only witness.

your friend Pedo: Albinovanus Pedo is a 'friend' to Martial's Muse because he is one of Martial's important predecessors in Latin epigram, at least according to Martial (see prose preface to Book 1). The clear sense of this poem is that Pliny's house on the Esquiline (its location is mentioned in one of Pliny's own letters) was once Pedo's.

the Hundred Men: the Centumviral Court, which met in the Basilica Julia and heard private cases.

Arpine pages: works by Cicero, Arpinum's most famous son.

10.23 *fifteen completed Olympiads*: an Olympiad is five years in Martial's reckoning, making Primus seventy-five years old.

10.25 *the proles of Abdera*: a Thracian polis on the mainland close to Thasos; trade made it rich; the Athenians said there was something in the air there that made its inhabitants stupid, although it did claim some famous intellectuals. Cicero, *Letters to Atticus* 4.17.3, 7.7.4, is our source. Martial's gloss on this not-quite-fatal charade is thus strikingly different than at 1.21 and 8.30.

the Shirt of Woe: the 'troublesome tunic' (*tunica molesta*), a coat soaked in pitch in which criminals were burned alive.

10.26 *Quirinus*: a synonym for Romulus, here standing in for the city he founded.

10.31 *a three-pound mullet*: the fish weighs four pounds in Martial's Latin, but the Roman pound only weighed three-quarters of our own.

10.33 *dipped in green verdigris*: verdigris (*aerugo*) was used figuratively for envy or jealous ill-will because, like rust, envy seeks to consume and ruin what it sees.

10.35 *Sulpicia*: the known Sulpicia of Latin poetry ('Sulpicia I' in the reference works) was, if real, a contemporary of Tibullus; a 'Sulpicia II' is adduced on the basis of 10.35 and of some decidedly thin late testimonia that 10.35 may have inspired. See note on 'Cinna' at 3.9.

Colchian's frenzy . . . Scylla and Byblis: myths of terrible acts provoked by sexual immorality. Medea of Colchis murdered and cut up her own brother to slow the pursuit as she eloped with Jason; Thyestes committed adultery with the wife of his brother Atreus, who took revenge by serving up Thyestes' own children to their unknowing father. Martial probably looks to Ovid as his main source for horrific mythological tales: Scylla was turned into a hideous sea-monster by a jealous love-rival (*Metamorphoses* 13–14); Byblis passionately pursued her own brother, Caunus (*Metamorphoses* 9.446–55).

Egeria . . . in Numa's dripping cave: these legendary figures establish a fairly obvious intertext with Juvenal, *Satire* 3. Numa was an early king of Rome; the nymph Egeria his supernatural mentor. A modern Italian mineral water is named after her.

her dear Calenus: his name means 'Hottie', and he reappears along with Sulpicia a few lines later at 10.38.

10.38 *Niceros' perfumes*: Niceros is named as a perfumer again at 12.65 (not in this selection). His Greek name ('Winsexy') vouches for the power of his merchandise; cf. note on 10.43, 'Phileros'.

10.43 *Phileros*: this Greek name ('Lovesexy') is too good to be true; and note his similarity to Niceros at 10.38, a few poems earlier.

10.53 *Jealous Lachesis*: one of the three Fates in Greek mythology. Clotho spins the thread of our lives; Lachesis measures it out; Atropos cuts it.

10.61 *Here rests Erotion*: Erotion's death was the subject of 5.34 and 37.

10.63 *Roman Tarentos*: see 4.1. All this solemnity makes the twist in the final line all the more delicious.

10.68 *ah m'sieu!. . . mon âme!*: the use of French mimics Laelia's predilection for lover's endearments in Greek. A straightforward translation into English ('My lord! My sweet! My soul!') would not convey either the change in sound or the connotation, inherent in the language-shift, that Laelia is putting on airs and endangering her reputation. Greek culture was still suspect, at least within the socially conservative world-view espoused by Roman satire.

twerking: the Latin, *criso*, means to make sexually suggestive motions with the hips, often in a squatting position. It is used only of women. Adams (1982: 137) has a useful discussion.

Lais: the fabled courtesan of fifth-century Corinth, and a byword for her trade; cf. 11.104.

10.76 *no knight off the Cappadocian runways*: a *catasta* was a scaffold or stage on which slaves were paraded for sale. As often, Martial is denigrating foreign-born freedmen who have risen through trade: equestrian status had a minimum wealth requirement.

Incitatus: the muleteer shares his name with the favourite horse that Caligula supposedly intended to make a Consul.

BOOK 11

11.1 *you book*: Martial's book is here addressed in its physical form as a book-roll (*liber*). This choice allows *libellus* to carry its alternate sense of 'petition'; see note on 8.31.

Pompey . . . the first ship: Martial alludes to the Porticos of Pompey, Europa (see note on 3.20), and the Argonauts (the *Argo* was the first ship, cf. *Xenia* 72); but prefers the portico of the temple of Quirinus, near his house.

Scorpus and Incitatus: Martial's readers were introduced to Scorpus at 10.53; Incitatus, or *an* Incitatus, at 10.76.

11.2 *Fabricia the ploughman's daughter*: her father was Fabricius, a famously austere and incorruptible hero of the old Republic (see note on 7.68 and cf. 11.5, 11.16).

Nerva: flagged up as a poet of real talent at 8.70, and now emperor. Rimell (2008: 167–8) has interesting things to say about Ovidian revisionism in this and the following poem, 11.3.

Santra: otherwise unknown as a poet, and a good example of a name recycled in multiple situations. His awfulness is dissected at length in 7.20, but there he is a greedy dinner-thief; elsewhere (6.39) he is a black cook. A real-life Santra is attested, but he was a grammarian in the Late Republic who published on the history of Latin literature.

11.3   *My recondite Muse*: the allusion (*Pimpleide*) is certainly recondite. Pimpla in Pieria (modern Litokhoro) had a spring sacred to the Muses. See note on 8.70.

11.5   *as was Numa's*: the proverbially rich Croesus aside, the poem's allusions are to exemplary figures from Rome's past. The overall point is that Domitian is a paragon of fair and enlightened autocracy whose virtues as a ruler even the staunchest of Republicans would admire. Numa (cf. 10.35, 11.104) was a famously just early king of Rome; Camillus, the early Republican general who saved Rome from the Gauls, was repeatedly made Dictator but was always quick to renounce dictatorial powers when the crisis had passed. Fabricius (cf. 11.2) was proverbially incorruptible and indifferent to wealth (see note on 7.68); Brutus led the conspirators who assassinated Julius Caesar because they feared he would declare himself king. The next set of examples left more ambiguous legacies. Sulla was the utterly ruthless general who during the republican-era civil wars twice marched armies into Rome, setting a shocking precedent, but who then (81 BC) surprised everyone by voluntarily resigning his Dictatorship and restoring constitutional rule. The great general Pompey, young upstart Julius Caesar, and the famously wealthy Crassus formed the First Triumvirate in 60 BC; it ended in further civil war, from which Caesar emerged victorious. Cato took Pompey's and the Senate's side and, though he lost the war, scored a lasting moral victory for Stoic virtue and Senatorial *libertas*.

11.6   *the sickle-bearing ancient*: Saturn. In Martial, a sickle usually identifies Priapus, guardian of orchards.

       mix them, Dindymus: Dindymon or Dindymus was a mountain in Phrygia sacred to Cybele, so the reader is probably meant to think of the poem's Dindymus as a eunuch (the distinguishing feature of Cybele's male priesthood).

       I'll slip you Catullus' Sparrow: Martial's (deliberate mis-)reading of Catullus' sparrow as a *double entendre* for 'penis' has become notorious.

11.13 *every Venus and every Cupid*: a deliberately very close echo of Catullus, *Carmen* 3, all about Lesbia's dead . . . sparrow (11.6).

11.16 *Curius and Fabricius*: see note on 7.68. Curius reappears as an exemplar of starchy virtue at 11.104.

       Dullsville: Patavia (modern Padua) was proverbial for its stuffy morals. 'Your philosophic cloak': the *pallium*, associated especially with philosophers.

       Brutus: this is not Brutus the assassin of Caesar, but his famous ancestor, who avenged Lucretia's rape by leading the revolt that overthrew Rome's Etruscan kings and ushered in the Republic. Lucretia's heroic suicide enshrined her as an object-lesson in female virtue.

11.18 *Cosmus' leaf*: see note on 3.82.

a snail-shell: used as a small measure in cooking, the equivalent of a modern teaspoonful.

Ranch . . . lunch: in Martial's play on words, only a single letter distinguishes *praedium* from *prandium*; the effect is hard to replicate.

11.20 *plain Latin speech*: *Latine loqui* (cf. prose preface to Book 1) is to speak bluntly and to the point. The quoted poem may well be genuine.

11.43 *The Hero of Tiryns*: Hercules; his wife was Megara. In myth, Tiryns in the Argolid was ruled by Eurystheus, the scheming king who assigned the hero his famous twelve labours to cleanse him of the blood-guilt that arose from slaughtering Megara and their children in a fit of madness.

the Oebalian boy: the reference is unhelpfully vague. Oebalus was a king of Sparta (father of Tyndarus and grandfather of Helen), and 'Oebalian' is used of Helen at Ovid, *Heroides* 16.126; it is frequent in Ovid and Silver Latin as a general synonym for 'Spartan'. But the boy is clearly Hyacinthus, as at Ovid, *Metamorphoses* 13.396.

Aeacus' son: Achilles; rather against the testimony of the *Iliad*, Patroclus is here presented as his youthful beloved.

11.48 *Silius*: the poet Silius Italicus (cf. 4.14). His assiduous care for Virgil's tomb is also attested in a letter of Pliny the Younger.

heir: in more of a figurative than literal sense: Silius is 'heir' to Cicero's genius as an orator and Virgil's as an epic poet. Compare 12.43 (see note).

11.52 *the eighth hour*: cf. 4.8 and Juvenal 1.49. The Roman day was divided into twelve hours of light, and night into twelve of darkness; the length of the hour thus depended on the time of year, but the eighth hour will always be two-thirds of the way through the daylight, i.e. early-to-mid afternoon. Martial is saying Cerialis will not have to give up too much of his afternoon in order to attend.

lizard-fish: it is not known what kind of fish the *lacertus* was; *lacerta* is Latin for lizard. Apicius (10.2.7) has a recipe for a sauce with which to serve it.

11.53 *her three children*: the British woman Claudia Rufina has been a good Roman wife and improved her husband's standing. On the *ius trium liberorum*, see note on 4.27.

11.69 *Erigone's hound, or the dog of Dictaean bloodline*: Martial invokes three mythical *exempla* of doggish excellence. Erigone's dog, Maera, led its mistress to the body of her murdered father, King Icarius of Athens; when Erigone hanged herself, Maera jumped off a cliff. Zeus turned Cephalus' unerring hunting-dog, Laelaps, into the constellation Canis Major, but the episode alluded to by Martial is obscure. The 'Dulichian dog' a few lines later is Argus, the faithful hound that recognized Odysseus on his return home after twenty years' absence.

11.86 *a throat condition*: a play on the meaning of the Latin *gula*: the throat, but also the throat as the seat of taste and appetite.

11.97   *Telesilla*: the Telesilla of Lucillius, *AP* 11.239 (see note on 6.7) smells vile, which is presumably why Martial refuses to sleep with her (cf. 4.4).

11.99   *the Symplegades*: the Greek name for the Clashing Rocks, also known (as in Martial's Latin at their second appearance) as the Cyanean Rocks. Jason and the Argonauts successfully passed between them.

11.104   *a Curius, a Numa, or a Tatius*: three upright leaders of early Rome in the good old days. Tatius was the Sabine king who reconciled with Romulus; on Curius, see note on 7.68. Numa (cf. 10.35) succeeded Romulus, married Tatius' daughter, and established many of Rome's most lasting institutions.

the Ithacan: Odysseus.

a Lucretia . . . a Lais: the Lucretia of Livy's early history of Rome killed herself rather than live with sexual dishonour (cf. 11.16); Lais (cf. 10.68) was a famous courtesan.

11.108   *clear my slate*: the Latin *soluo* can simply be 'let me go', 'dismiss me' (and the reader has now reached the end of the book); or, to release someone from an obligation or debt.

BOOK 12

PREFACE

sitting on my arse: *desideo*, 'sit idle', can have the more particular meaning 'sit on the toilet'.

not so much . . . through and through: i.e. provincial and backward. Cf. Velleius Paterculus 2.51 on Cornelius Balbus, 'not just born in Spain, but Spanish through and through' (*non Hispaniensis natus, sed Hispanus*).

12.1   *the barking Molossians*: a breed of hound native to Greece and much prized by Romans who enjoyed hunting.

a whole hour: on Roman hours, see note on 11.52: winter hours were shorter. There is an untranslatable play of words whereby *hora* carries two senses: hour, and season of the year.

12.4 (5)   *read these poems*: Martial's instruction points the notional addressee (Caesar) towards the 'condensed' edition of Books 10 and 11 described at the outset, but of course the actual reader of the present poem is *not* reading 'those' poems at all—he or she is reading Book 12 instead. Fitzgerald (2007: 159) astutely comments: 'As readers of Book 12, some of whom have read through books 10 and 11, we are made aware of a privileged reader of the same material moving on a separate, swifter track. We have a walk-on part in his reading as the *vacui* [unoccupied] to whom he has awarded the necessary *otium* [leisure] to read the uncut Martial.'

12.16   *three small fields*: a variant on 9.21's agricultural metaphor for sodomy.

12.17 *expensive balsam*: *Amomum* was an aromatic from the East, probably of the cardamom family: see Dalby (2000: 197).

Dama: a stock name for a slave or freedman in Plautus; when Horace at *Satire* 2.7: 46–67 disguises himself as a slave, 'Dama' is the name he naturally plumps for.

12.18 *the hill of our lady Diana*: there was a temple of Diana on the Aventine (a modern piazza is named after it).

12.31 *after seven lustra*: the *lustrum* is a sacrifice carried out by the censors every five years.

Nausicaa: the daughter of King Alcinous of Phaecia, where the ship-wrecked Odysseus is given hospitality in Homer's *Odyssey*; the beauties of his palace garden are extolled early in the epic's seventh book.

12.33 *a fig-orchard*: as at 12.16, an agricultural metaphor: the 'figs' are the sodomized behinds of Labienus' cute boys. The fig is used metaphorically for the anus already in Greek sources: Adams (1982: 113). Later in the book (12.96), Martial explains that some 'figs' are better than others, and boys' are the choicest variety, the small and tender 'Chians' (cf. 7.31).

12.43 *Didyma's girls*: the transmitted text has *Didymi . . . puellae*; SB is surely right that this must be emended to *Didymae*. Didyma was the most important sanctuary in the territory of Miletus, a city that was a byword for top-drawer whoring.

12.52 *[But you are better . . . he reclaimed her.]*: the square-bracketed lines are not Martial's, but an inept later interpolation.

12.56 *a shower*: Martial's term, *soteria* (with a long 'e'), is transliterated out of the Greek. For Romans as for modern British readers, the proper times for presents are birthdays and Saturnalia (Christmas); Martial's use of foreign terminology is meant to grate on his Roman readers' ears, and to suggest the unwelcome infiltration of alien cultural values.

12.57 *Spanish gold-dust*: the word used, *alux*, is from Martial's native Spain.

Bellona: the Roman (originally Sabine) goddess of war. Her traditional worship involved ecstatic self-mutilation.

the magic rhombus: a trapezoidal noise-maker, twirled on a string during magical rituals. 'An eclipse was attributed to witches, and the clashing of brass vessels was in order to drive away evil demons' (SB); many local Italian *feste* still involve making lots of noise with pots and pans.

your runabout: an *essedum*, a light, fast carriage based on a Gaulish war-chariot design.

12.62 *Great King of the heavens of old*: Saturn, patron god of the Saturnalia.

the piñata: 'a cord hung with gifts for the populace' (SB on 8.78.7). The 'tickets' are vouchers exchangeable for gifts and party favours, like those described in the *Xenia* and *Apophoreta*.

12.73 *You say I'm your heir, Catullus*: not the 'real' Catullus, but then again, in the Martialverse, who is? Certainly, Martial's talk of being this Catullus' 'heir' raises the issue of literary inheritance ('in writing'). Martial effectively turns himself into a metafictional version of the ever-hopeful legacy-hunters whom he mocks so heartily elsewhere (see note on 2.32).

12.94 *Calabrian Muses*: Horace is the poet of the 'Calabrian lyre' at 5.30.2.

   How low won't you go?: this poem presumes a familiar hierarchy of literary genres, with epigram right at the bottom (or must Martial sink even lower to ditch his rival?).

12.96 *I want a Chian fig*: on figs as a sexual metaphor, see note on 12.33, with which the present poem is clearly in dialogue.

   leave the boys their part: in Latin as in English, 'part' (*pars*) can mean a person's proper role, or serve as a euphemism for genitalia (private parts); here it does double duty.

12.97 *shameless prayers*: a close echo of the phrasing of 11.80 (Martial wishing he could be with Julius Martial at Baiae).

XENIA/PARTY FAVOURS

1   The critical consensus is that this and poem 2 (not in this selection) do not belong in the *Xenia*. Poem 3 does indeed look like a likely 'Poem 1'.

   Whitebait need their jackets: recycling a book-roll as kitchen paper is a Catullan gambit that declares the worthlessness of its contents: see note on 3.2.

3   *there are headings*: on poem-headings in ancient books of epigrams, see note on Book 1 preface. Early in the *Apophoreta* (poem 2) Martial goes further, ironically suggesting that the reader in a hurry can just read the headings and ignore the poems they are attached to. Tryphon the bookseller was previously encountered at 4.72.

5   *Pepper*: pepper was a Saturnalia gift in the list at 4.46, as were the beans of *Xenia* 7.

9   *Pelusium*: stands here for Egypt generally, known as a source of lentils. Dal was generally a poor person's food (Leary 2001: 55), though capable of being elevated to fine dining: Apicius has some tasty recipes.

14 *Lettuces*: see note on 3.50.

32 *the Velabrum*: a low-lying area between the Palatine and Capitoline hills, known as a commodities market. Greeks seem to have recognized smoked cheese as a Roman speciality: Athenaeus 3.113C.

41 *Aetolian boar*: Aetolia was the mythic location of Meleager's boar-hunt; see 7.27. *Apophoreta* 93, another poem on a boar, revisits it. Roast suckling-pig (*maialino*) is still a favourite Roman dish.

50 *Truffles*: these will be the superior white truffles of northern and central

Italy. Apicius (7.14.1–6) includes six recipes for truffles served in various sauces.

72 *the Argo's hold*: the *Argo*'s historic status as the first ship, ushering in an age of trade that was bound up with the loss of the autarkic Golden Age, was a poetic truism; combining it with the particular export for which the voyage's destination (Colchis) was to become widely known is quite a clever twist. On pheasants and Phasis, cf. 3.38.

82 *sozzled in Baiae's Lucrinus*: on Lake Lucrinus and its oysters, see note on 3.20.

  the very best garum: cf. *Xenia* 102.

92 *Hares*: hare was a gift to be prized, as at 5.29; Apicius gives fourteen ways of serving it.

99 (98) *waving their togas*: SB offers a note explaining (on what seems slender evidence) how the crowd in the arena signalled with their togas; he adduces 12.28 (29).8, where the spectators wave their napkins to indicate a gladiator should be spared. The gazelle is intended for eating (Leary 2001: 162) but its recipient has second thoughts.

102 *Garum of the Associates*: *garum sociorum* was recognized as the best and most expensive kind. Attributing its invention to Apicius, Pliny the Elder (*Natural History* 9.30) specifies the livers of red mullet, and explains that Apicius liked to cook mullet in a sauce made from others of their kind, hence 'Associates'. If Pliny's explanation is right—and there are good reasons for doubting it (Leary 2001: 166)—then what Martial describes is not proper *garum sociorum* at all. Still, it is better than the *muria* of the paired poem.

103 *Muria*: a fish brine; it was quicker to make than regular *garum* and used cheaper fish.

107 *Romulus himself*: SB has a note on 'Romulus', a genuine Gallic wine-maker known from inscriptions. On resinated wine in antiquity, see Leary (2001: 171).

111 *there weren't any*: in other words, the wine is amazingly old—from the days of the kings, before Rome was even a republic.

126 *will all that stuff to yourself*: for dinner-parties while one lives; if any is left, it will come in handy at the funeral (pouring libations and anointing the corpse).

127 *forced garlands, Caesar*: Domitian's new hothouse blooms outdo winter roses shipped from Egypt; 6.80 (not in this selection) treats the same topic. A garland is of course also a collection of epigrams, like Meleager's *Garland*, and the position of this poem at the very end of its book encourages a metapoetic reading. Leary (2001: 194–5) points out that these 'forced' garlands are so called using the exact Latin term (*festinatas*) that Martial uses self-deprecatingly of his 'rushed' *libelli*, at 2.91 ('hastily assembled little books') and 10.2 ('I rushed before in putting my tenth little book together').

APOPHORETA/DOGGY-BAGS

1   *the aedile*: the magistrate responsible for limiting gambling activity to Saturnalia; cf. 5.84.

2   *over and done with in two lines*: this four-line poem, preceded by a twelve-line poem, says that all the poems in the book are two lines long.

    you can just read the titles: on poem-headings, compare *Xenia* 3 and its note.

28   *if it's windy*: awnings (*uela*) kept the sun off the crowd in an amphitheatre or theatre; evidently they couldn't be spread on windy days.

52   *A Flask Made of Horn*: a rhino-horn flask is an accessory for wealthy bathers at Juvenal 7.130.

53   *Rhinoceros*: is this second 'rhinoceros' another flask, or a child's toy? Ambiguity deepens with context: 52 is a flask, so, flask; 54 is a child's toy, so, toy.

98   *Porsena*: Lars Porsena was an Etruscan king who made war on Rome in the early sixth century BC. The story of Mucius (see note on 8.30) is an important part of this semi-legendary history. Arretium (modern Arezzo), the home of moulded terracotta Arretine ware, is 40 miles north of Porsena's Clusium (Chiusi).

124 '*Lords of Nature, the toga-wearing race*': any Roman schoolboy would instantly recognize the first line as a quotation from Jupiter's anticipation of the rise of Rome early in the *Aeneid* (1.282).

    who gave his great father the stars: Domitian's temple to the Flavian *gens*; cf. 9.1.

162 *Pallid care steers clear of hard bunks*: worries come with wealth and station.

172 *Lizard-Slayer*: the reference is to the *Sauroktonos*, a famous statue by Praxiteles in which a youthful Apollo lounges against a tree-trunk, about to kill a lizard. It is known through Roman copies such as the one described by Martial.

185 *when you've put away your nuts*: i.e. when Saturnalia is over; nuts are associated with the festival in the opening poems of both the *Xenia* and the *Apophoreta*.

186 *Virgil on Parchment*: a travel-sized parchment codex, of the kind advertised in 1.2 and 1.44.

194 *Lucan*: Martial praises his fellow Spanish author at 5.74 and 7.23.

203 *made a wanker of Hippolytus*: the legendary misogynist who abstained from all sexual contact; his exclusive devotion to Diana, goddess of the hunt, so angered Venus that she orchestrated his death. The story is the subject of a famous play by Euripides. On the terminology of masturbation in Martial see note on 9.41, and cf. 11.104.

205 *pumice*: used to depilate; Martial wants a boy who does not yet have body

hair. At 1.117 (see note), in a programmatic allusion to Catullus, *Carmen* 1, Martial's *libellus* was 'smoothed with pumice'.

217 (216) *the bird-catcher's slave*: this poem is placed between a poem on a bird-catcher and one on a caterer (*opsonator*), a clear example of Martial using sequencing to imply a narrative connection. Birds were a delicacy; game-birds were hunted, as here, while other kinds were farmed in aviaries.

INDEX

American Literature

British and Irish Literature

Children's Literature

Classics and Ancient Literature

Colonial Literature

Eastern Literature

European Literature

Gothic Literature

History

Medieval Literature

Oxford English Drama

Philosophy

Poetry

Politics

Religion

The Oxford Shakespeare

A complete list of Oxford World's Classics, including Authors in Context, Oxford English Drama, and the Oxford Shakespeare, is available in the UK from the Marketing Services Department, Oxford University Press, Great Clarendon Street, Oxford OX2 6DP, or visit the website at www.oup.com/uk/worldsclassics.

In the USA, visit www.oup.com/us/owc for a complete title list.

Oxford World's Classics are available from all good bookshops. In case of difficulty, customers in the UK should contact Oxford University Press Bookshop, 116 High Street, Oxford OX1 4BR.

THOMAS AQUINAS	Selected Philosophical Writings
FRANCIS BACON	The Major Works
WALTER BAGEHOT	The English Constitution
GEORGE BERKELEY	Principles of Human Knowledge and Three Dialogues
EDMUND BURKE	A Philosophical Enquiry into the Sublime and Beautiful Reflections on the Revolution in France
CONFUCIUS	The Analects
RENÉ DESCARTES	A Discourse on the Method Meditations on First Philosophy
ÉMILE DURKHEIM	The Elementary Forms of Religious Life
FRIEDRICH ENGELS	The Condition of the Working Class in England
JAMES GEORGE FRAZER	The Golden Bough
SIGMUND FREUD	The Interpretation of Dreams
G. W. E. HEGEL	Outlines of the Philosophy of Right
THOMAS HOBBES	Human Nature and De Corpore Politico Leviathan
DAVID HUME	An Enquiry concerning Human Understanding Selected Essays
IMMANUEL KANT	Critique of Judgement
SØREN KIERKEGAARD	Repetition and Philosophical Crumbs
JOHN LOCKE	An Essay concerning Human Understanding

	An Anthology of Elizabethan Prose Fiction
	Early Modern Women's Writing
	Three Early Modern Utopias (Utopia; New Atlantis; The Isle of Pines)
FRANCIS BACON	Essays The Major Works
APHRA BEHN	Oroonoko and Other Writings The Rover and Other Plays
JOHN BUNYAN	Grace Abounding The Pilgrim's Progress
JOHN DONNE	The Major Works Selected Poetry
JOHN FOXE	Book of Martyrs
BEN JONSON	The Alchemist and Other Plays The Devil is an Ass and Other Plays Five Plays
JOHN MILTON	The Major Works Paradise Lost Selected Poetry
EARL OF ROCHESTER	Selected Poems
SIR PHILIP SIDNEY	The Old Arcadia The Major Works
SIR PHILIP and MARY SIDNEY	The Sidney Psalter
IZAAK WALTON	The Compleat Angler

	Travel Writing 1700–1830
	Women's Writing 1778–1838
FRANCES BURNEY	Cecilia Evelina
ROBERT BURNS	Selected Poems and Songs
JOHN CLELAND	Memoirs of a Woman of Pleasure
DANIEL DEFOE	A Journal of the Plague Year Moll Flanders Robinson Crusoe
HENRY FIELDING	Jonathan Wild Joseph Andrews and Shamela Tom Jones
WILLIAM GODWIN	Caleb Williams
OLIVER GOLDSMITH	The Vicar of Wakefield
SAMUEL JOHNSON	The History of Rasselas
ANN RADCLIFFE	The Italian The Mysteries of Udolpho
SAMUEL RICHARDSON	Pamela
TOBIAS SMOLLETT	The Adventures of Roderick Random The Expedition of Humphry Clinker
LAURENCE STERNE	The Life and Opinions of Tristram Shandy, Gentleman A Sentimental Journey
JONATHAN SWIFT	Gulliver's Travels A Tale of a Tub and Other Works
HORACE WALPOLE	The Castle of Otranto
MARY WOLLSTONECRAFT	Mary and The Wrongs of Woman